# Situating Sartre
IN TWENTIETH-CENTURY
THOUGHT AND CULTURE

# Situating Sartre
## IN TWENTIETH-CENTURY THOUGHT AND CULTURE

EDITED BY
Jean-François Fourny
and Charles D. Minahen

MACMILLAN

© Jean-François Fourny and Charles D. Minahen 1997

All rights reserved. No reproduction, copy or transmission of this publication may be made without written permission.

No paragraph of this publication may be reproduced, copied or transmitted save with written permission or in accordance with the provisions of the Copyright, Designs and Patents Act 1988, or under the terms of any licence permitting limited copying issued by the Copyright Licensing Agency, 90 Tottenham Court Road, London W1P 9HE.

Any person who does any unauthorised act in relation to this publication may be liable to criminal prosecution and civil claims for damages.

First published 1997 by
MACMILLAN PRESS LTD
Houndmills, Basingstoke, Hampshire RG21 6XS
and London
Companies and representatives
throughout the world

ISBN 0-333-71358-3

A catalogue record for this book is available from the British Library.

10   9   8   7   6   5   4   3   2   1
06   05   04   03   02   01   00   99   98   97

Printed in the United States of America by
R.R. Donnelley & Sons
Harrisonburg, VA

*In Memory of Our Fathers,*

*Henri Fourny and Charles N. Minahen*

## contents

Acknowledgments .................................................... ix

Introduction: From a Post-imperial Point of View
    *Jean-François Fourny* ................................................. 1

1. Search for a Method: *Le Scénario Freud*
    *Rhiannon Goldthorpe* ............................................... 11

2. Flaubert's Blind Spot. The Fetishization of Subjectivity: Some Notes on the Constitution of Gustave in Sartre's *L'Idiot de la famille*
    *Christina Howells* .................................................. 29

3. Ethics and Revolution in Sartre's *Les Mains sales*
    *Charles D. Minahen* ................................................ 39

4. Freedom at Work: Sartre on Ponge
    *Natascha Heather Lancaster* ........................................ 53

5. Sartre and the Age of the American Novel
    *Anna Boschetti* .................................................... 71

6. The Narrative of Return in "Orphée noir"
    *Marie-Paule Ha* .................................................... 93

7. Freedom and Flirtation: Bad Faith in Sartre and Beauvoir
    *Toril Moi* ........................................................ 111

8. Snails and Oysters: Sartre and His Homosexualities
    *George H. Bauer* .................................................. 129

9. Adrift in the Realm of the Senses: Sartre and Fusional Being
    *Robert Harvey* .................................................... 147

10. A Revisionary Account of the Apotheosis and Demise of the Philosophy of the Subject: Hegel, Sartre, Heidegger, Structuralism, and Poststructuralism
    *Philip R. Wood* ................................................... 165

Notes on Contributors ............................................... 197

Works Cited ......................................................... 199

Index ............................................................... 209

## acknowledgments

We are grateful to Blackwell Publishers for permission to include a revised version of a chapter of Toril Moi's book, *Simone de Beauvoir: The Making of an Intellectual Woman* (Oxford: Blackwell Publishers, 1993). Maria-Teresa and David Vanderboegh very kindly took time out from busy schedules to complete an English translation of Anna Boschetti's essay, and we thank them for it. We have also very much appreciated the advice and encouragement of our colleague in the Department of French and Italian at Ohio State University, Charles G. S. Williams, who has supported this project from its inception. Margaret Bolovan, too, has been involved since the beginning, and we are especially indebted to her for shepherding the manuscript from stage to stage with the dedication of a true professional. Her expert research and editorial assistance, perceptive reading of the text, and meticulous attention to detail have proven invaluable, as the initial collection of formally diverse essays has been transformed into a consistent and cohesive whole. Finally, we have benefited greatly from our collaboration with Maura Burnett and Wendy Kraus of St. Martin's Press, whose combined editorial expertise has enabled us to complete the publishing process in a very constructive and productive manner.

INTRODUCTION

# From a Post-imperial Point of View
## Jean-François Fourny

**THE FAMILY IDIOT?**

Just over fifty years after the publication of *Being and Nothingness* in 1943, Jean-Paul Sartre remains by all accounts the most studied French author in the world, as was demonstrated by a recent bibliography listing more than six thousand Sartre-related items.[1] In fact, a quiet but intense activity around Sartre's work never ceased in the seventies and eighties, especially in the English-speaking world, precisely when poststructuralism seemed to be gaining formidable momentum. As early as the sixties Sartre was on the defensive, quarreling with a new generation of writers (the New Novelists) and philosophers and critics (the so-called structuralists), and his publishing and intellectual empire appeared to be crumbling. To many it was clear that once the symbolic father was murdered all the sons would divide up his legacy among themselves. Sartre's destiny was felt to be that of many celebrated but somehow old-fashioned authors whose work has bored high-school students to tears in France generation after generation.

Now, it so happens that a certain brand of poststructuralism is itself on the defensive as it is increasingly challenged by the political and materialist readings it always discarded as irrelevant or naïve. Ironically, it is the subject, which the New Novel and poststructuralism wanted so badly to erase once and for all, that is returning. Likewise, those who were once so harsh with Sartre are the very ones who began resuscitating the subject, for example, Michel Foucault in philosophy or, in fiction, Claude Simon.[2] The subject discussed these days is not of course the European, male, bourgeois subject of thirty years ago. What I am referring to is a renewed concern through various approaches for a subjectivity once deemed dead. The collapse of communism and the threat of neofascism across the world have once again brought the very old question of individual freedom to the fore. Whatever was said during the seventies about the absence of absolutes and the impossibility of freedom and justice, the fact still remains that all persons, sophisticated or simple, male or female, Caucasian, Asian, or people of African descent, do know freedom and lack of freedom, justice and injustice, fairness and oppression when they see them, albeit differently.

The return of the subject is no mere fashion, since those who contributed so much to the advent and subsequent hegemony of poststructuralism and did so much to erase or conceal the subject in the name of undecidibility had themselves obviously made in previous lives "individual" decisions that were just plain wrong (Heidegger, for example), if not bordering on the criminal as in Paul de Man's case. In terms of moral responsibility, the bill for this most sinister episode of intellectual history would claim more than six million lives along with innumerable unspeakable crimes.

A recent book argues that poststructuralism was no more than the intellectual translation of all the fears generated by the Cold War that were rekindled by Jimmy Carter when he interrupted the relative détente favored by Richard Nixon, thereby reintroducing fear and undecidibility into international relations.[3] Whether the author of this challenging book is right or wrong I do not know, but it is true that a new critical space now exists in which one already finds more diversity, more tolerance, and more research avenues than under poststructuralist hegemony. The indispensable task of historicizing this episode, like any moment in intellectual history, must be left to others. Poststructuralism will eventually be judged according to its own very real merits and equally real limitations and given a fair review. While this is not the task here, we may nonetheless observe that a wide array of critical tools has emerged during the last fifteen years and has engaged in what the Cold War vocabulary would have called a relatively "peaceful coexistence." But one may ask what all this has to do with Sartre. This is precisely the point.

## ONE IS RIGHT TO REVOLT

Who would have thought fifteen years ago that biography and autobiography would enjoy the current revival that has drawn renewed attention to what the French call *le personnel*? Well, from his autobiography to his monumental, unfinished *The Family Idiot* through his own relationship with Simone de Beauvoir supported by a huge body of correspondence, Sartre has much to offer. To take another example: by bracketing the context and freezing (some used to say "saving") the text in the American poststructuralist manner, a taboo on the study of the material conditions of the possibility of this very text was instituted. This move also very conveniently made it unsavory to pay attention to the material and institutional conditions of the possibility of criticism itself. Carefully shielded, in the continuation of metaphysics, behind the fetishization of a discourse that had replaced the Hegelian "Spirit," the critic was then free to ignore not only race, gender, and class, but also the devastating correlations that can be established between personal income, geographic location, former graduate studies, academic pecking order, career history, and/or the refusal of political positions, which is itself a political position.[4]

New historicism and cultural studies, along with a reinvigorated French sociology as represented in the works of Pierre Bourdieu, made this field of inquiry legitimate again. But this invigorating liberation of *le personnel* not only contributed to further and welcome developments in already well-established fields such as feminism, but also encouraged the emergence of new ones. If gender studies, as a promising and distinct American academic specialty, is to do for men what feminism did and is still doing for women, Sartre has helped to initiate the process through his absolute frankness and refusal of the bourgeois private/public distinction that allowed him to talk and write openly about the personal, the body, and (homo)sexuality. And who will one day write a treatise on the probably very real influence of Mrs. Heidegger on major developments of Western philosophy in the twentieth century? Finally, the emergence of postcolonial studies, one of the major intellectual events of a *fin de siècle* full of sound and fury, calls for a pressing revision of our beliefs, values, and, above all for those of us who are of European descent, good intentions. Here, also, Sartre cannot be avoided.

The postcolonial condition is a fact. However, the concept of a post-imperial condition might also need to be introduced one day so as to understand better *fin-de-siècle* French intellectuals. French thought today clearly has to readjust after (and come to grips with) the "loss of the empire." This may be why there might never again be "great" intellectual gurus like Sartre, or even Michel Foucault. In other words, France is not the Center nowadays, but just one regional center among many others in a polycentric world. And this shift is probably a very good thing. American-style multiculturalism (whatever this may mean) may not be the universal answer to the problems faced by European (or other) societies; but reverting to the past, exclusion, denial, or just ignoring the issue will not help France precisely when its intellectuals should come up with creative and workable solutions.[5]

## NO EXIT

In a way, Charles de Gaulle negotiated decolonization so as to maintain the French imperium in a new guise. There was perhaps an intellectual emperor like Sartre only because there was another emperor like de Gaulle who prolonged the fiction of the empire. This is where Sartre's view of the third world becomes crucial. While his personal sympathy for the oppressed cannot be doubted, it is obvious that he projected a European (that is, Marxist) vision onto other cultures. Sartre's third world is to some degree reduced to Cuba, Vietnam, and parts of Africa, because of their Marxism. Was Sartre then reproducing the traditional Marxist neglect of religion and native cultures? In a way, yes. But there is also another side to the story to be found in his dealings with African and Caribbean writers. There, another Sartre appears, against all odds, as the cold-blooded political activist turned sensual and lyric. In fact, the author of dry books like the *Critique of Dialectical Reason* or of dogmatic essays like *What is Literature?* was also an adept interpreter of poetry—the only literary genre he did not practice himself—interested in Stéphane Mallarmé and Aimé Césaire.

Structurally speaking, Michel Foucault inherited what Pierre Bourdieu would call Sartre's *poste*.[6] Just like Sartre, Foucault mustered an impressive moral authority, and like Sartre, he involved himself in all the generous causes of his time. And just like Sartre, Foucault practiced intensely the very modern art of the personal interview. However, considering his stature as one of the leading intellectuals teaching at the leading intellectual institution—the *Collège de France*—of one of the post-imperial metropolises, Foucault's silence on non-European cultures (other than Khomeini's Iran) is astonishing. After all, since France harbors less than one percent of the world's population, how the many rich multicultural responses to the experience of life could be left aside or ignored I also do not know. This, I believe, is an area that the emerging field of postcolonial studies must investigate. However, I do know that there is no point in building postmortem cases and trials when there were no malicious intentions. We all live in a historically very limited horizon, and no individual can be asked *a posteriori* to give more than he or she could give. To think otherwise would amount to calling for a revisitation of the Stalino-Freudian dogmas of the thirties. And if I may paraphrase the late Supreme Court Justice Thurgood Marshall, it is left to all of us to do everything we can with the little we have.

## THE DEVIL AND THE GOOD LORD

The currently fashionable, though highly suspect, assimilation of fascism and communism as an unholy dyad would have us believe that these were no more than two sides of the same coin. It has been recently suggested that Sartre implicitly partook in Stalinism by refusing to denounce the former Soviet Union.[7] This accusation forgets the Cold War, its destructive and sadistic psychological climate, and the extraordinary arrogance of a segregated America organizing witch hunts. Forgotten too were Sartre's noble and generous intentions, whatever his mistakes. And who has never had to choose between two evils? Is the road to hell paved with good intentions? Sometimes, yes, but not always, and this applies to all of us, including Jean-Paul Sartre and America. Was Sartre a Stalinist when he was taking his life in his own hands by denouncing the Algerian war? Sartre, I believe, also did everything he could, and even more, with what he had.

This last issue bears directly upon both the intense hatred and adulation Sartre generated, which seem to constitute a feature of intellectual life in the twentieth century and a questionable French export of the intellectual star system to the United States. There was Sartre, there was Foucault, and there was Jacques Lacan. Then there was, in the United States, Jacques Derrida, Paul de Man, and today, as an indirect consequence of this cult-like mentality, the anti-intellectual and gallophobic writings of Camille Paglia.[8] What I am talking about here is the total loss of distance and critical sense among intellectuals who are supposed to know better. Why was Sartre so revered and hated? Why do so-called intellectuals need so much to adore and worship? It may very well be that psychoanalysis holds the key to this morbid question.[9] It might also be the case that in the future a rigorous sociology of intellectuals will ruthlessly investigate the Catholic, Jewish, and Protestant roots of this patriarchy-based search for a father, a leader, a *duce*, a shaman, or a guru. Maybe one was a poststructuralist ten years ago, just like she was a communist a generation before and just like he was a Catholic another generation before.

In light of the transformations the intellectual landscape is undergoing today, situating Sartre can doubtless help us evaluate or reevaluate the new, or not so new, critical methodologies. But it is at the same time a narcissistic enterprise, because it means situating ourselves: it is not only the generation of Roland Barthes or Michel Foucault who had somehow reluctantly to admit that Sartre made them what they were, but also, I believe, those who came after and well after.

## HE CAME TO STAY

The following essays are meant to cast a new light on Sartre's work and reassess its relevance to our *fin de siècle*. The volume opens with Rhiannon Goldthorpe's study of *Le Scénario Freud*. Sartre's massive screenplay for John Huston's film, *Freud: The Secret Passion*—commissioned in 1958 but eventually withdrawn—was not published until 1984, but its different versions throw fascinating light on Sartre's intellectual development during the period of its composition. The originally anti-Freudian Sartre, as he dramatizes the themes of self-discovery, self-deception, freedom, responsibility, and constraint, and as he develops his own "progressive-regressive" method, transforms Freud into an existential hero, while his interpretation of Freud's insights in terms of the methodology of the human rather than the natural sciences revives the controversies of a broader intellectual tradition. The essay, "Search for a Method: *Le Scénario Freud*," assesses the originality and significance of Sartre's screenplay and its revaluation of Freud's most creative years.

Sartre's characterizations of subjectivity have often been misunderstood and distorted, if not turned into a parody of Cartesianism. According to the legend, Sartre theorized a homogeneous Eurocentric ego that would simply reflect his own ethnic, sociological, and gender-informed background. Through a subtle interpretation of *The Family Idiot*, Christina Howells argues that Sartre's definition of subjectivity is not very different from Lacan's, which was conceptualized at the same time as the mirror stage. What this unfinished book on Flaubert shows is that Sartre's subject is split, but also constituted by this very *Spaltung*. And it is precisely because the Sartrean subject is alienated and divided against itself from the origin that it can escape the "deterministic" process, as Howells's rereading of *The Family Idiot* proposes.

Recognizing that Sartre's philosophical works leave the question of ethics theoretically unresolved, Charles (Dennis) Minahen finds in the moral dilemmas depicted in the literary works the kinds of specific situations that resist systematic explanation but lend themselves to the analysis of individual choices that Sartre's ethics of freedom is predicated upon. While the author does not offer a ready-made solution to each dilemma, an implied judgment often emerges when the dishonesty or hypocrisy underlying an action is exposed. But the task is often complicated by the characters themselves, who cannot be relied upon to sort out the problem of culpability. Focusing on *Les Mains sales*, where the ethical dilemma is rendered all the more ambiguous by the context, a revolution, Minahen resituates the Hugo-

Hoederer relationship in an attempt to clarify, through a new look at revealing textual details, the controversial ethics of the situation that provoked Sartre himself uncharacteristically to express his own authorial intention.

For somebody like the poet Francis Ponge the world is inside us. For Sartre, as the next essay in this volume also demonstrates, what matters is to expel man and the world from himself. The Sartre-Ponge dialogue could not be more uncanny at first sight. However, it is Natascha Lancaster's contention that Sartre's reading or willful misreadings of Ponge's poetry lead to a crucial reinterpretation of dehumanization as a paradoxical exercise of human freedom. If active contemplation (like reading) involves the risk of dehumanization and of the subject's disappearing into objects, it may be because of our desire to fly from reality or our wish to disappear so as to reemerge later. Thus the question becomes: how can we exercise our aesthetic sense without being "possessed" or invaded by objects? Sartre's answer, Lancaster tells us, is that we will always be able to keep objects at bay and remain ourselves through the exorcism of writing and naming.

Sartre's intellectual trajectory is exemplary in illustrating the importance of the United States for modern European culture. In his conception of the novel and narrative structures, Sartre accorded a central role to the American novel, which he enthusiastically promoted in his critical and theoretical writings. In his *Situation* essays, Sartre consecrated the status of the American novel in European letters by proposing it as a model to the new generation of writers. Anna Boschetti's essay shows how crucial Sartre's work on American writers such as John Dos Passos or William Faulkner was for the emergence of the New Novel. And as I mentioned at the beginning of this introduction, it was these very New Novelists who were later to oppose Sartre so bitterly.

From L. S. Senghor to Aimé Césaire to Frantz Fanon, Sartre remained an avid reader of postcolonial intellectual production. The focus of Marie-Paule Ha's postcolonial rereading of *Orphée noir* is on the narrative of return that frames Sartre's discussion of the *négritude* movement. Ha's contention is that this narrative of return, which rests on a manichean reading of the colonizer and colonized power relations, fails to account for the highly complex and ambivalent character of the colonial and postcolonial predicament. In a way, like any other condition, the post-imperial condition offers both blindness and insight as all identities become problematic.

The return of *le personnel* makes it now possible to put the personal and the philosophical on equal footing, and what is more personal, after all, than flirting? Through flirting serious heterosexual business takes place both in Sartre's *Being and Nothingness* and de Beauvoir's first published novel *She*

*Came To Stay*. Toril Moi's interpretation of Sartre's philosophical treatise and de Beauvoir's novel, both published in 1943, is based on the human drive to seduce. This refreshing approach subverts reactionary hierarchies that would rank Sartre's philosophical opus magnum above a semi-autobiographical narrative written by a woman. Or that would rank the philosophical above the personal because they might very well be one and the same thing. And was it not Marx himself who claimed that the philosopher's relation to philosophy is no more than the philosopher's relation to himself?

Since its early Greek origins, Western philosophy has been pervaded by male homosexuality, although this connection has been repressed and concealed for most of its official history. Perhaps then Sartre was never more a philosopher than when he openly discussed homosexuality or promoted Jean Genet to literary stardom. The late George Bauer's essay addresses what appears to be a highly complex issue in Sartre's works. His fiction and philosophical writings offer an imposing array of homosexual characters, while his personal diaries tend to relate earthly pleasures such as friendship, food, and sex in an ambivalent manner. Sartre very much valued friendship and male bonding, but he also confessed to choosing his male friends for their physical beauty, turning Paul Nizan, among others, into *hommes-femmes*. Bauer links this taste for handsome men to Sartre's obsessively elaborate discussions of food. This highly original and provocative essay treats us to a complex set of menus and culinary metaphors—involving shellfish (which Sartre hated) and sausages (which Sartre preferred by far)—that all display his ambiguous feelings and opinions concerning homosexuality.

The next essay, by Robert Harvey, also deals with mollusks, but of the giant sort that terrorized the young Sartre as he was reading *Twenty Thousand Leagues Under the Sea*. According to Harvey, it was the philosopher's well-known repulsion by viscosity and mud, shaped by Jules Verne's fantasies about underwater life, that made him the land-bound thinker he became. As a consequence, Sartre's characters often go to the beach or travel to seaside resorts but rarely venture into the ocean because, for Sartre, there is no safe passage. By the same token, Harvey unveils the submarine intertextuality that unites Sartre, Marcel Proust, and Marguerite Duras through their contradictory treatments of the sea.

Finally, Philip Wood takes Sartre's progressive-regressive method seriously: Sartre can only be understood today in terms of his successors—a relationship that Wood argues has been bedeviled by constant confusion. Thus, Wood undertakes a massive rewriting of French thought of the last fifty years. He points out that the "subject," for Heidegger and the poststructuralists, never meant something like *consciousness,* but rather *ground.*

In the course of demarcating Derridean *différance* from the Hegelian system, maintaining that the stakes of the infamous "death of the subject" have been fundamentally misunderstood, Wood takes issue with defenses of Sartre on the grounds that he was not an "essentialist" (e.g., Fredric Jameson)—for Wood this was never the point of poststructuralist attacks—as well as with structuralist criticisms of Sartre on the grounds that he was an individualist and humanist (e.g., Louis Althusser and early Gilles Deleuze).

We hope that these highly insightful and diverse essays will contribute to rediscovering a thinker who proves to be much more complex than was believed just a few years ago. If I may paraphrase Sartre, this volume was meant to show that *les jeux ne sont pas faits.*

## NOTES

1. Michel Contat and Michel Rybalka, eds., *Sartre: bibliographie 1980-1992* (Paris: CNRS Editions, 1992).
2. See, for example, Michel Foucault, *The Use of Pleasure,* trans. Robert Hurley (New York: Pantheon, 1985) and Claude Simon, *L'Acacia* (Paris: Minuit, 1989).
3. Tobin Siebers, *Cold War Criticism and the Politics of Skepticism* (Oxford: Oxford University Press, 1993).
4. I realize one might ask why, for example, weight and height should not be listed as factors. And why not, since the endless and impossible task of criticism is to rebuild the context. See Gerald J. Prince, "On Narratology: Criteria, Corpus, Context," *Narrative* 3 (1995): 73-84.
5. I first thought of a post-imperial condition while attending a conference held at Rice University in the spring of 1993. The topic was terror, consensus, and the singularity of French thought. A dozen or so prominent French academics were to speak. After a while I was far from being the only one to identify a very real disarray in the papers we were hearing. There was an unmistakably nostalgic ring for the times when French thought reigned unchallenged. Moreover, laments of the demise of the former French strategy of integrating immigrants (by demanding that they become French through secondary education and military service, while renouncing their own cultures) were uttered. Thus, the implication was that the identity-related uncertainties postcolonial studies have been dealing with are both shared and mirrored in the post-imperial condition.
6. Pierre Bourdieu, *Questions de sociologie* (Paris: Minuit, 1980).
7. Tony Judt, *Un Passé imparfait* (Paris: Fayard, 1993).
8. Camille Paglia, *Sex, Art, and American Culture* (New York: Vintage Books, 1992).
9. As Niilo Kauppi reminds us in his *French Intellectual Nobility: Institutional and Symbolic Transformation in the Post-Sartrian Era* (Albany: State University of

New York Press, 1996): "It was not strange to hate Sartrian philosophy in the 1960s: everyone had to be either 'for' and 'against' concepts, which were the property of groups. The followers of Sartre—an intellectual totem—would use certain concepts and schemas, different from those of the followers of Lévi-Strauss, for instance. Robbe-Grillet's comment on some of his friends' attitudes toward Sartre exemplifies this: 'Moreover, I believe that Duras and Simon really hate Sartre'" (22).

# 1

# Search for a Method: *Le Scénario Freud*

**Rhiannon Goldthorpe**

The title of this essay perhaps needs a little explanation. The second part, *Le Scénario Freud,* is, of course, very easily explained. It refers to the synopsis and screenplay that Sartre wrote between 1958 and 1960 for John Huston's film *Freud: The Secret Passion,* which remained unpublished until it appeared posthumously in 1984.[1] The choice of Sartre as a scriptwriter was an odd one: in his early writing Sartre had explicitly argued against Freud, elaborating, instead, his own version of existential psychoanalysis, and there is very little mention of Freud in Sartre's work between *L'Etre et le néant* (1943)[2] and the *Scénario*. It was not Sartre's apparently anti-Freudian stance, however, that led to his eventual withdrawal from Huston's project. Huston had Sartre's text rewritten by two professional scriptwriters, with the result that Sartre refused to have his name appear in the credits. And although the *Scénario* itself is much more interesting than the version eventually filmed, Huston's position deserves some sympathy. It would have taken five hours to screen Sartre's original script; when it went back to him for cuts an even longer version returned. Huston's film did retain some of the most powerfully cinematic scenes mainly as Sartre had written them, including two of his largely fictional case histories. One of those memorably developed in Sartre's second version is that of Karl Schwartz, the general's son: under hypnosis he works out his Oedipal phantasies on a dressmaker's dummy which, in a highly condensed image, symbolizes both father and mother. He reappears in a powerful nightmare sequence in which Freud's mother is represented as an impassive, Byzantine empress, with a live snake writhing around her wrist. The other case is that of Cecily Körtner, whose hysterical paralysis, strabismus, and various other symptoms signal the repression of what she knew about the death of her father in a brothel and her desire for her mother's death. Much of the rest of the film is perfunctory: it loses the specifically Sartrean analysis of how Freud came to be what he was and do what he did.

The first part of my title, "Search for a Method," is less straightforward. The first version of the *Scénario* followed very closely upon Sartre's essay "Questions de méthode" (translated as "Search for a Method"), which was to become part of the first volume of the *Critique de la raison dialectique* (1960).[3] It is therefore not surprising that the screenplay shares, as we shall see, some of the methodological preoccupations of that essay. Then, of course, the *Scénario* is concerned precisely with the period when Freud was moving toward the discovery of his own doctrine and his own method. This in turn suggests that the *Scénario* marks a crucial stage in Sartre's sometimes overstated rapprochement with Freudian psychoanalysis or in his own continuing "search for a method." However, what I primarily wish to argue in this essay is that the remarkable degree of identification with Freud that Sartre seems to achieve in the *Scénario* does not imply a movement toward Freudian theory, still less an unconditional acceptance of that theory. It marks, rather, an assimilation of Freud into Sartre's own system and into the intellectual tradition to which Sartre himself subscribed throughout his career. Sartre presents Freud's search for a method in his, Sartre's, terms, but they are terms that allow him to resolve his own hostility to Freud.

Why was it, then, that Sartre, in 1958, felt able to write about Freud in a way that, while short of hero-worship, was not unsympathetic? The early Sartre was, as I have already suggested, explicitly anti-Freudian, a stance that was particularly apparent in the theories of *Esquisse d'une théorie des émotions* (1939),[4] of *L'Etre et le néant,* and in the application and development of those theories in *Baudelaire* (1947) and *Saint Genet* (1952). A number of implications may be drawn from Sartre's by now well-documented position.[5] Freud's theory of the unconscious in the first topography is at variance with Sartre's own ostensible commitment to the transparency, freedom, and spontaneity of consciousness—a commitment that had led him, in his earliest philosophical essay, *La Transcendance de l'ego* (1936),[6] to take issue even with Edmund Husserl, the founding father of phenomenology. (For Sartre consciousness, as pure activity, was not substantial enough to contain the ego postulated by Husserl. The ego, far from being a constituent of consciousness, was a construct of consciousness, an object *for* consciousness.) Nor could he agree with the Freudian view that the unconscious exists as a domain separate from the rest of the psyche. He could not accept the spatializing theory of the mind in which elements within a separate region—the unconscious—exert causal pressure upon consciousness, thereby reducing it to a relatively secondary and passive phenomenon. What Sartre could not accept, either, was that Freud's theory gives priority to the past. Existential psychoanalysis attempts, instead, to account for the future-oriented projects through which the subject creates itself and tries to make sense of the world in which it finds itself but which it also, in part, creates. Sartre does acknowledge the fact that within the Freudian topography there is room for a theory of the sense-giving activity of the mind, but in the *Esquisse d'une théorie des émotions* he criticizes it in terms that already in 1939 have an anti-Lacanian ring: in psychoanalysis, Sartre complains, "the significance of our behavior lies wholly outside that behavior itself or, if you like, the *signified* is entirely cut off from the *signifier*" (ET, 33; ST, 51, translation modified). He rejects, too, the resulting reduction of consciousness, in his view, to the status of an object, controlled by the same deterministic forces as those that, he acknowledges, govern the world of objects. He also takes exception, with considerable over-simplification, to the rigid system of symbolization associated, he believes, with the Freudian emphasis on mechanistic causation: Why, he asks, should a pincushion always be taken to represent a woman's breast? This implies another Freudian notion that Sartre could not accept: the idea of the censor. For Freud the distortion involved in symbol or symptom formation arises from the activity, itself unconscious, of the censor, a function that operates as a selective barrier primarily between the unconscious system on the one hand and the pre-conscious/conscious system on the other. Sartre takes issue with this in his most notoriously anti-Freudian passage: his analysis of bad faith in *L'Etre et le néant*. He fully accepts that some of our motives, or the implications of our behavior, may be concealed from us, but his theory is conceived precisely to argue that our consciousness consciously conceals them from itself: the censor must be aware of what it is concealing.[7] And the *Scénario* itself seems to dramatize a riposte for those who wish to psychoanalyze Sartre by suggesting, for instance, that his early insistence on the autonomy of consciousness may be attributed to his father's early death, which created the central lack in his life. (Sartre rather knowingly takes these critics on: the Freud of the *Scénario* has several fathers, as he himself acknowledges, and as Josef Breuer, one of the major paternal surrogates along with Meynert and Fliess, points out with resigned amusement.) Others attribute Sartre's insistence on the autonomy of consciousness to the fact that his authoritarian grandfather compensated oppressively for the absent father. Or his apparent privileging—often exaggerated by critics—of mind at the expense of body and his early and no doubt mistaken criticism of Freud's pansexualism are attributed variously to his own ugliness or to the fact that he had been feminized by his mother.

What Freudian critics forget, however, when they reduce Sartre's theories to an expression of his own contingent traumas, is that Sartre was in fact writing, and knowingly writing, within a well-established non-Freudian intellectual tradition. And I do not refer here to again well-documented phenomenological theories of consciousness. Sartre's views are firmly grounded in the dual and controversial allegiances of two distinct traditions, of *Erklären* (explanation) versus *Verstehen* (understanding), a controversy which, originating in Germany, dominated much late nineteenth- and twentieth-century thinking, and which is still very much a live issue in the methodology of the human and social sciences and in which the status of Freud is very much at stake. As the terms indicate, the *Erklären* tradition emphasized the role of scientific explanation, based on mechanistic or biological models, in the investigation of human behavior. This tradition is familiar through its close association with positivism, as it claimed that the epistemology of the exact natural sciences provides the only valid methodological model for the human sciences. (The past tense seems appropriate in considering such features of the *Erklären* tradition, since its epistemological postulates have been revised more rapidly with recent advances in scientific theory than those of the *Verstehen* approach.) The *Erklären* method involved a commitment to the principle of universal causality and subsumed individual cases under general laws of nature, including "human nature"—a notion that is anathema, of course, to committed existentialists. Its emphasis was a mechanistic and determinist one, and in its approach to human behavior it stressed that the force of motives lies in the fact that agents are disposed to follow characteristic patterns of behavior, such patterns providing the "laws" that link the motives to the action in the individual case. Behavioral symptoms were caused either by organic disturbances or by a trauma affecting psycho-sexual development, which the subject cannot cope with and which is therefore relegated to the unconscious: as a result, the analyst must work back from the symptom to the cause. The opposed tradition of *Verstehen* seeks to understand social and psychological phenomena in terms of distinctively human intentions or meanings apprehended either through empathy and intuition or by rational or imaginative reconstruction. These are all modes of apprehension that Sartre explicitly practices from his earliest writing, having adopted or adapted them from the time of his involvement in the 1928 translation of Karl Jaspers's *General Psychopathology* and from his knowledge of the philosopher of history, Wilhelm Dilthey, probably acquired during his stay in Germany from 1933 to 1934.[8] In the *Verstehen* tradition the patient's behavior is a goal-directed attempt to cope with a situation that frustrates the realization of implicit aims. This approach implies, and is motivated by, a pre-reflective understanding of the situation, which will not have been explicitly formulated but which will be made explicit through the understanding and interpretation of the therapist. On the other hand, the attitude in the *Erklären* tradition toward attempts to account for facts in terms of intentions, goals, and purposes is either to reject them as unscientific or to show that they can be transformed into causal explanations. Freud's notion of the "purposive idea" as it is developed in the second volume of *The Interpretation of Dreams*[9] is interestingly ambiguous from this point of view: it can either be seen to be subject to causal explanation through its relation to the mechanism of the censor, or it can be seen to take the form of an unconscious intention. It is in the latter sense that Sartre chooses to take it in the *Scénario,* in which, as we shall see, he seems particularly anxious to harness Freud to the *Verstehen* tradition. Be that as it may, there can be little doubt about Freud's early and ineradicable debt to the school of the great physicist Hermann Helmholtz and, through him, to the *Erklären* approach.[10] The mechanistic emphases of Freud's *Project for a Scientific Psychology,*[11] which he never repudiated, and his allegiance to the constancy principle and to theories of bound and free energy place him firmly in that school. So does his view that psychological phenomena exhibit many of the same characteristics and characteristic patterns as the neuro-physiological phenomena on which they are causally dependent and in terms of which they may be analyzed and explained. In one of the first dramatic conflicts of the *Scénario,* Sartre chooses to show Freud in early revolt against the Helmholtz tradition, which his mentor Meynert represents, and against the mind-body relationship that it implies. Rather than considering the mind to be subject to physical mechanisms, Freud is shown to subscribe to the more Sartrean view that the body colludes with the mind in the realization of an "unconscious intention" and that patients have the capacity to *invent,* with apparent spontaneity, ways of escaping from their suffering. It is precisely in terms of intentions, goals, and purposes that the *Verstehen* school seeks to interpret, rather than explain, the behavior of the subject, whether in terms of individual psychology or as an historical agent. That interpretation implies a synthetic, rather than analytic, grasp of the phenomena under consideration. Sartre's attempt to achieve a totalizing understanding of the subject is clearly situated in this tradition, and his Freud is eventually seen to realize that the extirpation of specific symptoms, which may be explicable in terms of some past trauma, is subordinate to the comprehension of the individual's behavior as an integrated attempt to deal with a total situation.[12] This synthesizing ambition is, of course, particularly notable in

Sartre's existential biographies, including the *Scénario*. In Sartre's case it also owes much, though perhaps initially at second hand, to the already progressive-regressive method in historical studies of Wilhelm Dilthey, one of the major proponents of the *Verstehen* school. Dilthey's emphasis on understanding rather than on explanation led him to stress the importance of individual psychology and to feel that biography was the best mode of writing and reading history. This emphasis is already visible in Sartre's discussion of Kaiser Wilhelm II and the "causes" of the first world war in his *Carnets de la drôle de guerre* (written in 1939 and 1940, published in 1983),[13] while the direct debt to Dilthey remains in Sartre's use of the notion of the "objective mind" of a period in his account of the French Second Empire in *L'Idiot de la famille* (1971-72).[14] (For Dilthey, as for Sartre, the demystified "objective mind" signified the totality of the cultural and institutional features that embody the shared norms of a society.) Such points are far from tangential to the *Scénario*, in which, as we shall see, the integration of the individual and the socio-historical plays an important role. However, what one chiefly needs to remember is that when Sartre uses the term *compréhension*, whether in the context of existential psychoanalysis or in the interpretation of historical action, it has the status of a technical term. In notebooks dating back to 1935 he offers an early definition of *compréhension* as a preconceptual faculty for grasping the significance of objects and relations between objects as synthetic wholes. Through *compréhension* object and thought are one, and the implication is that the subject/object dichotomy is thereby resolved.[15]

The fact that Sartre is trying to draw Freud into his own camp is already apparent in Sartre's interpretation of Ernest Jones's massive biography of Freud, which was being translated into French as Sartre was beginning his own project. The biography was a revelation to him, as it portrayed a Freud very much after his own heart: hostile to the establishment, subverting bourgeois assumptions, exposing hypocrisies, obstinate, angst-ridden. But Sartre draws on this material with considerable chronological and dramatic license. This is equally true of his reading of the *Studies on Hysteria*,[16] *The Interpretation of Dreams,* and those letters from Freud to Fliess that were then available in *The Origins of Psychoanalysis* (1954; translated into French in 1956).

The *Scénario* begins in September 1885, while the twenty-nine-year-old Freud is still attached to Theodore Meynert's laboratory and psychiatric service: in three months' time he will leave for Paris to study J.-M. Charcot's experiments with hypnosis, which Meynert deplores. It ends about six months after the death of Freud's father Jakob in October 1896 and, achronologically, just after Freud's break with Wilhelm Fliess, which Sartre brings forward in time by several years. The *Scénario* therefore encompasses the transition from hypnosis and the hypnotic-cathartic method to the free association method, and, less legitimately, Sartre telescopes into the period Freud's discoveries of repression, the sexual aetiology of the neuroses, the seduction theory, infantile sexuality, the Oedipus complex, transference, the death wish, the significance of dreams, and his own self-analysis. A crowded program—but it is even further complicated by the inclusion of Freud's family situation, dream sequences of Sartre's invention, case histories—some fictional, some composite—and the highly dramatized conflictual relationships of Freud with his various mentors: Meynert, Breuer (from whom he derived the hypnotic-cathartic method and with whom he published the *Studies on Hysteria* in 1893), and Fliess. This compression serves a characteristically Sartrean purpose: it exemplifies his continuing preoccupation with freedom in that its major if implicit theme is Freud's self-emancipation and self-realization. These take precedence even over the discovery of an emancipating therapy. The screenplay begins—or almost begins—with Freud's destruction of the diary that symbolizes his past: an exemplary existentialist gesture. It ends with his equally exemplary assuming of the responsibility of intellectual fatherhood. And yet each of these acts is, like the acts of so many Sartrean protagonists, ambiguous: in destroying his diary Freud also destroys the records of the dreams that might already have provided the clues for future self-understanding—a gesture, perhaps, of suppression through bad faith. And the assuming of intellectual fatherhood may involve the restriction of the freedom of others. The interweaving of self-discovery and self-deception, and of freedom, responsibility, and constraint, is one of the major leitmotifs of the work, familiar from the early Sartre. But as a dramatized biography, the screenplay is also contemporary with, and an example of, Sartre's progressive-regressive method as it is outlined in a theoretically enriched form in the first volume of the *Critique de la raison dialectique*—an enrichment that owes much to Dilthey's approach in his *Critique of Historical Reason* (1927). In Sartre's "Questions de méthode," which introduces his own *Critique*, the development of the individual is shown to interact dialectically with his historical context through the mediation of his family, his economic situation, his class, and its ideology. Thus, Sartre explores Freud's responses to his father's apparent passivity and the poverty of his petit-bourgeois family, to current sexual taboos and double standards, and to his status as a Jew, not only in terms of the prevailing anti-Semitism of Vienna, but also in relation to the patriarchal implications of Jewish custom. This is exemplified not only by Freud's resentment of his father's meekness, but by the betrayal of Jewishness on the part of his surrogate fathers. The symbolic significance of Mosaic law as a patriarchal ideal soon becomes a leitmotif— in defiance of actual chronology. Freud is also shown reacting to the extremely hierarchical and conservative institution of medical education and practice prevailing at the time, and he is situated at a crucial turning point, Sartre suggests, not only, as can be taken for granted, in the methodology of psychotherapy, but in the history of science—a point of change that Freud then helps to precipitate. Freud internalizes, is changed by, and, it is suggested, freely changes the institutions that condition him in a curious synthesis of the active and the passive.

The threats to Freud's autonomy are not only external ones, whether familial or institutional. He has to come to terms with and project himself beyond his own capacity for destructive aggression, the resentment that betokens dependence, a streak of sadism (fear, he thinks, is salutary), his puritanism, his gullibility, and his initial lack of self-awareness. But the tenacious working through has its own heroism and its own dialectic: psychoanalysis, dramatized in specific case histories, is, when successful, a mutual process that heals both patient and analyst. However, the dominant thrust of Sartre's highly allusive portrayal of Freud is not concerned primarily with the humanitarian goal of allaying human misery, nor with the crucial discovery at this stage of sexual libido as the basis for all human drives. Sartre is obviously reluctant to abandon his own schema in which the ontological desire to *be* takes precedence, closely followed by the desire to *know*. What emerges from the *Scénario* is that, as far as Sartre's Freud is concerned, the primary motivation is not the *libido tout court,* but the *libido sciendi.* Moreover, this drive toward knowledge and truth is shown to be morally ambivalent in that, although ideally disinterested, it may also be associated with a thirst for power. Here, the movement within Freud's development from knowledge to understanding, from *connaissance* to *compréhension,* can be seen as a move from the negative to the positive. the thirst for power will itself have to be dominated, it is suggested, if self-knowledge and a recognition of the autonomy of others are to be achieved as by-products, so to speak, of the *libido sciendi.* And although the process of the pursuit of knowledge and self-knowledge may be associated with frustration, pain, and disgust, it is also seen ultimately to be the source of self-realization: the desire to know fosters, although it cannot fulfil, the desire to be. But it is also crucial, in Sartrean theory, that the *libido sciendi* is highly sexualized. For Sartre it can also be associated with eating, assimilation, surfeit, and nausea. It is therefore not surprising that he tends, in some contexts, to privilege spontaneous consciousness over reflective knowledge or that those who, like his Flaubert, suffer from a form of cognitive anorexia prefer to substitute the creation of imaginary worlds for knowledge of the real. In *L'Etre et le néant,* Sartre sets aside the biblical association of knowledge with the loss of sexual innocence by instituting what he calls the Actaeon complex: following up the images with which we usually express desire for knowledge he concludes that knowledge is a form of appropriative violation with dominantly sexual overtones. The hunter after knowledge is the Actaeon who surprises Diana at her bath. Sartre does not go on to say in *L'Etre et le néant* that Actaeon's punishment was to be torn to pieces by his own hounds. Freud, however—and much of the drama of the *Scénario* depends upon this topos—at first suppresses but eventually has to confront the potentially destructive and self-destructive power of the search for knowledge, which must not only violate the secrets of the other, but violate internalized sexual taboos. Knowledge is poised on a knife edge between creation and destruction, fascination and revulsion, concealment and revelation.[17]

Sartre's ambivalent attitude toward knowledge accounts for much of Freud's inner tension in the *Scénario*. Much of the external tension is created by the evidently dramatic patient-analyst relationship, in which the patient may be catalyst, victim, or collaborator. But the tension is certainly intensified by the way in which Freud's mentors—Meynert, Breuer, Charcot, and Fliess—frustrate or unknowingly abet his ambivalent progress toward knowledge. Each of them exemplifies a particular inadequacy, both intellectual and personal, that Freud must himself transcend in the interests of his own journey toward maturity. Space will not allow an exhaustive discussion of their individual contributions, but one of the strengths of the screenplay is Sartre's adroit creation of elaborate and economical, if often fictitious, intersections between these relationships and their implications. The presentation of Meynert is typical of these.

I suggested earlier that in focusing the Freud-Meynert drama upon Meynert's commitment to Helmholtzian mechanism Sartre is really grinding his own anti-positivist axe. But Meynert also serves to exemplify a Freud-Sartre drama. Since hysteria, and particularly male hysteria, cannot be explained in purely physiological terms, Meynert at first refuses to recognize it as a condition: it is a form of "comedy" or "lie." Yet he himself constantly exhibits a wide variety of hysterical symptoms, while maintaining, in the kind of Sartrean phrase that characterizes the transparency of consciousness itself: "I know myself: I am as clear as spring water" (SF, 45). Is this an example of Sartrean bad faith, the result of conscious censorship, or of Freudian repression? Sartre mischievously gives himself the benefit of the doubt by expanding into a whole character portrayal the following brief footnote from Ernest Jones's biography: "Meynert later confessed to Freud on his deathbed that he had himself been a classical case of male hysteria, but had always managed to conceal the fact; incidentally it is known that he was a very erratic and neurotic person and a heavy drinker. Some consolation for Freud," adds Jones, "if only a slight one."[18]

Meynert's deathbed confession in the *Scénario* is much more complex in its movement from acknowledged repression to understanding and reconciliation and in its anticipation, even *in extremis*, of a new future. For the confession is also a conversion: a recognition of Freud's greater insight and of the legitimacy of his vocation. Jones's reductive allusion becomes a source of multiple resonances in relation both to Freud's semi-fictional experience and to the reader's response. Meynert reveals that his life has been lived by an Other: "un Autre" with a capital "A" (SF, 157). It is not easy to see how the capitalized Other could be represented cinematographically: nonetheless, this revelation of self-alienation may be variously interpreted. It, too, is orientated toward the future in its intuitive sense of Freud's own ontological difficulties, and it marks a step forward in helping to confirm both his project and his sense of identity. The alienating "Other" may indicate the betrayal of mind by body in hysteria: Freud himself will outgrow such symptoms. It may, on the other hand, remind us of Lacan's view of the unconscious itself as the discourse of the Other. This might be confirmed by Meynert's exhortation to Freud: "My life has been lived not by me, but by an Other. . . . Break the silence" (157). The broken silence (foregrounded in the scene itself by the force of the unsaid) may betoken the translation of that discourse or Meynert's ultimate desire to communicate or the breaking of the conspiracy of silence which frustrates progress. Or Meynert's phrase may suggest that Lacan was himself echoing Sartre's contention in the closing section of *L'Etre et le néant* that consciousness is always inhabited by an Other: not by the empirical other who is implicated in the more familiar notion of our "being-for-others," but by the principle of alterity itself—a principle that we must recognize and existentially assume. (The passage in question is, incidentally, systematically suppressed by poststructuralist critics who wish to set Sartre up as the proponent of a simplistic theory of the unitary consciousness.)

Meynert's confession also confirms his earlier internalizing and betrayal of the power of authority, which he had abused in relation to Freud—at least in Sartre's version of their relationship. Meynert's room is dominated by a reproduction of Michelangelo's Moses (in defiance of actual biographical chronology), and one of his gestures is a convulsive parody of its pose. This discrepancy between an archetypal representation of law and paternal authority and its distorted imitation dramatizes one of the major themes of the *Scénario*: the gap between the power of the paternal imago and the shortcomings of its actual incarnation and the various tensions created by the experiences of this discrepancy at different stages in the development of the individual.

The dream-world, too, is implicated both prospectively and retrospectively in the significance of the Meynert episode. Freud, quite early on, dreams of himself, identified with Meynert, meeting the Emperor Franz-Josef. Sartre emphasizes the familiar Freudian equation of divine, royal, and paternal authority by having a voice intone: "Behold the Emperor, Father of the Fatherland, the Eternal Father" (65). Among the dreams created by Sartre this is one of the more perfunctory, as the Freudian symbolism and the mechanisms of condensation and displacement are at their most overt, but the dream nonetheless mobilizes abundant meanings. It alludes not only to Meynert but to the engraving of Hannibal and his father Hamilcar, which Freud consciously associated with a stand against anti-Semitism and, less consciously, with the father-son relationship: the waking Freud tended to identify himself with Hannibal. In Freud's dream, a Carthaginian soldier who resembles Hannibal shoots the Emperor, while the dream-Freud shouts "No!" (66). The reader (this episode was not included in the final film) will no doubt perceive the incongruity of the identity established between the Emperor figure and the feebly ineffectual Jakob Freud and may come to the apparently banal conclusion that the image of the father-son relationship owes very little to conscious experience and much more to the internalizing of archetypal social and cultural elements. Their development in Freud's later experience could be said to correspond more closely, however, to Sartre's progressive-regressive method than to Freudianism itself: the elements are dialectically changed as they integrate and transcend past experience, moving beyond it toward a synthesis in potential self-realization. This view is confirmed in a later dream, again of Sartre's composition. Its setting is a railway journey in which Meynert, Breuer, and Fliess, each of whom claims to be Freud's father, invite him to join a bizarre game of cards. Jakob Freud is the ticket inspector who later acquires the dignity of Moses. The dream alludes to Freud's railway phobia, generated, it is later revealed, by Freud's repressed childhood memory of the "primal scene," and neatly—perhaps too neatly—associates it with the more Sartrean contingencies of the game of chance. This in turn undermines the notion of the censor and the hollowness of the paternal mandate. The surrogate fathers exemplify inauthenticity and bad faith as they exhort Freud to cheat; each travels without a ticket (Sartre, in *Les Mots*,[19] uses the same image to symbolize his own lack of mandate on his journey through life). The arbitrariness of the authority that Freud's surrogate fathers exercise over him is thus implied; their dream-deaths and the displaced recognition of this arbitrariness signal Freud's growing autonomy. However, the interdependence, both inevitable and unjustifiable, of the traveler and the ticket inspector is not completely understood until later. Freud's resentment against his natural father, briefly revived at Jakob's deathbed, partly inspires but is eventually liquidated by his revision of his seduction theory, his acceptance of his own intuitions concerning infantile sexuality, and his forgiveness of Jakob's pusillanimous responses to anti-Semitism. It will fall to Freud, the latter-day Hannibal, to avenge the oppressed Carthaginians. Acceptance and *compréhension,* rather than scientific explanation (or the pseudo-scientific calculation peddled by Fliess and now rejected) reveal that it is essential for the subject to free himself of the irrationality of the created father image and recognize the natural father for what he is: a freedom and an acceptance that seem, in Sartre's view, to go beyond the recognition and liquidation of the Oedipus complex. It is this acceptance that, in part, heralds Freud's eventual transition to belated maturity and explains his earlier aggression as a son. The ineffectual Jakob ultimately proves to have been Freud's true but unwitting mentor.

The associated dreams of the Emperor and the railway journey and the two deathbed scenes—those of Meynert and Jakob—lead to the implicit recognition that Meynert had played the role of the Moses whom Freud would have wished his father to be. But Meynert's role indicates in yet other ways the dynamic and evolving structure that Sartre reads into Freud's experience. Freud's resentment of Meynert is ostensibly motivated, in part at least, by the fact that Meynert had denied the existence of hysteria and had both publicly and privately attacked Freud's espousal of hypnotic suggestion after his visit to Charcot's clinic. But Sartre shows this resentment to be itself in bad faith: Freud had abandoned this method because, in part at least, he was afraid of what it might reveal about his own psyche; and on his deathbed Meynert is as perceptive about Freud as he is about himself. Such revelations are precisely, he now insists, the risk Freud must take. Meynert had identified himself with God the Father; he now warns Freud, echoing a familiar Sartrean motif, that he must make, if necessary, a pact with the devil.

This eruption of Faustian hyperbole might suggest a touch of melodramatic overstatement on Sartre's part, if it were not for its basis in Freud's often expressed admiration for Goethe. As it is, it prepares us for the tongue-in-cheek zest with which Sartre characterizes Wilhelm Fliess as the Mephistophelian tempter. Fliess would now be regarded as a charlatan and eventually was so regarded by Freud, but, as their correspondence indicates,

Freud became extraordinarily dependent upon him and remained so until the age of about forty-five in what Jones described as a form of delayed adolescence. Sartre rightly portrays Fliess as subscribing to an extreme form of biological determinism, thereby reinforcing the influence of the Helmholtz tradition from which Freud, according to Sartre, had tried to free himself in rebelling against Meynert. Fliess was a specialist in diseases of the ear, nose, and throat who was convinced that all our vital activities, our illnesses, even the date of our death, are related to various types of sexual periodicity, which he calculated according to a complex numerological system. He also believed that there is a close relationship between genital activities and the mucous membrane of the nose, which led him to postulate a nasal reflex neurosis associated with sexual vasomotor disturbances. Sartre is quite right in attributing to Fliess a rather manic kind of pansexualism, which he earlier mistakenly attributed to Freud: he makes amends to Freud by allowing him to establish his theory of the death instincts during the Fliess period but independently of, indeed in defiance of, Fliess. (Freud in fact elaborated this theory much later, during the first world war.) Sartre omits the fact that the relationship between the death instinct and what Freud called the "demonic" tendency to repetition may itself be traced back to Fliess's theory of periodicity. But be that as it may, in the screenplay, Sartre, while dramatizing the undoubted fascination exercised by Fliess, is anxious to discriminate between Fliess's views and Freud's. Freud's theory of bisexuality may owe much to Fliess, but Fliess's hypotheses are shown to be crudely quantitative: Freud's are "lived," Sartre suggests, precisely in his relationship to Fliess; he approaches him with "an air of almost homosexual provocation" (365).

Freud and Fliess share, for a time, an attitude toward Freud's patients that implies that the patients simply offer experimental material that may be exploited for the verification, rather than falsification, of hypotheses. This attitude also implies that knowledge is valued as a source of power. But Fliess's thirst for knowledge is seen to remain at the level of a dehumanized pseudo-scientific curiosity, unaccompanied by any desire for self-knowledge, and to be methodologically flawed in its tendency to confuse hypotheses with facts. For Freud, on the other hand, epistemological issues are increasingly seen to be complicated by moral problems, including the rather basic but undoubtedly dramatic one of whether the revelation of the truth in analysis may prove to be therapeutic or destructive. This dilemma underlies the struggle for Freud's conscience that Sartre contrives between Fliess and the humane but perhaps pusillanimous Breuer, who believes that it may sometimes be necessary to lie to the patient. Breuer's moral ambivalence is compounded by the phenomenon of transference: he is so disturbed by the phantom pregnancy of his hysterical patient Cecily Körtner that he abandons her treatment, which is subsequently taken up by Freud. Breuer rationalizes his abdication by adducing the dangers of revealing the truth. For Freud, truth is precisely what is at stake.

Nonetheless, Freud, in Sartre's account, does not come well out of the case histories. His treatment of Cecily Körtner is, however, an exception. This cannot be accounted for entirely in terms of the inadequacies of the earlier hypnotic-cathartic method and the superiority of free association—the talking cure—which Freud, according to Sartre, learns from Cecily. The hypnotic-cathartic method is already, of course, an advance on the method of hypnotic suggestion, in which the patient is hypnotized and the physician then gives the patient instructions that will rid him of the symptom. In Sartre's portrayal of Charcot, he is shown to have complete mastery over his patients, who are reduced to puppet-like automata. There is a double denial of autonomy: hysteria eclipses their freedom, and the scientist reduces it still further. In the hypnotic-cathartic method, the patient is hypnotized but is then encouraged to talk, at the same time giving the doctor information and freeing himself of the symptom. In the fictional case of Karl Schwartz, the Oedipal son of a general, Sartre's Freud is horrified by the patient's verbal and symbolic enactment, under hypnosis, of his parricidal and incestuous desires—horrified, it is implied, because he is forced to recognize these impulses in himself. Although there are signs, when the patient wakes, of recovery from his neurosis, Freud is so disturbed that he refuses to continue with the case, and he orders the patient to be locked up again—"*double*-locked" (493)—a fairly obvious symbol of Freud's own repression. Failure here, it is suggested, is clearly the responsibility of the therapist. Even so, one is left with the sense, too, that the method is deficient in that it does not allow the significance of the patient's phantasies to become accessible to his consciousness. This, in Sartre's view, would be the advantage of the free-association method, as fictionally exemplified in the case of Cecily Körtner in the *Scénario*. Sartre is biographically correct in indicating that the method is, in a sense, the discovery of the patient: she refuses to submit to Freud's insistence that she should answer his questions and is therefore allowed to follow her own train of thought. In Sartre's version, this recognition of the patient's conscious initiative establishes a much more collaborative relationship between patient and analyst, involving mutual revelation through intuition, empathy, and reciprocity, rather than through power and violation or through reliance upon theories of the mechanics of energy and economy as an explanatory model. Sartre has so constructed this case history that it is invulnerable to the criticism he levelled against psychoanalysis in 1939: the signifier no longer stands in an external causal relationship to the signified. And Cecily is not the victim—or not simply the victim—of passively experienced traumas: it is also her *intentions* that remain unconscious for so long.

However, a certain ambivalence in Sartre's attitude toward Freud does seem to persist right to the end of the *Scénario*. The Freud who, in practice, refuses to impose any conceptual grid upon his treatment of Cecily presents his findings a little later to Fliess with cut-and-dried dogmatism (395). (Even so, Fliess is disappointed to find that the place of Science has been usurped.) Along with his growing sympathy for Freud as a man, Sartre continues to express skepticism concerning psychoanalysis as a system and a movement. The beginning of psychoanalysis as a system is conventionally thought to date from the discovery of free association; it is no accident that Sartre decides to close the *Scénario* at this point. Freud's assumption of intellectual fatherhood, which provides the closing lines of the *Scénario,* marks the beginning of the psychoanalytic movement. There is some irony in Freud's claim to fatherhood: it appears, on the one hand, as an affirmation of his emancipation from Meynert, Breuer, Fliess, and Jakob Freud. But the claim may also signify an internalizing of the other in a desire for established identity—an internalizing of the super-ego, of the father's command to the son, and an intimation, therefore, of bad faith. It may be read not only as an expression of emancipation but as an affirmation of authority. Then there is a further ambiguity. Sartre's synopsis ends with the words of the forty-one-year-old Freud: "It was my turn to play the role of the father" (570)—simultaneously a conscious assumption of and a distance from bad faith. In the final scene of the completed *Scénario* Freud asserts: "Now, I am the father"—a much more categorical and therefore less Sartrean affirmation of identity, an identity that is compromised, furthermore, by the inadequacies of Freud's own father figures.

It is clear that Sartre's relation to Freud, brought to vivid life again in the writing of the *Scénario,* becomes much more complex after this attempt at imaginative reconstruction. But it remains ambivalent. Its negative aspects are reinforced by Sartre's transcript of a tape-recorded session of analysis in which the aggression of the analysand is quite eclipsed by the aggression of the analyst.[20] Its positive potential is revealed in the rehabilitation of another Sartrean anti-hero and in an even more monumental synthesis of existential psychoanalysis and Freudian insight: the would-be totalizing understanding of Flaubert in *L'Idiot de la famille.*

## ABBREVIATIONS

ET: Jean-Paul Sartre, *Esquisse d'une théorie des émotions.*
SE: Sigmund Freud, *The Standard Edition of the Complete Psychological Works of Sigmund Freud.*
SF: Jean-Paul Sartre, *Le Scénario Freud.*
ST: Jean-Paul Sartre, *Sketch for a Theory of the Emotions.*

## NOTES

1. References will be given in the text to this edition: Jean-Paul Sartre, *Le Scénario Freud,* preface by Jean-Bertrand Pontalis (Paris: Gallimard, 1984), henceforth abbreviated SF; translations by the author. For differing accounts of Sartre's relations with Huston concerning the film, see Huston's autobiography *An Open Book* (London: Macmillan, 1981) and Sartre's letters to Simone de Beauvoir in *Lettres au Castor et à quelques autres,* vol. 2 (Paris: Gallimard, 1983), 356-62. For the vicissitudes of the genesis of the *Scénario* and for a stimulating interpretation in a different perspective, see Annette Lavers, "Sartre and Freud," *French Studies* 41 (1987): 298-317. The Sartre-Freud relationship was also the subject of Michel Favart's television program "Sartre contre Sartre" (25 and 28 September and 1 October 1991), in which some crucial scenes of the *Scénario* were screened. (See Michael Scriven, "Television Images of Sartre," *French Cultural Studies* 3 [1992]: 87-92.) I am grateful to Michael Scriven for having drawn this program to my attention.
2. Jean-Paul Sartre, *L'Etre et le néant: essai d'ontologie phénoménologique* (Paris: Gallimard, 1943); *Being and Nothingness: An Essay on Phenomenological Ontology,* trans. Hazel E. Barnes (London: Methuen, 1958; reprint 1972).
3. Jean-Paul Sartre, *Critique de la raison dialectique (précédé de Questions de méthode), I: théorie des ensembles pratiques* (Paris: Gallimard, 1960); *Search for a Method,* trans. Hazel E. Barnes (New York: Knopf, 1963); *Critique of Dialectical Reason, I: Theory of Practical Ensembles,* trans. Alan Sheridan-Smith, ed. Jonathan Rée (London: New Left Books, 1976).
4. Jean-Paul Sartre, *Esquisse d'une théorie des émotions* (Paris: Hermann, 1965); *Sketch for a Theory of the Emotions,* trans. Philip Mairet (London: Methuen, 1962), henceforth abbreviated, respectively, ET and ST.
5. For a particularly clear account of Sartre's complex attitude to Freud and its development, see Christina Howells, "Sartre and Freud," *French Studies* 33 (1979): 157-76.
6. Jean-Paul Sartre, *La Transcendance de l'ego: esquisse d'une description phénoménologique,* ed. Sylvie le Bon (Paris: Vrin, 1965); *The Transcendence of the Ego: An Existentialist Theory of Consciousness,* trans. Forrest Williams and Robert Kirkpatrick (New York: The Noonday Press, 1962).
7. Sartre's distinction between pre-reflective and reflective consciousness, between consciousness and knowledge, and between the "lived" *[le vécu]* and

the "known" are relevant to his arguments concerning bad faith and the censor. Space precludes more detailed discussion, but it is worth noting that the notion of the "lived," which is somewhat ambiguously related to the unconscious, is described in 1970 in terms that would not have been out of place in his description of bad faith in 1943. His later formula runs as follows: the "lived" is that mode of experience in which "consciousness is shrewd enough to decide to forget" (*Situations, IX* [Paris: Gallimard, 1972], 108). In this form of tactical and teleological forgetting, the *activity* of consciousness is still very much in the foreground. Even so, it is possible to detect in the early Sartre an acknowledgment of an element of opacity within consciousness, which is in tension with his general emphasis upon its transparency. In *L'Etre et le néant*, for instance, the fundamental project of the individual is "lived" rather than "known," which is why existential psychoanalysis may be required in order to bring it to light. The distinction between the lived and the known seems to prefigure Sartre's partial acceptance of Freudian theory.
8. For further discussion of Sartre, Dilthey, and the *Verstehen* tradition, see Rhiannon Goldthorpe, "Understanding the Committed Writer," *The Cambridge Companion to Sartre*, ed. Christina Howells (Cambridge: Cambridge University Press, 1992), 140-77.
9. Sigmund Freud, *The Interpretation of Dreams*, in *The Standard Edition of the Complete Psychological Works of Sigmund Freud*, vols. 4 and 5 (London: The Hogarth Press, 1953), henceforth abbreviated SE.
10. Freud's discovery of intentions and meanings in neurotic behavior might seem to bring him closer to the *Verstehen* school. However, as Gerald Izenberg points out, quoting from *The Interpretation of Dreams* (the emphasis is his): "'interpreting a dream implies assigning a "meaning" to it—that is, *replacing it* by something which fits into the chain of our mental acts as a link having a validity and importance equal to the rest' (SE, 4:96). The element to be interpreted was not to have its meaning drawn out of itself in terms of manifest contextual significance but was to be replaced by another element, itself meaningful, whose relationship to the first was a causal one and in fact mechanically causal" (Gerald N. Izenberg, *The Existentialist Critique of Freud: The Crisis of Autonomy* [Princeton: Princeton University Press, 1976], 18). The concepts of *Verstehen*, on the other hand, as exemplified, however diversely, in the work of Dilthey, Weber, and Jaspers, "rest on the idea of meaning as immanent in, not causally related to, the expression to be interpreted" (18). It might be added that while the word "interpretation" could be construed as relating to the hermeneutic tradition with which the *Verstehen* approach is closely associated, it does not correspond exactly to the German word *Deutung*, which, according to Laplanche and Pontalis, would seem to be closer to "explanation" or "clarification." See Jean Laplanche and Jean-Bertrand Pontalis, *The Language of Psychoanalysis*, trans. Donald Nicholson-Smith (London: The Hogarth Press, 1973), 228.
11. Sigmund Freud, *Project for a Scientific Psychology*, SE, vol. 1, (London: The Hogarth Press, 1966).

12. Sartre's appropriation of Freud for the *Verstehen* tradition anticipates Paul Ricoeur's philosophical study *De l'interprétation: essai sur Freud* (Paris: Seuil, 1965); *Freud and Philosophy: An Essay on Interpretation*, trans. Denis Savage (New Haven: Yale University Press, 1970). Ricoeur traces with particular subtlety the divergences and convergences between Freud's practice (as distinct from his metapsychology) and the hermeneutics of *compréhension*.
13. Jean-Paul Sartre, *Les Carnets de la drôle de guerre* (Paris: Gallimard, 1983); *War Diaries: Notebooks from a Phoney War*, trans. Quintin Hoare (London: Verso, 1984).
14. Jean-Paul Sartre, *L'Idiot de la famille: Gustave Flaubert de 1821 à 1851*, 3 vols. (Paris: Gallimard, vols. 1 and 2, 1971; vol. 3, 1972; revised ed., 1988); *The Family Idiot*, trans. Carol Cosman (Chicago: University of Chicago Press, vol. 1, 1981; vol. 2, 1987; vol. 3, 1989).
15. See "Le Carnet 'Dupuis,'" in Jean-Paul Sartre, *Œuvres romanesques*, ed. Michel Contat and Michel Rybalka, with the collaboration of Geneviève Idt and George H. Bauer (Paris: Gallimard "Pléiade," 1981), 1685. More elaborate definitions and applications are central to the *Carnets de la drôle de guerre*, the *Cahiers pour une morale [Notes for an Ethics]* (Paris: Gallimard, 1983), and the second volume of the *Critique de la raison dialectique: l'intelligibilité de l'histoire* (Paris: Gallimard, 1985). All are posthumously published works.
16. Sigmund Freud, *Studies on Hysteria*, SE, vol. 2 (London: The Hogarth Press, 1955).
17. More generally, knowledge is associated with the hermeneutic tradition of interpreting the hidden in terms of goals and means and ends, rather than causes. And here another distinction between knowledge and understanding may be noted: while the former is associated with sexuality, *compréhension*, for the Sartre of the *Cahiers pour une morale* (1947-48), is associated with love—with *agape* rather than *eros*.
18. Ernest Jones, *Sigmund Freud: Life and Work*, vol. 1 (London: The Hogarth Press, 1953), 253.
19. Jean-Paul Sartre, *Les Mots* (Paris: Gallimard, 1964); *The Words*, trans. Bernard Frechtman (New York: Braziller, 1964).
20. See Jean-Paul Sartre, "L'Homme au magnétophone," *Situations, IX* (Paris: Gallimard, 1972).

# 2

## Flaubert's Blind Spot. The Fetishization of Subjectivity: Some Notes on the Constitution of Gustave in Sartre's *L'Idiot de la famille*
### Christina Howells

Flaubert has a blind spot. It is his Ego. Sartre calls it "the blind spot of reflexivity."[1] This blind spot leads him down a blind alley into a trap—that of the fetishization of subjectivity.

What does this mean? And how does the blind spot relate to the fetish? To understand Sartre's somewhat sibylline pronouncements we must turn back from his last philosophical work, *The Family Idiot*, to his first, *The Transcendence of the Ego*.[2]

In *The Transcendence of the Ego,* Sartre lays down the fundamental tenet of existentialism. He argues against Edmund Husserl that there is no inner self, no core of personal identity. The ego is not transcendental, it is simply transcendent, an imaginary construct rather than an origin; it is not a core of being but an extraversion, a product; the ego is the self I make myself become, not the self that makes me what I am. The ego is not *in* consciousness, it is a product *of* consciousness. What is more, consciousness itself is not personal, it is impersonal or at most pre-personal. The ego has two faces, the I and the me, but neither of them can be identified with the subject (proper). The "me" is, as grammar correctly decrees, an object, not a subject. When I talk about me or myself, I am taking an outsider's viewpoint, the viewpoint of the other; the unity and selfhood I may detect in myself are the unity imposed from outside, part of the taming, objectifying processes that make of a *flux vital* (IF, 360) a relatively tidy synthesis.

The "I" is the subjective correlative of the "me." Like the body, it is usually transcended toward an external activity or focus: I am running, writing, talking—the ground to be covered, the subject of conversation are my focus, not the "I" who is the subject of my sentence. Indeed, this is the "I" which is my blind spot. For, Sartre argues, if I want to turn my attention reflexively back on myself, I am doomed to disappointment. I can sense, perhaps even imagine I glimpse obliquely, the "I" when I say, "I'm writing" or "I'm busy," but if I try to capture it for scrutiny, my gaze meets only a frustrating emptiness and obscurity. Sartre's explanation for this is technical—it is in terms of the different degrees of reflexivity involved in the different activities. The "I" who was writing or busy has in fact disappeared by the time I try to examine it. The "I" is now engaged in a new activity: the attempt to capture its essence (itself), and all it will be able to find therefore is its own (frustrated) attempt. I can never capture myself as subject, only as object. In Sartre's words: "the Ego only ever appears when one is not looking at it . . . *by nature* the Ego is fleeting" (TE, 70), so "the intuition of the Ego is a perpetually deceptive mirage" (TE, 69).

If the ego is a deceptive mirage that appears only when one is not looking at it, we can now understand in what sense it is Flaubert's blind spot: it is very literally what is outside his range of vision. At first sight this description appears to lack specificity—surely the ego is everyone's blind spot, a self we imagine we have but which, precisely because it is imaginary, can never be grasped. However, Sartre makes clear that the situation is both more disturbing and more complex in Flaubert's case, because, unlike most of us, Flaubert never feels any degree of identification with his ego (IF, 175). The normal construction of the ego involves a dialectic of passivity and activity, of otherness and selfhood, in which the necessarily objectifying views of me held by others are integrated within my view of myself and become part of my project of self-construction. "For most of us," Sartre writes, "passivity and activity are equitably involved: the dialectic of the Ego (Me—I—selfhood, alterity—action and play-acting) is a complex movement: and often the Self is simply the horizon of the *reflexive act,* in this case it is vision and oath but there is no play-acting. There is an objective reality of the Self, but this psychic object is . . . the pure correlative of reflexive selfhood—better still, selfhood is produced through the synthetic activity" (IF, 175-76). All these different determinants mean that the ego is a construct entailing internalization of the views of others but also reflexivity, spontaneity, and project. "The *person,*" Sartre writes, "is neither entirely undergone nor entirely constructed: moreover, it *is* not" (656). It may involve bad faith and error, but these terms necessarily imply the possibility of resistance—by recognizing the elements of alienation and mystification in my self-image.

Flaubert's ego, on the other hand, is more thoroughly alienated—he experiences it as coming to him only from others; he does not attempt to ratify it but rather to *act* it out (175). His self is introduced into his subjectivity, as it were, from outside. In Sartre's terms it is *allogène*, it is generated by the other, not the self.

This fundamental alienation, Sartre maintains, is a consequence of Gustave's lack of valorization by his parents and in particular his lack of maternal love. I cannot explore here Sartre's enormously lengthy examination of the various features of the young Flaubert's upbringing and family life. But I will sketch out briefly the theoretical framework of his argument about mother-love. Put simply, it is mother-love that induces in infants a feeling of necessity and justification and makes the world appear meaningful. The unquestioning love that babies experience from their mothers is what gives them the impression that their existence is significant and that they have a purpose. This is, in Sartre's view, an illusion. Indeed, by masking contingency, mother-love is a form of alienation, but, says Sartre, it is an "aliénation heureuse," not just a happy but also a *fortunate* alienation. It confers on children their "mandate to live" and gives them an illusion of necessity, which is itself a necessary illusion. This is precisely what Flaubert lacks—the illusory security that will allow him to abandon it *as* illusory in later life in order to advance beyond meaninglessness to construct his own meaning. Like Mallarmé, Flaubert discovers the bitter "truths" of existential anguish prematurely. "Happy children discover plenitude as an original given; negation, absence and all the forms of Nothingness appear to them afterwards as local insufficiencies, provisional lacunae, fleeting contradictions: in short Nothingness is posterior to Being."[3] Mother-love is an essential element in the child's future transcendence of his alienation and contingency.

In a sense, then, Flaubert may be seen as an anti-Roquentin. In *Nausea* Roquentin starts from a comfortable position of ontological security, which is unexpectedly shattered in adult life by an increasing painful awareness of contingency, absurdity, and alienation. We do not see where Roquentin eventually goes after his illusions have been destroyed, but we do witness his attempt to understand and come to terms with the new truths he is uncovering. Flaubert, on the other hand, will never come to terms with these truths, for he lacks the basis from which to do so. He will spend his life fleeing from the abyss of nothingness precisely because it was never hidden from him, even at the earliest stages of his life.

Flaubert, then, does not share the common human delusion of self-identity and self-coincidence. He experiences himself almost entirely through the eyes of others. It is as if he were not himself, but rather an alter ego (IF, 311, 407), a product of others and in particular of his family.[4] This childhood alienation prevents Flaubert from participating in the bourgeois individualism of his age—he has no conception of the incomparable specificity of selfhood on which to construct the common myth (IF, 347-48). The young Gustave is estranged from himself. Sartre describes his inability to reconcile his experience with any real notion of his own identity: the child makes no real connection between what Sartre calls "le flux vital sans Ego," a vital ego-less flux—the flux of consciousness, on the one hand, and on the other, the "absent Ego that other people call Gustave" (360); "le soi reste formel" ["the self remains formal"] (407). In a striking phrase Sartre writes of Gustave's "Ego martyrisé" (387), based, I suggest, not so much on the notion of religious martyrdom, but rather on the French phrase "un enfant martyrisé," an abused child.

But, of course, total self-alienation is not possible—Gustave may not identify with his ego as constituted by others, but he still necessarily participates in the reflexive self-consciousness of all conscious beings: "intimate experience," Sartre writes, "is characterized ontologically by doubling or self-presence" (394). And his reflexivity or *ipséité* (selfhood), may not be thetic, or fully self-aware, but it nonetheless constitutes an unseen, secret, (potential) subject that undermines the alter ego from which Flaubert is alienated. Indeed this non-thetic reflexivity lies hidden like a *ver rongeur* (408), a canker at the heart of his alienated ego:

> The true Gustave, the child without a Self, is only himself in secret by the adulteration of the ends imposed upon him (408). . . . a clandestine Ego, not seen . . . not understood, constructs itself like a lack in the Other . . . it is constituted reflexively *in order to remain unseen*, . . . on the horizon . . . vampirizing the Alter Ego. . . . (410)

And it is this clandestine canker, this secret vampire self, that in fact constitutes Flaubert's subjectivity. Just as we looked back at *The Transcendence of the Ego* to illustrate Flaubert's blind spot, so we will look now briefly at *Being and Nothingness*[5] to understand how precisely the *subject* should be understood before we see what it means for Flaubert to fetishize it. In *Being and Nothingness*, Sartre gives a complex account of what he understands by the notion of subject in its relation to consciousness. But just as the subject cannot be identified with the ego, which is only a construct, it cannot be identified with consciousness, which is precisely a "transcendental field without a subject" (EN, 291). Consciousness, we know, is intentional, always conscious of something outside itself. However, in its spontaneous self-consciousness, that is its reflexivity, consciousness becomes subjective; subjectivity is the "instantaneous *cogito*" (83), "consciousness (of) consciousness." This means that subjectivity is an immediate, untheorized self-awareness, the spontaneous reflexivity of consciousness when it is directed toward something beyond itself. It is never self-identical, even in its reflexivity. If it is *pour-soi,* for-itself, this is precisely because it is not *soi,* not itself (119-20). It is riven, split, it is its own negation (65). It is what it is not and is not what it is (97). Its very reflexivity, its presence to itself, is a mark of its lack of self-coincidence (120)—its being is always deferred. Consciousness is always elsewhere, it is *diasporique* (182). This is what enables it to escape identity (119). The subject then, like the ego, is a product. It is the product not of an imaginary synthesis but of the reflexivity of consciousness. No more than the ego is it an essential core of selfhood. It is not a *subjectum,* an underlying ground or foundation (Greek: *hypokeimenon*). It is rather the very lack of foundation or self-coincidence of consciousness that constitutes the subject. In this sense the Sartrean subject is *originally* split, or riven. (We might remark in passing that this philosophical explanation could provide the essential grounds for understanding the paradoxical notion—common to romanticism—of the "native wound," Flaubert's *plaie native.* The subject is not divided *après coup,* it is constituted precisely by division.)

In all this Sartre is, of course, very close to Lacan, especially the Lacan of the '40s and '50s (and we know that the famous paper on the Mirror stage was first elaborated in the same year as *The Transcendence of the Ego,* 1936). For Lacan, too, the ego is an imaginary synthesis that alienates the subject in its illusion of stable selfhood. It comes between the subject and its attempts at self-realization because of its "irreducible inertia" (LE, 109). It provides not truth or reality but merely a potential *alibi* (LE, 375). For Lacan "the true subject" is "the subject of the unconscious."[6] Lacan and Sartre both reject entirely the aim and purpose of ego psychology—"the reintegration of the subject with his ego" (LE, 453)—a reintegration that for Lacan would be "devastating" (LE, 454), for Sartre impossible. For Sartre and Lacan the riven nature of subjectivity may be experienced as a curse but is, in fact, rather a salvation, for it is what protects us from the worst ravages of self-identity and, indeed, the death of consciousness (TE, 23). In Lacan's terms it is the "happy fault of life where man, in being distinct from his essence, discovers his existence" (LE, 345).

How does this description of the Sartrean subject help us understand his account of Flaubert? Sartre, in fact, appears to view Flaubert as a kind of test case for his theory of subjectivity, the exception, perhaps, that proves the rule. For whereas most of us invest sufficiently in the ego we construct to feel we have a self of sorts, even if it can never be as secure as we would like, and many people invest excessively in their ego to the point of identifying almost entirely with it, Flaubert, on the contrary, fails to achieve even a minimal sense of stable selfhood. Gustave's feeling of alienation from himself and his lack of belief in the usual totalizing egoic constructs we use to synthesize the disparate elements of our lives mean that he experiences his life as episodic, his emotions as intermittent, and his perceptions as fragmentary. He feels multiple, not unified: "'I have lived many lives,'" he writes, "'thousands of lives'" (IF, 223). And Sartre explicitly uses him as a test case when he asks: "Can one imagine such an *effritement* [an erosion, a crumbling, a disintegration] of experience without destroying the idea of subject?" (IF, 223). His answer is revealing, apparently evasive ("yes and no," he replies); it in fact leads him to reject the terms of the question itself as "too Kantian" and "too intellectual." The Kantian "unity of apperception" cannot be identified with the self-divided Sartrean subject. Indeed, the Kantian "I think," which can accompany all my representations, *need* not, in Sartre's view, and frequently *does* not, do so (TE). Reflexivity and the sense of self, or subjecthood, that accompanies it is always possible but is certainly not always present or actual. Much of my experience is accompanied by no thetic sense of selfhood whatsoever.

It is the very fragility of subjectivity that lies at the root of what Sartre calls Flaubert's fetishization of it. The elements of his constitution—that is, the alienation of his ego, his sense of the fragmentary nature of experience, and his premature awareness of his own lack of self-identity—lead him to fetishize what in fact is not susceptible to objectification or thoroughgoing unification. Sartre uses Octave Mannoni's article on *Verleugnung, dénégation* or denial (disavowal), to explain his use of the term fetish. Mannoni's well known paper, entitled "Je sais bien ... mais quand même" ["I know well ... but even so"] shows how this kind of denial (disavowal) arises when a cherished belief (a desire) is threatened by reality. The subject repudiates the experience and attempts against the evidence to sustain his belief. He may deny reality but he cannot eradicate it, and his belief can henceforth subsist only in a modified form. (In the classical Freudian account, the revelation to the child that its mother has no penis is not fully accepted by the child who ultimately adopts a fetish as a substitute for the missing maternal phallus [IF, 427-28].)

Sartre's discussion of Flaubert's "fetishism" involves necessarily an account of the latter's sexuality, in particular a fascinating analysis of his private letters, including his homosexual experiences and masturbatory fantasies. Fortunately this material is outside the domain of my paper, so we must stay with the perhaps drier topic of subjectivity. Flaubert denies the real and valorizes the imaginary (720). His awareness of his own contingency and lack of identity leads him to "*fetishize* subjective experience" (432), lack is transformed into plenitude. *Dénégation* (440) lies at the heart of his choice of the imaginary, but the reality—that his self is *un*real and imaginary—will undermine all his attempts to deny it. Even at moments when Flaubert tries hardest to free himself from alienation and alterity, it is still evident between the lines of his very denial of it. Sartre takes the example of Flaubert's images of subjectivity—Gustave repeatedly uses the metaphor of the mirror to express his most intimate relation with himself (680). What he *intends* to say is apparently that we do not need other people to valorize us—we can be our own best judges. But what he *implies* through the metaphor of the mirror is precisely the opposite of this. "Gustave chooses as image of the *pour-soi* the object which manifests, in a mirage, his *being-for-others*," Sartre writes (681). He may think he is seeking in the mirror to see himself as he is, but the mirror can never be more than "un *ersatz* figé de l'autre" ["a frozen *ersatz* of the other"] (761). The mirror can neither show him himself as subject nor yet confirm him externally as would the other. The mirror provides an imaginary realm that can only ever reflect unreal images and further abysses of specular alienation.

It is not only from his ego that Gustave feels alienated; he is equally alienated from himself as acting subject: "the subject which inhabits him is not himself but a closed being, impenetrable, absent, which takes on consistency through his gestures without thereby ceasing to be a stranger to him" (728). Gustave cannot assume his own agency. Action cannot be differentiated from play-acting. Sartre refers to his "sujet-autre," subject as other (730). Gustave's ego, then (defined now as "pôle de la psyché, quasi objet"—pole of the psyche, quasi object) has no being: and he imagines his own subjectivity rather than experiencing it (731-32). Sartre's analysis shows him living on three levels of unreality—firstly attempting vainly to make his play-acting real, secondly internalizing his permanent derealization, and thirdly assuming it (735). But the final assumption is never possible without external justification and valorization, the lack of which has been precisely the cause of the problem. Flaubert lives his relation to his self as a vicious circle, a prey to his "imaginary Ego" (737) and in a false relation to his subjectivity. His *Je* is no more than a disguise (765), a mask that conceals any incipient experience of *ipséité*, or spontaneous reflexivity, rather than focusing it.

We can now understand better the implications of Sartre's remarks about "the true Gustave" as a clandestine canker, remaining unseen, and vampirizing the alter ego. The terms convey the depths of Flaubert's alienation—not only is his ego alienated, his very subjectivity is vitiated, transformed from a spontaneous product of reflexive self-awareness into a kind of alternative Self, dependent on its opposition to the self others have constructed for him. And this is the "fetishization of subjectivity" of Sartre's striking phrase. The private self that Gustave seeks to retreat to in his intimate tête-à-tête with himself or his mirror is, as he recognizes, no more than an *image*. "Le *soi* . . . est une pure image" ["The *self* . . . is a pure image"] (915). Consequently it is inflated with all the attributes an imaginary subject might aspire to—an image of divine, solitary creativity. All his inadequacies and failures are transformed into signs of election, his weaknesses into strengths, not through the struggle with the real, which genuine self-transformation would involve, but simply in the unreal, imaginary domain. As a child and adolescent, then, Gustave does precisely *nothing* to achieve the spiritual greatness he yearns for. Nothing can be trusted to survive the ravages of the reality-principle. Gustave's *Verleugnung,* denial (disavowal), is very deep-seated. Sartre describes his fetishization in the following terms: "Gustave attributes to himself in the imaginary the sublime and heroic subjectivity of his fictive Ego" (917). He fills what he feels to be the infinite lack he holds within him with an imagined infinite plenitude (918). He compensates for his failures by inventing a "sublime Ego" out of the reach of any real assaults.

The final chapter of this story would involve an analysis of Flaubert's relations with language, through which he ultimately frees himself from his alienation to the imaginary by bringing the imaginary back into the domain of the real in the form of writing. But this would take us too far beyond his blind spot and his fetishization of subjectivity. Indeed, it would take us further into Sartre's relations with Lacan, which I have referred to very briefly here and explored at greater length elsewhere but which need a far more intensive treatment than anyone has accorded them so far. I will simply close by remarking that Sartre's analysis of Flaubert's *personnalisation,* the stage that follows his *constitution,* on which I have been focusing, the stage that in Marxist terms is the point at which Flaubert makes something out of what has been made of him, is very close to the Lacanian notion of subject. For the Lacanian subject, split and derelict as it may be, is never entirely abandoned; indeed, in a form of paradoxical (and typically Sartrean) *loser wins,* it is constituted through a synthesis with language, itself dependent on a lack of self-identity and an alienation to the imaginary. Sartre's Flaubert could be the prototype for the *man* of my final quotation from Lacan: "Without that gaping lack that alienates [man] to his own image, this symbiosis with the symbolic, in which he is constituted as mortal subject, could not have been produced" (LE, 552). But Sartre is not simply close to Lacan, his notion of subjectivity could also be the prototype for what Derrida has described as a possible way forward for a reinterpretation and reinscription of the subject. In an interview with Jean-Luc Nancy in 1989, Derrida makes the following striking remarks:

> We were speaking of dehiscence, of intrinsic dislocation, of *différance*.... Some might say: but precisely, what we mean by "subject" is not absolute origin, pure will, self-identity or the self-presence of consciousness, but rather this non-coincidence with self. This is a response to which we should return. By what right may this be called a subject? Conversely, by what right may we forbid this to be called a "subject"? I am thinking of those who want to reconstruct, today, a discourse on the subject that no longer has the form of self-mastery, of self-adequation, center and origin of the world, etc., but which would rather define the subject as the finite experience of non-self-identity.[7]

Derrida is clearly not thinking of Sartre, but he could, nonetheless, be describing the Sartrean deconstruction of the subject as he attempted it in various forms in all his major philosophical works, from *Being and Nothingness* through to *The Family Idiot*.

For however fragile the Sartrean subject may appear, however far from the ideal, creative, self-determining agent, a subject of sorts still remains. It may be alienated or non-self-identical; its very fissures and cracks are what lets it escape the deterministic process.

### ABBREVIATIONS

EN: Jean-Paul Sartre, *L'Etre et le néant*.
IF: Jean-Paul Sartre, *L'Idiot de la famille*, vol. 1.
LE: Jacques Lacan, *Ecrits*.
TE: Jean-Paul Sartre, *La Transcendance de l'Ego*.

### NOTES

1. Jean-Paul Sartre, *L'Idiot de la famille* [*The Family Idiot*], vol. 1 (Paris: Gallimard, 1971), 411, henceforth abbreviated IF. Here, as elsewhere, page references to works originally written in French are to the French editions, and translations into English are the author's.
2. Jean-Paul Sartre, *La Transcendance de l'Ego: esquisse d'une description phénoménologique*, first published in *Recherches Philosophiques*, vol. 6, 1936,

reprinted in edition by Sylvie Le Bon (Paris: Vrin, 1965), henceforth abbreviated TE.
3. Jean-Paul Sartre, *Mallarmé: la lucidité et sa face d'ombre* (Paris: Gallimard, 1986), 102-3.
4. Cf. Jacques Lacan, *Ecrits* (Paris: Seuil, 1966), 374-75, henceforth abbreviated LE.
5. Jean-Paul Sartre, *L'Etre et le néant: essai d'ontologie phénoménologique* (Paris: Gallimard, 1943), henceforth abbreviated EN.
6. Jacques Lacan, "Introduction au commentaire de Jean Hyppolite sur la 'Verneinung' de Freud" (1954), LE, 372.
7. Jacques Derrida, "Il faut bien manger, ou le calcul du sujet: entretien (avec J.-L. Nancy)," *Cahiers Confrontations* 20 (winter 1989): 98.

# 3

# Ethics and Revolution in Sartre's *Les Mains sales*

## Charles D. Minahen

The question of ethics in Sartre's philosophical and literary works is one of the most controversial (and fascinating) issues that the author left tantalizingly unresolved. It is also one that obsessed him but that he was never fully able to found phenomenologically. The end of *L'Etre et le néant* is full of promise concerning the subject, and the work's analyses of the now familiar yet ever elusive concepts of "good faith," "bad faith," and "authenticity" seem to move, however sketchily and inconsistently, in that direction.[1] But Sartre was never able subsequently to realize a systematic theory of ethics, due, in no small part certainly, to the emphasis on praxis in his existential phenomenology and its even greater relevance to a study of specific human actions and situations.[2] He did fill some notebooks on ethics, left incomplete in 1948 along with other discarded *fausses pistes*. Two of these that have survived were published posthumously under the title *Cahiers pour une morale*[3] by his heir, Arlette Elkaïm-Sartre, although contrary to Sartre's wishes, his biographer-godson John Gerassi states,[4] raising doubts about the reliability of a work that the author clearly had abandoned and, by his own account, "renounced finishing" (SX, 207).

Sartre's departure from the individual-centered focus of his earlier works and his subsequent adoption of a Marxist view must have rendered the *Cahiers*, to some degree at least, moot. This evolution did, in any case, inspire a revaluation of his early hostile portrayal of "the Other." If the Benny Lévy conversations with Sartre, published in *Le Nouvel Observateur* just before Sartre's death can be believed—Gerassi thinks not[5]—Sartre continued to be concerned with the problem of ethics but had totally rethought the "soi-autrui" ["self-other"] dilemma and had come to place greater value on shared consciousness and fraternity.[6] This was really not, though, a new development. As early as *Les Mains sales* (1948),[7] the specific focus of this study, Sartre fashioned a hero who unhesitatingly sacrifices his own self-interest (and ultimately his life) in an astonishingly genuine and generous act of human compassion, to emerge a veritable paragon of existential virtue and authenticity.[8]

Significantly, this ethical example is presented not in a treatise or essay, but in a play divided into seven tableaux, which draw attention to the setting as a space of human action and conduce readily to the depiction of situations.[9] Like Cicero's practical approach in *De Officiis,* whose discussion of stoic ethics inevitably turns to an analysis of case histories, Sartre's emphasis on praxis in his situational conception of ethics finds a particularly cogent and effective form of exposition in literary (and, in this case, dramatic) representation. In Cicero, particularly when it is a question of difficult moral decisions, each incident is considered on its own merits, and certain basic principles of right and wrong, rooted in common sense or "nature," are applied to an analysis of circumstances, including motives. For Sartre, in situations requiring a moral choice, the determination of good and bad faith rests upon an intuition of the truth or falsity of an intention or act (predicated on "faith" in an unproved or unprovable sense of certainty) and the execution of that act (or inaction) in consonance (good faith) or dissonance (bad faith) with that intuition. Even though Sartre, unlike Cicero, does not explicitly express a solution to each dilemma, an implied judgment often emerges when one considers the situation from the perspective of the ethical theories he was able to elaborate and analyze.

A particularly trenchant example of such a case occurs in *Les Mains sales,* where the question of authenticity is applied to acts committed in the acutely ambiguous moral context of a communist revolution. The situation the author proposes is *in extremis,* since revolution involves by definition a radical overthrow of established orders and systems, thereby isolating actions from any absolute or easily identifiable ethical standard or code. The two main characters of the play, Hugo and Hoederer, are by virtue of their revolt outlaws, and yet this in no way insulates them from accountability for what they do. Their freedom is merely all the more apparent and the responsibility for it all the more explicitly their own. In *Les Mains sales,* the drama turns about an assassination, an act presented as "ownerless" due to the circumstances under which it is committed. Sartre makes it clear that we cannot rely upon the characters themselves to sort out the problem of culpability, since bad faith often masks itself as sincerity. Nevertheless, when words are scrutinized in light of deeds, the hypocrisy that is an unmistakable sign of bad faith is inevitably exposed.

The fact that the play has elicited contradictory responses and judgments corroborates the author's stated unwillingness to impose solutions. Early audiences' empathy for Hugo and certain critics' identification of him as the author's *porte-parole* compelled Sartre, as he embraced more and more fully and passionately the Marxist view, to express his own reading, which came down unequivocally on the side of Hoederer.[10] Since then, the critics have tended to fit their readings to this belated expression of authorial intention, which, when the play is read carefully, does seem to be the most compelling view. Hoederer is authentic and Hugo is "de mauvaise foi" ["in bad faith"], even if the latter, dubbed "un intellectuel anarchiste" (54), that is, a bourgeois convert to the proletarian cause, resembles, albeit superficially, Sartre himself. But the critics, while getting the judgment "right," have not always convincingly and exhaustively explained why it is so, and they have tended to dwell too much on authorial intention at the expense of an open, unprejudiced reading of the text, which, even if it corroborates the author's reading, must ultimately stand by itself and be evaluated on its own terms.

Of the play's two central characters, Hoederer, who exemplifies the important existential distinction between seeming and being, is the least problematic. He is first presented, by means of hearsay reports and opinions of the other characters that precede him on stage, as a traitor to the party's cause, since he is willing to compromise principles for practical gains. His policies seem altogether Machiavelian in his readiness to use any means (to "dirty his hands" as needed) in order to accomplish his ends. This is at first contrasted unfavorably with Hugo's "pure" devotion to the party's revolutionary ideals. It is not the party's ultimate vindication of Hoederer's strategy that reveals his authenticity but rather his unflinching commitment to the course of action he has decided upon, despite the risk of assassination that it engenders. In this respect, he is a clear example of what Sartre terms "pure reflection," the authentic mode of consciousness in which self-reflection and action are integrated and simultaneous. His repeated demonstrations of strength, self-confidence, and integrity are clear signs of such authenticity, which also manifests itself as courage (when for example he turns his back to Hugo knowing he conceals a revolver) and compassion (when after Hugo's failure to act he specifically avoids taking action that would further humiliate him). His repeated assurances of "confiance" ["confidence"] are not a pose or a devious strategy aimed at manipulation. They are sincere, and he is willing to take life-threatening risks to prove it. The lie he blurts out in his dying breath to protect his friend-turned-assassin testifies to his capacity to transcend the Machiavelian *Realpolitik* he practices as a revolutionary, in order to affirm a higher and more essentially human love and generosity. The immediate, unhesitating nature of the act is consistent with Sartre's analysis of pure reflection, and although seemingly spontaneous, it is a word-act wholly consistent with the communistic humanism he advocates in contrast to Hugo's idealistic interest in what men "pourront devenir" ["will be able to become"]. "Et moi," Hoederer states,

> je les aime pour ce qu'ils sont. Avec toutes leurs saloperies et tous leurs vices. J'aime leurs voix et leurs mains chaudes qui prennent et leur peau, la plus nue de toutes les peaux, et leur regard inquiet et la lutte désespérée qu'ils mènent chacun à son tour contre la mort et contre l'angoisse. Pour moi, ça compte un homme de plus ou de moins dans le monde. C'est précieux. (211)

> [And I, I love them for what they are. With all their filth and all their vices. I love their voices and their warm hands that take, and their skin, the nudest skin of all, and their uneasy gaze, and the desperate struggle they wage, each one in turn, against death and against anguish. For me, one man more or less in the world counts. It's precious.]

Although his example will haunt Hugo and inspire in him one last attempt at an imagined authenticity, the diametrical difference between the two men is clear from the start. Hugo's bad faith is so integral to his being that it manifests itself in nearly everything he does. He joined the party to spite his family's bourgeois pretensions, and he cares not a whit that he may be responsible for his father's death. His relationship with his wife amounts to a game in which "playing" has become altogether indistinguishable from reality. The verb "jouer" ["to play"], as many critics have noted—how could one miss it?—recurs over and over again, and Hugo and Jessica have made such play so essential to their marriage that they cannot "sortir du jeu" ["get out of the game"].[11] The absurdity of the situation is no more ironically apparent than when, in response to Hugo's demand, "Sois sérieuse" ["Be serious"], Jessica replies, "Je n'aime pas le sérieux mais on va s'arranger. Je vais jouer à être sérieuse" (75) ["I don't like seriousness, but that can be arranged. I'll play at being serious"].

Life for Hugo is in fact nothing but a "comedy," as he first intimates to Hoederer ("Est-ce que je ne suis pas en train de me jouer la comédie?" [111]) ["Am I not just kidding myself?"] and thereafter repeatedly to Jessica regarding their relationship (118, 193) and the assassination he proposes to accomplish (120). In his drunken display before Georges,

Slick, and Jessica, he reasserts his feeling of entrapment in the game ("Je joue la comédie du désespoir. Est-ce qu'on peut en sortir?" [168]) ["I'm acting out the comedy of despair. Will it ever end?"], and later, recalling his crime to Olga after his release, he wonders "Si toute était une comédie?" (245) ["If it were all a comedy?"].[12] The suggestion of entrapment and hopelessness is a self-deceptive, guilt-relieving ploy aimed at raising his plight to the level of tragedy, and his belated claim that "je vivais depuis longtemps dans la tragédie. C'est pour sauver la tragédie que j'ai tiré" (242) ["I'd been living for a long time in tragedy. It was to save the tragedy that I fired"] is merely a responsibility-shirking alibi. There is nothing tragic, that is, pre-determined, inescapable, noble, or heroic about his act.[13] It was, rather, comic in the Aristotelian sense of grotesque and ludicrous, a comedy on the verge of degenerating into "farce," the very word Hugo himself ultimately employs when he realizes hysterically the utter senselessness of his act, now viewed politically as an embarrassment that must be repudiated and forgotten (254).

The insistence upon the theatrical metaphor to describe Hugo is thus as relentless as it is appropriate, since his entire existence is predicated upon an illusion. What he admires in Hoederer is that he is "vrai" ["real"], while he himself "vi[t] dans un décor" (132) ["lives in a stage set"]. He has been acting a part, rehearsing empty gestures for so long that he has lost any sense of identity beyond that of a role. In this sense, he is like the *garçon de café* described in *L'Etre et le néant*, "[qui] joue à *être* garçon de café" ["who is playing at *being* a waiter in a café"], just as Hugo "[joue] bien au révolutionnaire" (67) ["is indeed playing at being a revolutionary"]. Sartre's analysis of the former is clearly applicable to the latter:

> Et c'est précisément ce sujet que *j'ai à être* et que je ne suis point. Ce n'est pas que je ne veuille pas l'être ni qu'il soit un autre. Mais plutôt il n'y a pas de commune mesure entre son être et le mien. Il est une "représentation" pour les autres et pour moi-même, cela signifie que je ne puis l'être qu'en *représentation*. Mais précisément si je me le représente, je ne le suis point, j'en suis séparé, comme l'objet du sujet, séparé *par rien,* mais ce rien m'isole de lui, je ne puis l'être, je ne puis que *jouer à l'être,* c'est-à-dire m'imaginer que je le suis. (EN 96)
>
> [And it is precisely this subject who *I have to be* and who I am not. It is not that I do not wish to be him nor that he be an other. But rather there is no common measure between his being and mine. He is a "representation" for others and for myself, which signifies

that I can be him only *in representation*. But precisely if I represent him to me, I am not he; I am separated from him, as the object from the subject, separated *by nothing,* but this nothing isolates me from him. I cannot be him, I can only *play at being* him, that is, imagine that I am he.]

Such a separation of consciousness into subject and object introduces a dualism into consciousness by means of which a "self" is constructed as a reified object, that is, a reflecting subject set in opposition to a reflected object. This inauthentic mode of consciousness is what Sartre terms "impure reflection," which creates conditions for the possibility of fleeing being "dans le 'ne-pas-croire-ce-qu'on-croit'" (EN 107) ["into the 'not-believing-what-one-believes'"] that is by definition bad faith.

That Hugo exemplifies a state of impure reflection[14] is signified throughout the play by his narcissistic obsession[15] with his reflected image, whether in the photos of himself that he guards secretly in his suitcase or in furtive glances of his reflection that he catches in mirrors (42, 167). Like Estelle in *Huis clos,* Hugo seems to need to see a perceptible image of himself in order to be sure he exists. Even Hoederer remarks to him that "tu t'occupes beaucoup de toi" (114) ["you pay a great deal of attention to yourself"].

His penchant for talking too much, noted by Olga—"Tu as besoin de parler pour te sentir vivre" (20) ["You need to talk to feel alive"]—is another symptom of his inauthenticity, since he allows words to suffice in place of deeds. The many allusions to the Hamletic quandary, such as the observation of Hoederer that "tu réfléchis trop" (227) ["you think too much"], coupled with a desire to act that is constantly thwarted by a failure to take advantage of opportunities to do so, only serve to compare him unfavorably with Shakespeare's hero. Whereas Hamlet spurns suicide in favor of pursuing a calculated course of action he knows will cost him his life, Hugo leaps to action in a fit of rage and murders the only friend he has ever known for reasons he does not understand, only to kill himself later when remorse and self-hatred provoke a similarly impulsive and desperate act.

It seems to me, however, that there is a deeply repressed motive for these two puzzling acts, constituting still another manifestation of his bad faith. Many details of the play expose Hugo's insecurity about his masculinity. The stage directions that describe him as *"Un grand garçon de vingt-trois ans"* (12) ["A tall (big) boy of twenty-three"] already suggest his immaturity. Moreover, his admission to Hoederer that "je donnerais ma main à couper pour devenir tout de suite un homme" (142) ["I'd let my hand be cut off to become a man immediately"] not only expresses an ostensibly urgent desire to pass from adolescence into manhood, but also seems to betray, in the allusion to the severed member, an unconscious and equivocal castration fear and/or wish. Hoederer's burly bodyguard, Georges, had previously noted that Hugo "a l'air délicat" (84) ["seems delicate"], and we have only Hugo's word that his sexless relationship with his wife is due to her frigidity, even though she later warms up and seems quite ready to yield to Hoederer. Is it, in fact, a repressed homosexual urge coupled with self-disgust for that urge that causes Hugo twice to shrink from Hoederer's touch, for fear of having to face and admit his sexual attraction to the man (only to have circumstances, the second time, ironically impel the older man physically upon the younger in protective reaction to an explosion)?[16]

In the search scene, Hugo seems quite awed by the bodyguards' macho prowess and invites Jessica to feel Georges' muscles. The stage directions stipulate, however, that first *"Il les tâte"* (86) ["*He* feels them," my emphasis].[17] At the opening of the fourth tableau, moreover, Hugo is discovered alone in Hoederer's room handling (fondling?) the latter's penholder and coffee pot. That these gestures are vicariously erotic is clearly suggested by the guilty way in which, as the directions state, *"Hugo repose précipitamment la cafetière"* (122) ["Hugo hastily sets the coffee pot down"] and by his evasion of Jessica's repeated query, "Qu'est-ce que tu fais [faisais] avec cette cafetière?" (122-23) ["What are (were) you doing with that coffee pot?"].

When the Hugo-Hoederer interaction is examined closely, distinct homoerotic overtones are readily discernible, but their respective expressions of their affective proclivities could not be more dissimilar. Hoederer, who admits to Jessica, "je ne sais pas parler aux femmes" (217) ["I don't know how to talk to women"], is frank about his preference of men over women. He tells Hugo, "Quand j'ai à choisir entre un type et une bonne femme, c'est le type que je choisis" (137) ["When I have to choose between a man and a woman, I choose the man"], confiding to him right after, "c'est toi que j'ai choisi" (138) ["I chose you"], and later, "je te garderai près de moi et je t'aiderai" (229) ["I'll keep you near me and I'll help you"]. Hugo, by contrast, is indirect, misleading, and hypocritical. He assassinates Hoederer almost immediately after nervously admitting to him that "je sais à présent que je ne pourrais jamais tirer sur vous parce que . . . parce que je tiens à vous" (233) ["I know now that I could never shoot you because . . . because I like you."][18] Only in retrospect, when it is too late, is he finally able to come to grips with his love for the man: "J'aimais Hoederer, Olga. Je l'aimais plus que je n'ai aimé personne au monde. J'aimais le voir et l'entendre, j'aimais ses mains et son visage et, quand j'étais avec lui, tous mes orages s'apaisaient" (246) ["I loved Hoederer, Olga. I loved him more than

I ever loved anyone in the world. I loved to see him and hear him, I loved his hands and his face, and when I was with him all my turmoils were calmed"]. Now the true motive for his "crime passionnel" (253) ["crime of passion"] is clear. When asked if he was jealous, he replies, "Jaloux? Peut-être. Mais pas de Jessica" (243) ["Jealous? Perhaps. But not of Jessica"]. The assassination was indeed the result of jealousy directed at Hoederer but not for trying to seduce Jessica whom Hugo never loved. In killing Hoederer he has jealously murdered the actual object of his love for showing affection to a rival (ironically his own wife) who threatens to supplant him.

The many critics who see the father-son paradigm predominating in the Hoederer-Hugo relationship seem to overlook or attenuate the homoerotic element, perhaps because of the incest taboo implied in such an attraction (combined with the homosexual taboo). But it is precisely because Hoederer is not Hugo's blood father and Hugo not Hoederer's blood son that they can harbor a more libidinal desire for one another, although it still is stigmatized by the comparatively less intimidating homosexual taboo alone. Philip Wood's point that Hoederer "inevitably represents to Hugo, as an object of phantasmatic fulfillment, a father figure who can now be slain in the flesh"[19] is true for the authoritarian traitor Hugo originally agreed to assassinate (and who was symbolically a hostile father-oppressor). But the man he met turned out to be someone he found himself falling in love with, as did simultaneously his wife with whom, at least subconsciously, he suddenly had to compete. So it was a potential father-lover (not a father-oppressor) that Hugo ultimately encountered, who was outside the patricidal imperative of the Freudian Oedipus complex and thus not a target for slaying. Why, then, did he slay him? Marc Buffat attributes Hugo's initial failure to kill Hoederer to "love of the one he must slaughter" (40), when ultimately just the opposite is true: it is this love turned instantaneously into jealousy-hate when it perceives itself betrayed that actually spurs the killing.

Charles Hill's claim, in his attempt to rule out jealousy as a motive, that Hugo, when he avows love for Hoederer, "is not suggesting, of course, a homosexual attraction" since "Sartre always treats this phenomenon explicitly,"[20] seems to understate and underestimate Sartre's complex approach to homosexuality, a pervasive theme in his works, which is often quite nuanced and ambiguous, as is here the case with Hugo and Hoederer. That Sartre, perhaps half-unknowingly, recognized and depicted a homoerotic dimension in relations between men—even in the form of homophobia, which he apparently had to deal with himself[21]—testifies to his remarkably keen, open-minded, and dispassionate insight into human behavior. The homo/bisexual level, in *Les Mains sales,* is only one among others (and a rather subtle one), but it does, I believe, affect the outcome of events, redounding once again to Hoederer's credit (he is openly honest) and Hugo's disgrace (he continues to dissemble and repress).

One has every right, then, to be suspicious of Hugo's ostensibly courageous last gesture to give a revolutionary meaning to his and to Hoederer's death by delivering himself to his executioners, as it cannot be taken seriously. He is giving one last "performance," so well played in fact that even he mistakes it for real. The truth is he is once again fleeing from responsibility into, in this case, the safe haven of death by a cowardly surrender to suicide that, in an angry moment of intolerable shame and disgust, as rash and emotional as the murder he now wants to efface, finally accomplishes the self-annihilation he has always sought.

Sartre later agonized over misinterpretations of his implied criticism of party zealots like Hugo (and Olga), who justify their actions in the name of ideology and relegate responsibility for them to an entity outside themselves. While it may seem that "everything is permitted" in a revolution, this is clearly not the case. Every act in every context has an "owner" and must be accounted for "in situation." It is ludicrous to claim, as does Hugo, that a murder is "abstrait" (186) ["abstract"] or committed by "le hasard" (243) ["chance"]. This does not mean that one cannot be at the same time revolutionary and ethical. Hoederer illustrates the case of a strategist who is Machiavelian yet authentic and courageous. He acts deliberately and confidently, without hesitation or regret. Hugo, by contrast, plays roles, vacillates indecisively and surrenders unthinkingly to impulse, shameful of everything he is and does. He proves the point that the authenticity of a project, even one of revolutionary social change, is only fully known *in praxis*, since it may also serve as a mask or a scapegoat for actions committed in bad faith.

## ABBREVIATIONS

CV:  Stuart Z. Charmé, *Vulgarity and Authenticity: Dimensions of Otherness in the World of Jean-Paul Sartre.*
EN:  Jean-Paul Sartre, *L'Etre et le néant.*
SX:  Jean-Paul Sartre, *Situations, X.*

## NOTES

1. Jean-Paul Sartre, *L'Etre et le néant* (Paris: Gallimard, 1943), 95, henceforth abbreviated EN. Quotations from this work will be accompanied by English translations I made after consulting (and often disagreeing with) Hazel E.

Barnes's edition, *Being and Nothingness* (New York: Washington Square Press, 1992). (In my translation, I have used "him" instead of "he" for some predicate nominatives, in keeping with common usage and to avoid odd-sounding syntaxes.) Here as elsewhere, when comparisons could be made with available preexisting translations, I have not hesitated to select my own renderings, which, as a general rule, privilege when possible the literal over the figurative. All of the texts expressly written by Sartre are presented in bilingual form, with the English in brackets following the French. The French precedes, because it is the French text I am analyzing, and there are many crucial (and often highly nuanced) French words that do not translate fully or accurately into English. Brackets are used for translations to distinguish them clearly from parenthetical expressions. I am ultimately responsible for all of the English translations of French texts and, in the case of those not by Sartre, have replaced the original with my translation, although page numbers, as in the Sartre, refer to the original French editions.
2. In his conversation with Paolo Caruso, Sartre very clearly affirms the relative ethics of praxis over moral absolutism: "La morale n'est pas autre chose qu'un certain auto-contrôle que la *praxis* exerce sur elle-même, mais toujours à un niveau objectif; elle est, par conséquent, fondée sur des valeurs constamment dépassées, parce que posées par la *praxis* antérieure" ["Morality is nothing other than a certain self-control that praxis exercises over itself, but always on an objective level; it is consequently founded on values that are constantly superseded, because posited by previous praxis"]. Jean-Paul Sartre, "Entretien sur *Les Mains sales* avec Paolo Caruso (1964)," *Un Théâtre de situations,* ed. Michel Contat and Michel Rybalka (Paris: Gallimard "Idées," 1973), 263-64; the English version is entitled *Sartre on Theater,* trans. Frank Jellinek (New York: Random House, 1976).
3. Jean-Paul Sartre, *Cahiers pour une morale [Ethics Notebooks]* (Paris: Gallimard, 1983).
4. John Gerassi, *Jean-Paul Sartre: Hated Conscience of His Century,* vol. 1 (Chicago: University of Chicago Press, 1989), writes that "Sartre certainly expected Castor [Simone de Beauvoir] to decide which of his unpublished works to publish posthumously and not Elkaïm (or me, for that matter, though he gave me or asked Castor to give me copies of many of them). Thus Elkaïm decided to 'present' Sartre's *Ethics* (which he never wanted published at all)" (158).

In the opening words of her preface to *Cahiers pour une morale,* Elkaïm-Sartre states, on the other hand, that "Sartre always wished that the unfinished philosophical texts of his mature years be published only after his death" (7) and quotes in support a brief excerpt from the 1975 Contat interview, revised and reprinted as "Autoportrait à soixante-dix ans" ["Self-portrait at Seventy"] in *Situations, X* (Paris: Gallimard, 1976), 207-8, henceforth abbreviated SX. When, though, the full context of Sartre's remarks is considered, it seems more accurate to say that he saw no point in publishing them, especially the outdated remnants of his "Ethics," comprising what little remained of a "first part" that was to introduce a "principal idea" he never wrote down. The *inédits* were, in effect, "completely dead" for him. He probably would not even recognize them or only recognize them with "surprise," as if written by a stranger. He knew, though, that they doubtless would be published after his death—Contat's own long interest in publishing them was obvious proof of that—but he did not want them published while he was living and still controlled them. He thought that works belonged to the author while alive but then passed to the heirs and editors to whom they inevitably must be entrusted, and he did so without much concern (SX, 207-9). That he refrained from destroying the few remaining *inédits* tells me that his ambivalence toward them led him, in the end, to decide not to decide what to do with them.

5. Two citations from the Gerassi biography are pertinent (given the characterization of Benny Lévy in the second passage, the obvious inference is that he is considered by Gerassi to be one of the late "fake disciples" referred to in the first passage): (1) "In the last two years of his life, Sartre was made to seem to repudiate his total achievements. Out went his dialectic. Out went his revolutionary fervor. Out went his defense of the counterviolence of the violated. . . . He even started searching for his 'Jewish roots,' according to some of his fake disciples, who had by then convinced France's reactionary left-wing tabloids that they, and only they, spoke for the master. Surrounded by petty Stalinists, Sartre's history was totally rewritten even before he died. To his old 'family,' to Simone de Beauvoir, to me, it was all one hell of a manipulation" (22); and (2) "all civil contacts between Elkaïm and Castor and other members of 'the family' were destroyed, mostly by Elkaïm's former mentor, the fanatic onetime Maoist leader turned rabbinical and Talmudic scholar Benny Lévy (aka Pierre Victor or Pierre Bloch), who keeps trying to prove that Sartre was really a Jewish philosopher all along" (158). Of course, it must be noted that Gerassi, by his own account (11-12) designated by Sartre to be his "official biographer" in an "exclusive agreement" written on paper supplied by a waiter at La Coupole, would appear to have his own stake to protect in the Sartrean legacy. For a different (more positive) view of Sartre's relationships with Lévy and Elkaïm-Sartre, see Stuart Z. Charmé, *Vulgarity and Authenticity: Dimensions of Otherness in the World of Jean-Paul Sartre* (Amherst: University of Massachusetts Press, 1991), 224 ff., henceforth abbreviated CV.

6. See Jean-Paul Sartre and Benny Lévy, "L'Espoir maintenant . . . ," parts 1-3, *Le Nouvel Observateur* 800 (10 March 1980): 18-19, 56-60; 801 (17 March 1980): 52-58; 802 (24 March 1980): 55-60. See also Herbert Spiegelberg's article, "Sartre's Last Word on Ethics in Phenomenological Perspective," in *Sartre: An Investigation of Some Major Themes*, ed. Simon Glynn (Aldershot, UK: Avebury, 1987), 37-54.

7. Jean-Paul Sartre, *Les Mains sales* (Paris: Gallimard, 1948). Numbers in parentheses, unless otherwise identified, refer to page numbers of this edition. For

the English version, I have consulted and often opted for a modified version of Lionel Abel's translation, *Dirty Hands*, in *No Exit and Three Other Plays* (New York: Vintage Books, 1955).
8. Simone de Beauvoir notes in *La Force des choses* [*The Force of Things*] that "Henceforth [after the war], instead of opposing individualism and collectivity, he no longer considered them anything but linked one to the other"; cited in Marc Buffat, *Les Mains sales de Jean-Paul Sartre* (Paris: Gallimard, 1991), 20.
9. Each tableau is further divided into scenes according to the classic pattern of a scene change corresponding to a change of characters on stage. Abel's English translation presents a simplified and, to me, diminished and confusing version in seven "acts" with no scenic subdivisions.
10. His statements in this regard are frequently quoted by the critics and can be found in *Un Théâtre de situations,* 249, 259.
11. Hugo's exact words are, "Nous n'en sortirons pas" (76), with *en* clearly referring to their game playing.
12. The meaning of the French word *comédie* can be both specifically comic ("comedy") and generic ("play"). The word is also used in a variety of common, idiomatic expressions that connote acting, role playing, dreaming, self-delusion, and so forth (see *Le Nouveau Petit Robert* [Paris: Dictionnaires Le Robert, 1993]). Sometimes the theatrical nuance is lost in English translations of phrases employing *comédie* and/or the related words *jouer* and *jeu*.
13. Jean Alter's remark, in *"Les Mains sales,* ou la clôture du verbe," *Sartre et la mise en signe,* ed. Michael Issacharoff and Jean-Claude Vilquin (Lexington, KY: French Forum, 1982), that the central part of the play (the flashback) "evokes a classical tragedy in five acts, marked by fatality, since one already knows its outcome and it only tells the why and the how" (69–70) implies that foreknowledge has a causal effect on the necessity of the outcome, when, as Philosophy demonstrates to Boethius in *The Consolation of Philosophy,* foreknowledge does not itself impose necessity on future events. The knowledge here, in any case, is from after the fact, not before, and has no bearing on the dénouement of events. The tragic conception of fatality assumes an unalterable and inescapable predetermination, which is precisely what Sartre denies in *Les Mains sales*—Hoederer might not have been shot—as he did in *Les Mouches* [*The Flies*], where an all-out assault is launched against the Greek concept of predetermination due to inherited guilt (I discuss this last point in "*Crime:* A Floating Signifier in Sartre's *Les Mouches,*" *Sartre,* ed. Christina Howells [London: Longman, 1995], 93). Sartre's theater, as Buffat points out, is actually "an antitragedy" that depicts, however paradoxically, "a universe in which *freedom is destiny*" (65) (cf. Christina Howells's book, *Sartre: The Necessity of Freedom* [Cambridge: Cambridge University Press, 1988], where the very title evinces the importance of this idea). While it is true that human experience is determined by certain ineluctable facts, like death, freedom is that essential mode of human will and being that constantly seeks to control, change, exceed, or overcome conditions arising from the facticity of being-in-the-

world. See the excerpt from *Cahiers pour une morale* (447-49) reproduced by Buffat (203-6), which obviously develops ideas from *L'Etre et le néant*.
14. See Rhiannon Goldthorpe's analysis of Hugo in *Sartre: Literature and Theory* (Cambridge: Cambridge University Press, 1984), 110-14.
15. According to Pierre Verstraeten, *Violence et éthique: esquisse d'une critique de la morale dialectique à partir du théâtre politique de Sartre* (Paris: Gallimard, 1972), Hoederer offers Hugo a way out of "the profound narcissism of his attitude" (61).
16. Hugo's first recoil from Hoederer's advance ("je n'aime pas qu'on me touche" (112) ["I don't like being touched"] is in response to Hoederer's placing a hand on his shoulder. The second one ("Ne me touchez pas" ["Don't touch me"]) is followed in rapid succession by the detonation of the bomb, Hoederer's cry "A plat ventre!" ["Hit the ground!"], and the stage direction, *"Il saisit Hugo par les épaules et le jette par terre"* ["He seizes Hugo by the shoulders and throws him to the ground"] (159).
17. Curiously, Abel translates this "Il" as "She," as if unwilling (consciously or unconsciously) to accept the homoerotic nuance and thus predisposed to treating the original French as a misprint.
18. I have reproduced Abel's more or less neutral "I like you," even though the expression *tenir à* is more nuanced and ambiguous than a simple "je vous aime bien." The semantic depth of "je tiens à vous," which makes it difficult to translate by a single English term, can be seen in the following dictionary citations: (1) "Tenir à, to set value [or] store on, to be attached to, to value, to care for, to prize" and, drawing from the examples offered, "to be keen on, to mean a great deal to" (*Larousse dictionnaire moderne, français-anglais anglais-français* [Paris: Librairie Larousse, 1960]); (2) "Tenir à qqn, à qqch., y être attaché par un sentiment durable" ["to be attached (to someone or something) by a durable feeling"] (*Le Nouveau Petit Robert*). The affective attachment connoted by both definitions makes such an admission on the part of uptight, unsure-of-himself Hugo all the more emotionally charged and revealing.

Yet Hugo also underscores the ambiguity of the relationship and maintains some distance from Hoederer by his persistent use of "vous." Earlier, in the third tableau, Hoederer told Hugo to use "tu" with him, in direct response to Hugo's "vous" (93). The latter's reaction is left in suspense over several pages of dialogue, and when it comes, it is a rejecting "vous" (101). Thus, even as late as scene two of the sixth tableau, Hugo is staving off Hoederer's "seduction" (represented by his relentless "tu," which is also ambiguously paternal) by taking refuge in the French language itself, sheltered by the code of compelling social distinctions and expectations that are so deeply ingrained in the French concept of "you."
19. Philip R. Wood, *Understanding Jean-Paul Sartre* (Columbia: University of South Carolina Press, 1990), 214. A similar view is expressed by Robert Harvey, *Search for a Father: Sartre, Paternity, and the Question of Ethics* (Ann Arbor: The University of Michigan Press, 1991), for whom "[Hoederer's]

position as a surrogate father . . . [transforms] Hugo's murder of the Trotsky look-alike into a symbolic patricide" (191).
20. Charles G. Hill, *Jean-Paul Sartre: Freedom and Commitment* (New York: Peter Lang, 1992), 176.
21. Sartre was not so much fearful of homosexuals—he was actually quite fascinated by them and their "marginality" (CV, 171). He feared rather his own possibly "repressed homosexuality" (CV, 159), although he did admit to Simone de Beauvoir that he felt a "macho" attraction to women and very much preferred their company to men (SX, 118-20), whom, by contrast, he did not like as a "species" and with whom he felt personally embarrassed by any sort of tenderness, confidentiality, or intimacy (CV, 159).

# 4

# Freedom at Work: Sartre on Ponge

## Natascha Heather Lancaster

Jean-Paul Sartre's literary criticism needs to be situated within a study of the effects that Sartre's writings are designed to have on readers. In his works on literature, Sartre's aim is to empower readers to act and to extend the limits of human freedom. To this end, Sartre reveals the means required to modify the reader's relationship with literature and reality. In other words, Sartre's critical writings attempt less to explain an author's texts than to incite the reader to become an active participant in the shaping of literature and the world. I shall demonstrate the above assertions, using one of Sartre's earlier essays, "L'Homme et les choses" ["Man and Things"],[1] which is devoted to the poetry of Francis Ponge.[2]

In his essay on Ponge, Sartre discloses the effort human beings make *to conceal* the fact that dehumanization is a form of work. By revealing the energy we expend to disguise this particular type of labor, Sartre establishes the basis for an ethics that he develops in subsequent critical writings such as *Saint Genet, Actor and Martyr*[3] and *The Family Idiot*.[4] Because, in Sartre's view, dehumanization is not a given but the result of intense human labor, it is a fundamentally human process involving a person's freedom. This process produces various effects. For instance, it can make a person seem robot-like or as passive and inert as a thing. Whatever the case, the human agency involved is generally not noticed. Since we tend to perceive only the results of the process, we may be aware of certain individuals' passivity or of the mechanical nature of their gestures, but remain oblivious to the work involved in creating and maintaining these ways of being-in-the-world. In short, the dehumanized product often blinds us to the process of dehumanization and prevents us from seeing that dehumanization is indeed a human process.[5]

This social phenomenon has many ramifications, the most obvious of which is the belief that some individuals are born passive and are predisposed by nature to be something other than human. This belief lies at the root of oppression. Oppression can be defined as the work human beings perform on themselves and others in order to disguise the fact that oppression is a specific type of labor. The more we conceal the means of oppression, the more we protect oppression's survival.

In "L'Homme et les choses," Sartre reveals the effort and skill that go into creating and maintaining oppression.[6] In so doing, he performs a potentially revolutionary act by inciting readers to make an informed choice: faced with the fact that oppression is a form of action that conceals human agency, will they go on using their energy and skill to destroy and deny human action in themselves and others? That is the first alternative. Or conversely, will the readers redirect their energy and skill toward other goals and affirm openly that human beings are *always* active even when they seem passive?

In their respective works, Ponge and Sartre express a similar wish, namely, that reading will incite readers to act. In other words, the primary objective of these two writers is less to communicate a message for readers to decipher than to have a practical effect on their way of life. Thus, in "L'Homme et les choses," Sartre expresses admiration for the way Ponge's poetry makes the reader restless:

> It is this constant fluttering between interiority and exteriority that defines the originality and power of Ponge's poems; these small disintegrations within an object that reveal *states* beneath its *properties,* and then the sudden returns that unify states of being into behaviors and even into feelings; it is this frame of mind that he awakens in the reader, making the latter incapable of settling anywhere and leading him to wonder whether matter may not be animated and whether the movements of the soul may not in fact be shudderings of matter. (263)

Ponge voices a similar aim with regard to the reader in his poem, "The Washing Machine": "Of course, I would not go so far as to claim that the example or the lesson of the washing machine ought strictly speaking to galvanize my reader—but I would probably despise him a little for not taking it seriously."[7] The key expressions in these two passages are to "galvanize" the reader and to "awaken" in the reader a feeling of restlessness.

In "L'Homme et les choses," Sartre compares Ponge with a number of other writers, such as Gustave Flaubert, Guy de Maupassant, Colette, and Virginia Woolf. Sartre uses these comparisons to distinguish between two ways of relating to reality. On the one hand, one can observe reality from a distance and describe its external appearance. According to Sartre, this is what Flaubert, Maupassant, Colette, and Woolf do. Concerning the two women writers, Sartre states:

> It is not a question of *describing* things. In [Ponge's works], there are very few of those brilliant snapshots with which the likes of Virginia Woolf and Colette render the exact appearance of an object. [Ponge] talks about a cigarette without saying a word about the white paper in which it is rolled, about a butterfly with hardly a mention of the patterns adorning its wings: he is not concerned with qualities but with *being*. (242-43)

About Ponge, Flaubert, and Maupassant, Sartre remarks:

> It has been said that Flaubert used to tell Maupassant: "Put yourself in front of a tree and describe it." The advice, if it were indeed given, is absurd. The observer can measure things—and that is all. The thing will always withhold its meaning from him—and its being. Ponge no doubt looks at the mimosa; he looks at it attentively and for a long time. But he already knows what he is seeking in the flower. (227)

Alternatively, one can actively involve oneself in reality to the point of virtually setting up residence in things. These are the terms Sartre uses to define Ponge's way of relating to the world. According to Sartre, the poet thereby has a more direct access to the Being of objects. "In short," he states about Ponge's "Introduction to the Pebble," "it is a question not so much of *observing* the pebble than *of installing oneself in its heart [en son coeur]* and looking out at the world through its eyes, just like the novelist who, in order to portray his heroes, eases himself into their consciousness and describes things and people the way they appear to those heroes" (HC, 242, emphasis added).

The important point is that Ponge's relation to things involves his blending with the Other. Sartre describes this process in typically existentialist terms: "For man is not huddled up within himself, but out there, always out there, all the way from the sky down to the earth. The pebble has an inside, man does not: but man loses himself so that the pebble can exist" (268). This is not to say that Ponge never looks at things, but that his look is highly active since it transports him into objects. Sartre notes that "Ponge has called 'contemplation' the moment of ecstasy when he has got himself out of himself *[où il s'est établi hors de soi]* at the very heart of things" (245-46). For Sartre, this type of contemplation is active for various reasons. I will list these reasons and discuss them later. Sartre states: "Firstly, I would willingly call it 'active contemplation' because, far from suspending all involvement with the object, it supposes on the contrary that one should adapt oneself to it through a great number of activities *[une foule d'entreprises]* which need only satisfy the criterion of not being utilitarian" (246). Sartre considers Ponge's way of looking at reality active also because it fulfills a political function: "His contemplation is active, because it destroys the social order which is reflected in and on things" (247). I will show that the social order in question is the one that conceals that dehumanization is the effect of human work.

Lastly, Ponge's way of looking at the world is active, in Sartre's view, because it keeps people grounded in reality. Contemplation, as the poet practices it, has nothing to do with escapism. As a matter of fact, it serves as an antidote to the desire to flee from reality. Sartre quotes Ponge who states, in "Introduction to the Pebble," "Every time we want to escape, let contemplation and its resources stand in the way. No sense in going: transfer yourself into things" (PL, 77; HC, 247).

The transfer of the self to things precipitates a temporary loss of human identity. In other words, "active contemplation," as Sartre calls it, has dehumanizing effects on the person who performs it. According to Sartre, Ponge reproduces these effects in many of his poems. Sartre does not criticize the poet for doing this but seeks to ensure that the reader is fully aware of the work dehumanization implies.

For instance, Sartre analyzes Ponge's poem, "The Young Mother," which describes an anonymous young woman who has just given birth:

### The Young Mother

Shortly after childbirth a woman's beauty is transformed.

The face often bent over the chest lengthens a bit. The eyes, attentively lowered on a nearby object, seem to wander when they look up from time to time. They reveal a glance full of trust, while soliciting continuity. The arms and hands curve and strengthen. The legs which have greatly thinned and weakened are willingly seated, knees drawn up. The belly is distended, livid, still tender; the womb placidly yields to sleep, to night, to sheets.

. . . But soon upright again, this whole great body moves about hemmed in by a lanyard within easy reach of streaming white linen squares, which every so often her free hand grasps, crumples, wisely fingers, to hang back or fold away depending on the result of this test. (TST, 52-53)

In his commentary on "The Young Mother," Sartre underlines the progression throughout the poem, showing that dehumanization is not a given but a carefully created effect, and then he points out the technique Ponge employs to make the woman look like a thing: "Here the organs go their separate ways and each of them leads a slow-moving existence. Human unity has dissolved. We are dealing with a polyp rather than a woman. And then in the last lines everything comes together. But what is constituted is not a person but a great blind body *[un grand corps aveugle]*" (HC, 235).

Dehumanization as human work is also the focus of Sartre's comments on "The Gymnast," but this time Sartre stresses the ways in which the poet transforms acquired human skill into something supposedly innate. Sartre's remarks are based on the following excerpt from Ponge's poem:

> Pinker than nature and less agile than a monkey, he leaps on the rigging, possessed by pure zeal. Then, his body stuck in the ropes, he queries the air with his head like a worm in its mound.
> To wind up, he sometimes drops from the rafters like a caterpillar, but bounces back on his feet. . . . (TST, 52; HC, 234)

In his commentary on this passage, Sartre first shows that Ponge produces the effect of a dehumanized man by concealing human labor, and then he defines the technique the poet uses to hide human work:

> The artifice of the description lies mainly in the fact that Ponge presents the gymnast as the representative of an animal species. He describes him the way Buffon used to design a horse or a giraffe. What was obtained through work, he gives to us as the congenital property of the species. "Less agile than a monkey," he says—and these words are all that is required to transform what is an acquired skill into a sort of innate gift. (HC, 235)

In his analysis of both "The Gymnast" and "The Young Mother," Sartre reveals the type of work required to dehumanize a person. And above all, he stresses the fact that work is indeed required to achieve that end.

The importance for Sartre of the problem of concealed human work in the process of dehumanization is nowhere more manifest than in the closing paragraphs of "L'Homme et les choses." Sartre is writing about "The Washing Machine," mentioned previously. First, Sartre quotes from Ponge's description of this machine:

> The washing machine is conceived in such a way that once it is filled with a pile of ignoble linen, the inner emotions and the

boiling indignation it feels as a consequence, as they are channelled towards the upper half of its being, come down again as rain onto the pile of disgusting material which turns its stomach—more or less constantly—and may this end with a purification. (GR3, 83; HC, 269-70)

Sartre's remarks on "The Washing Machine" are light-hearted. Thus, he playfully chastises Ponge for using the metaphor of the washing machine instead of just referring to human consciousness: "I am afraid I may be one of those readers who cannot take the lesson at all seriously. Is it not obvious that we are dealing with a pure and simple metaphor? Do we really need a washing machine to achieve the structure of purification that is in every consciousness and whose origin is much older and much more deeply rooted within us?" (HC, 270). Then, he points out with marked irony a major inaccuracy in Ponge's description of the washing machine. Washing machines do not operate all by themselves. In order to function properly, they require a human hand:

> And then, the comparison is inaccurate—even from the point of view of simple observation: it is not the dirty linen that makes the water in the washing machine boil. Without the heat from the hearth, the water would remain inert and get progressively dirtier without cleaning the materials. And Ponge must have known that better than anyone else, since he was the one who put the washing machine on the hearth. (270)

Yet again, Sartre's approach is to emphasize the poet's technique of transforming what is human into a thing—the technique in this instance being a metaphor—and to highlight the human effort required for there to be movement. In the example of "The Washing Machine," human work is needed to carry the machine over to the hearth.

In each case, Sartre shows that human freedom is at work even in circumstances where it appears absent. He thereby contributes to the success of Ponge's process of galvanizing the reader into action. The more varied the techniques used by the poet to conceal human action, the more pointed and direct are the means deployed by the critic to reveal the work of concealment. The degree to which the reader is galvanized depends on the combination of these two factors.

I stated at the opening of this essay that Sartre's procedure in "L'Homme et les choses" had an ethical and political dimension. I will now explain and justify this assertion. Contemplation, as practiced by Ponge, entails certain risks. Given that it involves transferring the self into things, there is a danger of the self totally losing itself in the objects it contemplates. As the psychiatrist R. D. Laing would put it, there is a risk of "engulfment."[8] The fear of engulfment is the fear of totally disappearing into the object of contemplation and forever losing one's human attributes. In other words, it is the dread of dehumanization becoming something absolute and final. Ponge refers to this danger in "Introduction to the Pebble": "But for a contemplative individual, what is most important is the progressive *nomination* of all the qualities that he discovers; those *qualities* that TRANSPORT him should not transport him further than their measured and exact meanings" (PL, 79; HC, 243). I will return later to the importance of naming as a means of protection against the risk of engulfment after first situating the origin of this risk and the dread it produces.

In "L'Homme et les choses," Sartre demonstrates that this fear threatens only when we forget that our relation to things and others is dynamic and dialectical and requires our active participation. Paradoxically, the fear of engulfment makes some individuals perform the dreaded act of projecting themselves into what is Other, in order to alleviate their fear of disappearing into things; that is, they take the initiative of engulfing themselves. In Sartre's view, this paradox animates Ponge's work, as well as the writings of other twentieth-century authors. According to Sartre, these writers share a common desire to view themselves and the world through the eyes of a nonhuman species: "We have already come across it a hundred times and in different guises, this attempt to see oneself through the eyes of a foreign species and to rest from the painful duty of being a subject. We have seen it in Bataille, Blanchot, the surrealists. It defines the direction taken by modern fantastic literature and the very particular materialism of [Ponge]" (HC, 266).[9] In a footnote appended to this statement, Sartre provides a causal and historical explanation for the attitude these writers adopt: "While God was still alive, man had nothing to fear: he knew he was being watched. Now that man is the only God there is, and now that his gaze brings all things to life, he strains his neck in an effort to see himself" (266). Sartre does not elaborate on the relevance of "the death of God" to this question, but it is relatively easy to deduce.

The presupposition behind Sartre's statement is that religion fosters the belief that our definition as human beings depends for its preservation on the look of an omniscient Other.[10] To the person who lends credence to this belief, "the death of God" is potentially devastating, since it raises questions concerning who or what will guarantee one's identity as a human being while "outside oneself," as Sartre puts it, and "installed in the heart of the pebble" or of any other thing, animal, or being. If no one can read my thoughts while I contemplate the world, and if contemplation implies my disappearance into things, will I stay merged with the object forever? Who will ensure that I stay human?

By revealing that dehumanization requires human work, Sartre dissolves the paradox described above and alleviates the fear of engulfment. He demonstrates to the readers that they already have the energy and skill necessary to guarantee their identity as human beings without the assistance of a superior power. Moreover, he shows the readers that they are all constantly using this skill and energy in their day-to-day lives.

The main point is that individuals who project themselves into things as a protection against the danger of engulfment are agents who are actively exercising their freedom. They choose the time and place for the dreaded event to occur and act accordingly. In other words, human freedom is at work even when the performed act is motivated by fear and a wish to escape from a disturbing reality.

The problem is that individuals who project themselves into the Other often devalorize the work they are performing or otherwise fail to recognize that they are being active. They tend to see themselves in a negative light, feeling that they are merely *acted upon* rather than *active*. When this negative perception of the relation between the self and things comes to dominate, there is a risk of psychosis, which is characterized by, among other things, the belief that one can literally be engulfed by the Other and stripped of all sense of oneself as a separate being with a specific reality.

However, there is an important shift in perspective once we recognize that our relation to things and others requires our active involvement. Projection of the self into the Other no longer seems a negative way of being, with connotations of danger and madness, but rather a positive, healthy, and even joyous way of life. For, if my transfer into the Other is the effect of my own labor and choosing, then my removal from that same Other and my return to myself are also within my power. I am empowered to choose when and where I blend with and reemerge from the things or others I actively contemplate. In short, I own the means necessary for preventing engulfment by the Other. Those means are identical to the ones I used to merge with the Other in the first place.

In the context of Ponge's poetry and Sartre's essay, the means concerned are writing and naming. I refer once again to the passage from Ponge's "Introduction to the Pebble," but this time in its larger context:

> For an individual who has a contemplative disposition, the whole secret of happiness is not to consider *as an evil* the invasion

of his personality by objects. In order for that experience to avoid becoming a mystical one, it is necessary (1) to arrive at a precise inventory of each thing that one has made the object of one's contemplation; (2) to change objects of contemplation rather frequently to assure a degree of equilibrium. But for a contemplative individual, what is most important is the progressive *nomination* of all the qualities that he discovers; those *qualities* that TRANSPORT him should not transport him further than their measured and exact meanings. (PL, 79; HC, 243)

"Thus," comments Sartre, "the imposition of the name acquires the status of a religious ceremony. First, because it corresponds to the moment of recovery: through naming, man, who had been diluted in the object, withdraws, gathers himself up, and recovers his human attributes" (HC, 243).[11]

Many new horizons open up for those who assimilate the lessons advocated by Ponge and Sartre, according to which we all own and constantly use the energy and skill needed to guarantee our human identity and autonomy. Liberated from the fear of engulfment, the readers will be able to enrich their way of relating to the world: "Man loses himself," Sartre states, "so that the pebble may exist," and "all those 'disgusting' men from whom Ponge wishes to flee or whom he wants to remove, they, too, are 'rats, lions, nets, diamonds.' They are those things precisely because they 'are-in-the-world'" (HC, 268). In other words, once the fear of engulfment is overcome, we can relate to things and beings that would otherwise have seemed too repulsive or too "foreign" to approach. This is a vital precondition for constructing a society in which differences between ourselves and others are respected, explored, and enjoyed.

Furthermore, the readers will be able to increase vastly their stock of energy and make informed choices concerning its use. According to Sartre and Ponge, we all have choices regarding the ways we use our energy. Ponge underlines this in his title "Taking the Side of Things,"[12] while Sartre emphasizes it at the very beginning of his essay when he writes: "Those who believed they could tear ideas away from words did not worry too much [about the status of language] or applied their revolutionary energies to other tasks" (HC, 229).

In short, to return to the question I raised at the beginning, are readers going to continue to expend energy and skill disguising their status as active and autonomous human agents, or are they going to affirm this status in a positive and frank way and redirect their energy and skills toward other goals? In the first instance, oppression and a feeling of malaise would likely dominate. In the second instance, new vistas could open up in which, for example, the traditional and oppressive oppositions between the "active heterosexual male," on the one hand, and the "passive female" and gay person on the other, would be overcome, thus paving the way for a new ethics. Reading the works of Ponge and Sartre could serve as a starting point for such an enterprise, since reading exemplifies the concept of active passivity that I have been discussing here and that Sartre defines in *What Is Literature?*:

> The belief which I accord the tale is freely assented to. It is a Passion, in the Christian sense of the word, that is, a freedom which resolutely *puts itself* into a state of passiveness to obtain a certain transcendent effect by this sacrifice. The reader *renders himself* credulous; he *descends* into credulity which, though it ends by enclosing him like a dream, is at every moment conscious of being free. . . . I can awaken at every moment, and I know it; but I do not want to; *reading is a free dream*. (35, emphasis added)

There are other obstacles to action that Sartre seeks to remove in "L'Homme et les choses." Most important is the inhibiting myth according to which human beings can be inhabited by things. In Sartre's view, Ponge, as well as Charles Baudelaire, Jean Genet, and Gustave Flaubert, all suffered from belief in this myth, that is, they all thought they were occupied from within by a foreign presence at once material and active. According to Sartre, the person who pays credence to this belief is deeply alienated.[13] The nature of the internal presence varies according to each individual. For some, it is an object, an idea, an image, or language itself. For others, it is one or more persons: in the case of Genet, the inner presence is the self-righteous bourgeois; in Flaubert's case, it is the father.[14]

Liberation in the Sartrean context involves expelling the so-called internal reality from the individual. This expulsion is a precondition for active and positive relationships between individuals themselves and between individuals, objects, and animals.[15] In philosophical terms, Sartre expresses the need for overcoming the belief in a material and animated internal reality by saying that we must all accept the "diasporic being" of the for-itself. The question is by what means we are to forge this acceptance. Sartre provides answers to this question in his critical writings.[16]

In the first part of "L'Homme et les choses" Sartre gradually creates tension between various passages of Ponge's work. Rather than dissolve the tension, he changes its poles, thereby providing a practical remedy to the alienating belief described above. He refers to this belief at the opening of his essay, as he is defining the nature of Ponge's activity as a poet. Basing his view on "The Mimosa," Sartre states that "[Ponge] is much more concerned at present with *fishing deep down inside him* for swarming and flowery monsters and bringing them up *[et pour les rendre]* than with determining their properties through careful observation" (HC, 227, emphasis added).[17] Prior to the decision to write, the poet is inhabited by things. There are objects inside him, in his stomach to be precise, since digestion is mentioned as well as "to bring up" *(rendre)*, that is, to vomit. Through the act of writing, the poet will then vomit the object that he believes is lodged inside him.

In another passage, Sartre notes that in Ponge's work, there is no mention of "thought." The poet describes humans only from the outside, in the manner of a behavioral scientist. The implication here is that there is nothing inside the head of the Pongean person: "Let us note for the moment this bias *[parti pris]* in favor of looking at man from the outside, in the manner of the behaviorist. Nowhere in his work do we find any references to *thought*. Man is distinguished from the other species by the objective act we call speech, that original way we have of striking the air and of creating a resonant object around it" (228).

Lastly, Sartre quotes passages in which Ponge asserts that the social order and speech are synonymous and reside within us: "Unfortunately, to cap this horror, *within ourselves,* the same sordid order speaks" (PL, 69; HC, 230).[18] Thus, the human being as Ponge describes him is spoken from within by a sordid order of things and words.[19]

How is human identity defined in these excerpts from Ponge's texts? There is the outer surface, which the poet observes in the manner of the behavioral scientist, and nothing else; that is, there is no reality *around* human beings since objects, the social order, and speech are all situated *within* the individual. In this respect, the Pongean person is akin to "The Washing Machine," which boils all by itself, propelled by the dirty linen inside it. In his essay, Sartre turns the Pongean concept of the individual inside out by expelling the world from inside human beings and human beings from inside themselves. Of course, this is a purely metaphorical representation of things since, in Sartre's view, humans are never really inhabited by objects; this is the belief from which he wishes to free the reader.

As one progresses through "L'Homme et les choses," one is struck by the change in the way the relation between "man and things" is described. Thus, objects are represented as calling out to humans for the latter to express them: "The things are there, waiting. And what we notice first of all is that they demand to be expressed, 'the mute entreaties they make for us to express them, at their true value, and for themselves—beyond their usual value as meaning—without choice and yet with measure, but which measure: their very own'" (TP, 137; HC, 240).[20] In other words, objects are no longer described as being inside humans but outside them. About Ponge's description of the way things call out to humankind, Sartre states: "This passage should be taken at face value. This is not a poet's formula for characterizing the appeals made by the most obscure, the most hidden of our memories. Ponge's intuition is direct, and as untheoretical as can be" (240). Thus, Sartre emphasizes the fact that the objects' calls emanate not from a person's inner being—a Romantic theme exemplified by Baudelaire, for example, in the "Spleen" poems—but from the surrounding reality. There is therefore a marked contrast between this description of the relation between man and things and the one with which Sartre opens his essay. For, in the introduction to "L'Homme et les choses," Sartre clearly states the opposite, namely that things are inside the poet and lodged in his memory: "There is no better way to emphasize the fact that Ponge does not come to objects by chance; the things he speaks of are elected; they have inhabited him for many years; they populate him; they fill his memory; they were present in him long before he had any problems with speech" (227).

This new relation between man and things is the outcome of a substitution that Sartre makes in his essay. In a quotation taken from Ponge, he exchanges the term "thing" for the term "word": "[Ponge] wanted 'to open up a series of interior trapdoors; travels through the thickness of [words]; an invasion of qualities, a revolution or a subversion comparable to the one effected by the plow or the shovel, when, all of a sudden, and for the first time, millions of parcels, grains, roots, worms, and tiny beasts, up to then buried in the ground, appear in the light of day'" (PL, 79; HC, 233). Sartre does not disguise the fact that he has altered Ponge's text. He points it out in a footnote: "The passage which I have just quoted applies to *things*, and not *words*. However, the context, which establishes a perfect parallel between the depths of the one and the depths of the other, allows me to substitute the *word* for the *thing*" (233).

Sartre has expelled the objects from inside the poet. As readers, we move from the inner to the outer world. In the process, we free ourselves from the delusions of the former, which would have us believe that the outer world only exists through the images we have of it within us. To reveal to readers that we "are-in-the-world" therefore entails not only releasing us from the fear of engulfment by objects in the outer world, but also freeing us from the shackles of the objects of internalization.

We saw earlier that Sartre defines reading as an "active passivity," which implies an active effort on the part of readers to make themselves passive. There is also a second and dialectically related movement whereby readers transform passivity into activity. Sartre demonstrates this second movement when he frees the poet and the reader from the belief that live monsters exist in the mind and body: "And as activity has rendered itself passive in order for it better to create the object, vice versa, passiveness becomes an act; the man who is reading has raised himself to the highest degree" (WL, 36).

In "L'Homme et les choses," Sartre first defines Ponge's "doctrine" and then analyzes its application in the poet's writings. As I hope to have shown, in Sartre's view, the conformity of a theory to a practice has little value in itself. Sartre's aim is more complex. As he states in *What Is Literature?* the writer is like a doctor whose role is to cure specific forms of alienation that affect readers in day-to-day life: "It is this familiar world which the writer animates and penetrates with his freedom. It is on the basis of this world that [the doctor] must bring about his concrete freedom" (51).[21]

In Sartre's own words, the overall aim of criticism is to establish a "relation of trust" between the reader, the text, and things.[22] To achieve this goal, Sartre uses a variety of techniques, some of which I have illustrated here. Each technique is designed to liberate readers from a belief that keeps them at a distance or in a state of passive contemplation with regard to the text and the world. This process of liberation empowers readers to modify their ways of relating to themselves, literary works, others, and the world. In short, Sartrean criticism provides practical techniques for readers to use each time they read a literary work and also, in day-to-day life, as they deal with others and the world of objects. The role of the Sartrean critic is, therefore, less to define literature than to galvanize the reader into becoming an increasingly active agent in the shaping of texts and the world.[23]

### ABBREVIATIONS

AV:   Beth Archer, *The Voice of Things.*
GR3:  Francis Ponge, *Le Grand Recueil* 3.
HC:   Jean-Paul Sartre, "L'Homme et les choses."
PL:   Francis Ponge, *The Power of Language.*
TP:   Francis Ponge, *Tome premier.*
TST:  Francis Ponge, *Taking the Side of Things*, in AV.
WL:   Jean-Paul Sartre, *What Is Literature?*

### NOTES

1. Jean-Paul Sartre, "L'Homme et les choses," *Situations, I* (Paris: Gallimard, 1947), 226-70, henceforth abbreviated HC. Sartre's essay originally appeared in *Poésie* (July-October 1944) before it was reprinted in *Situations, I*. There is, to my knowledge, no translation of Sartre's essay. All page references will therefore be

to the French edition of Sartre's text, and all translations will be mine. In "L'Homme et les choses," Sartre refers mostly to the collection of poems by Francis Ponge entitled *Le Parti pris des choses*. This collection has been translated under the title *Taking the Side of Things*, in Francis Ponge, *The Voice of Things*, trans. Beth Archer (New York: McGraw Hill, 1972), henceforth abbreviated AV. Page numbers of translated poems quoted from this edition will be given in parentheses, preceded by the abbreviation TST.

2. Sartre has often been criticized for using the authors he studies as mere pretexts for voicing existentialist precepts and his personal political beliefs. See, for example, Steven Ungar, "Sartre, Ponge and the Ghost of Husserl" *SubStance* 8 (1974): 139-50. Ungar claims that Sartre is using Ponge to express antagonism toward the philosopher Edmund Husserl: "Sartre's exposition substitutes polemic for analytic concerns: the allegations against Ponge form a displaced act of violence whose intended victim is more likely Edmund Husserl" (140). Jean-Yves Debreuille argues a similar point about Sartre's aggression toward poets in "De Baudelaire à Ponge: Sartre lecteur des poètes," *Lectures de Sartre,* ed. Claude Burgelin (Lyon: Presses Universitaires de Lyon, 1986), 273-82. The articles of Ungar and Debreuille exemplify the type of criticism that has been addressed to Sartre for almost all the critical texts he has written. The point is not to defend Sartre against these criticisms: there is no doubt, for example, that he often moves from analytic concerns to polemical ones. It is also true that, in "L'Homme et les choses," Sartre pays little attention to the linguistic dimension of Ponge's work. See Michel Collot, *Francis Ponge entre mots et choses* (Seyssel, FR: Champ Vallon, 1991), 7. My aim in this study is not to judge Sartre's critical writings in terms of their value as truth. Rather, my objective is to show the performative thrust of Sartre's procedure and its effects on potential readers of literary works. Neither of the critics quoted above takes into account the relationship to the reader in Sartre's essay on Ponge.

3. Jean-Paul Sartre, *Saint Genet, Actor and Martyr,* trans. Bernard Frechtman (New York: Pantheon Books, 1963).

4. Jean-Paul Sartre, *The Family Idiot,* trans. Carol Cosman, vol. 1 (Chicago: University of Chicago Press, 1981).

5. Usually, the term "dehumanization" has negative connotations. Sartre's procedure in "L'Homme et les choses" changes this. From something totally negative, dehumanization is transformed into something potentially positive.

6. In this respect, Sartre anticipates the work of certain feminist writers, such as Dana Crowley Jack. In her book, *Silencing The Self, Women and Depression* (Cambridge: Harvard University Press, 1991), Jack questions the commonly held belief that depressed women are passive individuals. About certain women living in a patriarchal context, Jack writes: "From the outside, such a woman's behavior may look 'passive,' 'dependent,' and 'helpless.' But from the inside, the compliant role, adopted in the hope of securing attachment, requires *tremendous cognitive and emotional activity to curb* the self. The

woman must *actively* silence her negative feelings, which she (and society) considers unacceptable. Such self-silencing leads her to experience self-condemnation, inner division and depression" (49, emphasis added).
7. Quoted by Sartre in his essay (HC, 169) and originally drawn from Francis Ponge, "La Lessiveuse," *Pièces, Le Grand Recueil* 3 (Paris: Gallimard, 1961), 80-85 (translation mine), henceforth abbreviated GR3. Ponge expresses a similar aim in "Some Reasons for Writing": "I speak only to those who keep quiet *(a matter of arousing them)*, be it only to judge them afterward on their words"; in Francis Ponge, *The Power of Language,* trans. Serge Gavronsky (Berkeley: University of California Press, 1979), 67 (emphasis added), henceforth abbreviated PL.
8. R. D. Laing, *The Divided Self, An Existential Study in Sanity and Madness* (Harmondsworth, UK: Penguin Books, 1965), 43, 58, 73, 75, 77, 80, 83, 82, 163.
9. Sartre is most probably referring to his essays about these writers. On Georges Bataille, see "Un Nouveau Mystique," *Situations, I* (Paris: Gallimard, l947), 133-74. On Maurice Blanchot, see "'Aminadab,' ou du fantastique considéré comme un langage," *Situations, I* (Paris: Gallimard, l947), 113-32. (This essay has been translated as "'Aminadab' or the Fantastic Considered as a Language" in Jean-Paul Sartre, *Literary and Philosophical Essays,* trans. Annette Michelson [London: Rider and Company, 1955], 56-72). About the surrealists, see Sartre's assembled comments in *What Is Literature?* trans. Bernard Frechtman (Bristol, UK: Methuen, 1967), henceforth abbreviated WL.
10. The all-powerful Other can also, of course, be the father or any other authority figure.
11. There is a remarkable continuity between the attitude represented by Ponge and Sartre and the position of a little girl who is quoted by R. D. Laing in *The Divided Self*. In all three cases, the same issues are involved: the transfer of the self into things, the fear of engulfment, and naming as a remedy. The little girl quoted by Laing states:

> I . . . had to walk to my father's shop through a large park which was a long, dreary walk. I suppose, too, that I was rather scared. I didn't like it, especially when it was getting dark. I started to play a game to help pass the time. You know how as a child you count the stones or stand on the crosses on the pavement—well, I hit on this way of passing the time. It struck me that if I *stared* long enough at the environment that I would *blend with* it and disappear just as if the place was empty and *I had disappeared*. It is as if you get yourself to feel you don't know who you are or where you are. To blend into the scenery so to speak. *Then, you are scared of it because it begins to come on without encouragement.* I would just be walking along and felt that I had blended with the landscape. Then I would get frightened and *repeat my name over and over again* to bring me back to life, so to speak. (110, emphasis added)

There is also an allusion to a little girl in "L'Homme et les choses." Sartre uses it to establish a distinction between himself and Ponge, as men, and little

girls. What is at stake, it seems, is the legitimacy and rationality of Ponge's activities and the Husserlian epoche that Sartre had adopted into his philosophy. Sartre defends both Ponge and himself against being suspected of believing in the possibility of observing the thing as it is in-itself. In other words, Sartre is asserting that in the transfer of the self to things, men stay conscious of the fact they are men: "how could I, *a man,* see Nature as it is without men? I once knew a little girl who would leave her garden making a lot of noise and then creep back on tip-toe to 'see what the garden looked like when she was not there.' But Ponge is not as naïve as all that: he knows very well that his desire to reach the thing in-itself is just an ideal" (HC, 236, emphasis added). In using this comparison to a little girl, Sartre in effect underwrites the position expressed by the girl whom R. D. Laing quotes in his book. Yet, in Laing's view, the girl's behavior reflects a psychological imbalance that he calls "depersonalisation." In effect, Ponge and Sartre both describe this type of phenomenon—but, like the little girl quoted by Laing, they remove its negative associations by showing that this process is actually an act over which the individual has control through another act, naming.
12. *Le Parti pris des choses* is difficult to translate, given the different meanings this title connotes in French. As Beth Archer points out, it can mean both "taking the side of things" and "the side taken of things." According to her, Ponge uses his title to mean: "1) the poet's option for things over ideas, and 2) the will expressed by the things themselves" (AV, 10-11).
13. Sartre was already working on this question from a theoretical point of view in the nineteen-thirties. See Jean-Paul Sartre, *Imagination: A Psychological Critique,* trans. Forrest Williams (Ann Arbor: University of Michigan Press, 1962).
14. The protagonists in Sartre's theater are also vulnerable to this belief. "Hell is others" may be understood in this context to refer to mythic others the characters in Sartre's play believe are inside them.
15. The literary text is a thing in the reader's eyes. The presupposition is that the way readers relate to things around them will influence the way they react to a literary text.
16. Sartre considers this myth to be at work in such statements as "I am spoken" or "I am another." It is partly on these grounds that Sartre objected to certain aspects of structuralism and psychoanalysis. See Jean-Paul Sartre, "Sartre répond," *Sartre Aujourd'hui,* special issue of *L'Arc,* (Paris: Librairie Duponchelle, 1990), 87-96. In *Saint Genet, Actor and Martyr,* Sartre leaves us in absolutely no doubt concerning his attitude toward those who propound the myth that human beings are "inhabited souls": "I know that the man whom I hear utter the words 'We doctors . . .' is in bondage. This *we doctors* is his ego, a parasitical creature that sucks his blood. And even if he were only himself, there are a thousand ways of being delivered to oneself as to beasts, of feeding with one's own flesh an invisible and insatiable idol. . . . I don't like inhabited souls" (83).
17. Sartre is referring to the following excerpt from Ponge's "Le Mimosa," in *La Rage de l'expression, Tome premier* (Paris: Gallimard, 1965) (henceforth abbre-

viated TP): "[Of the mimosa], I have an idea deep inside me that I must bring out. . . . I wonder whether it was not through the mimosa that my sensuality was aroused. . . . On the powerful waves of its perfume, I floated, ecstatic. So that now the mimosa, each time it appears within me, around me, reminds me of all that and wilts immediately. . . . Given that I write, it would be inadmissible for there to be no written work by me on the mimosa" (308) (translation mine).
18. From "Les Ecuries d'Augias" ["The Augean Stables"].
19. See also "Some Reasons for Writing": "Ashamed of the way things are arranged, ashamed of all those vulgar trucks which pass *through us* . . ." (PL, 65).
20. From "Les façons du regard" ["The Ways of the Look"], in "Proêmes," translation mine.
21. In Bernard Frechtman's translation of Sartre's text, for "doctor" we read "reader." I have restituted the term "doctor" to this passage.
22. See the chapter "Why write?" in *What Is Literature?* (26-46).
23. A shorter version of this paper was given in French at the session "Ethics beyond Genres" held in March 1993 at the Tenth Annual International Colloquium on Twentieth-Century French Studies, University of Colorado at Boulder. I thank Steven Winspur for giving me the opportunity to speak at his session.

# 5

# Sartre and the Age of the American Novel*
## Anna Boschetti

How much did the American myth count in the imagination and in the behavior of the Europeans? And the American models in the evolution of Western literature in the course of this century? Only comprehensive, systematic research would allow an adequate answer. But Sartre's trajectory can be considered a particularly meaningful indicator: he was the most famous and influential intellectual of a generation that was formed and affirmed itself in the golden age of the American myth, between the end of the twenties and the beginning of the sixties.[1]

Sartre often mentioned the stages of his discovery of America, from the heroes of his childhood readings, Nick Carter and Buffalo Bill, to cinema, jazz, Paul Morand's books (probably in particular *New York*, which was printed in 1930), and the reading of John Dos Passos, William Faulkner, and Ernest Hemingway.[2] When he was young he shared the fundamental idea of the American myth, that the U.S.A. prefigured the future of Europe: "When we were twenty years old, around 1925, we heard of skyscrapers. They symbolized for us the fabulous American prosperity. We discovered them with stupefaction in films. They were the architecture of the future, just as the cinema was the art of the future, and jazz the music of the future."[3] In the late 1920s, Sartre and Simone de Beauvoir read the contemporary American writers as soon as they were translated, and de Beauvoir tells, in *La Force de l'âge*, how their attraction to these novelists was closely associated with a fabulous image of America, enhanced by the most popular products of American culture:

---

*Translated from the original Italian and French by Maria-Teresa Vanderboegh and David Vanderboegh.

American novels, all of them, had yet another merit: they showed us America. This country, we hardly saw it but through deforming prisms, we understood nothing of it; but with jazz and Hollywood films, it had entered our lives. . . . America for us was, first of all, on a background of raucous voices and broken rhythms, a saraband of images: the trances and the dances of the blacks in *Hallelujah,* buildings propped against the sky, prisons in revolt, blast furnaces, strikes, long silky legs, locomotives, airplanes, wild horses, rodeos. When we turned away from this bric-a-brac, we thought of America as a country where the most odious capitalist exploitation triumphed; we hated its exploitation, unemployment, racism, lynchings. Nevertheless, beyond the good and the bad, life over there had something gigantic and unchained which fascinated us.[4]

One must not take too seriously the legend created by Sartre's famous statement in *Les Mots*—"I started out with a handicap of eighty years"[5]—with which he underlined with humor the exceptional nature of his accomplishments.[6] In reality he was barely fifteen years old when, in 1920, he started to follow all the interesting news for young aspiring writers, stimulated by Paul Nizan and other friends with whom he formed an elite within the elite at the *Ecole normale.* Thus, far from being late, he was among the very few in his generation who at the end of their studies were already, in their literary consumption, perfectly in accord with the orientation of the narrow circle of editors, writers, translators, and critics that represented at that time the literary avant-garde. In fact, for those happy few, "the age of the American novel" was just beginning: in 1926 *The Great Gatsby* had just been published in French translation, and it is indicative that the first French book dedicated to the contemporary American novel, Régis Michaud's *Le Roman américain d'aujourd'hui,*[7] was also published in the same year. Then Dos Passos's, Faulkner's, and Hemingway's works were translated as soon as their original versions were published. Simone de Beauvoir, who understood English, read many books in the original version, getting a subscription at Sylvia Beach's bookstore; she spoke about them with Sartre and translated whole chapters for him (BF, 59). With the translation of *Manhattan Transfer* in 1928, and thanks to Nizan, they discovered Dos Passos and noticed the newness of his technique (BC, 268 f.). They obviously were among the most loyal readers of the *Nouvelle Revue Française (N.R.F.)*—it was at that time the institution that embodied and oriented the definition of literary excellence—and of its publications, and it is therefore natural that they immediately found out about the authors recommended as the most interesting and new, such as Dashiell Hammett, Hemingway, and Faulkner: translations of *Sanctuary* (in 1933) and *As I Lay Dying* (in 1934) were published by, respectively, André Malraux and Valéry

Larbaud, the two writers who undoubtedly represented the peak of modernity within the circle of the *N.R.F.* (BF, 212-15).

## THE ROLE OF AMERICAN MODELS IN THE SEARCH FOR ORIGINALITY

One could say that these American writers had in Sartre's literary trajectory a role analogous to the one that his discovery of Husserl and Heidegger had on his philosophical career. These experiences completed his formation and allowed him to assimilate recent acquisitions in each of the two fields in which he wished to affirm himself. According to a cumulative logic, the fruit of secular history, whoever aspires to real greatness must "surpass" the positions of his predecessors. Originality is defined in respect to the whole past—this implies, therefore, mastery of all the preceding patterns—so originality is never, in reality, absolute newness but is instead the capacity of reelaborating and transforming that heredity to the point of challenging it.[8] Thus, if it is true that "Sartre finds his uniqueness in his suppleness in seizing the languages surrounding him and brewing them" (Idt, SO, xxix), this apparently paradoxical way of reaching originality can be found among the majority of the great innovators of the twentieth century. It is inscribed in the exigency of "overcoming," which leads to a paroxysmal play with models: it is enough to think of the prodigious imitators that were, for example, Marcel Proust, Guillaume Apollinaire, and Georges Perec. Thus, if one comes out of the "biographic illusion"[9] that induces one to treat every trajectory as a unique case, there is no need to have recourse, as does Michel Contat (CR), to particular hypotheses, which, furthermore, are anything but convincing, in order to explain the movements of assimilation and the distancing that characterize Sartre's literary journey.[10] It is no surprise that the commentators always find this double tension in his behavior toward the models, and the more it is accentuated, the more the models count for him.[11] A structural exigency, as Jacques Deguy recognizes, allows that "in all criticism of creators, admiration and rivalry are unequally mixed" (CR, 213). But Michel Contat risks deforming even more seriously the sense of Sartre's literary project and the reconstruction that I proposed,[12] when he affirms that Sartre has directed his career "toward a conquest of the *N.R.F.* as a reception area for his work" and declares, "I am summarizing roughly the analysis that Anna Boschetti made of the route of Sartre in the literary institutions of the thirties" (CR 312). Yet Contat knows well that Sartre wrote to obtain something quite different from institutional recognition. Certainly, to be published by Gallimard was objectively important for him, as a means of acceding to literary life. In his research, however, since the beginning, he was not at all concerned with corresponding to the taste of Gallimard's reading committee, which in his eyes was already out-of-date. As he would explain later in *Les Mots*, for him, literature was an absolute; he wanted to be a great writer. To succeed in such a task, one has to be supported by an extremely elevated concept of one's own vocation. Sartre's biography, like those of many other writers, testifies to a precocious feeling of election and confirms what Sartre himself declared in criticizing writers who think of recognition and have limited ambitions: "Without an extravagant pride, one does not write. . . . One must want *everything* if one wants to hope to do *something*."[13]

Dos Passos, Faulkner, and Hemingway embodied in Sartre's eyes, during the thirties, the outposts of modernity, especially on the technical level, which he considered (justly so) decisive.[14] Thanks to their influence, he could relegate to the past the contemporary French models that his generation had to confront, from Proust, André Gide, Jules Romains, and L.-F. Céline to those who were almost his age like André Malraux and Louis Aragon.[15] At the same time, the Americans were the point of departure that had to be surpassed in order to reach originality: "I have tried to learn from the technical research that certain novelists of simultaneity such as Dos Passos and Virginia Woolf have done. I have taken up the question at the very point where they had left it and I hoped to find something new on that path."[16]

It may appear strange that James Joyce is not included among these masters of modernity. Although Sartre became interested early in Joyce and spoke of him and the technique of stream-of-consciousness in the conferences held in Le Havre in 1931-32, it is not clear if he read *Ulysses* in its entirety before the war, and it is not even certain that he did so afterwards.[17] What made him prefer the Americans to Joyce can be perceived in the declaration that inaugurated his activity as a critic in 1938, in the incipit of his article on *Sartoris*: "With some distance, good novels become very much like natural phenomena; we forget that they have an author, we accept them like stones or trees, because they are there, because they exist."[18] In 1947 (in *Qu'est-ce que la littérature?*) he confirmed this ideal: "We hope that our books hold themselves up in the air all by themselves and that the words, instead of pointing back toward the one who traced them, forgotten, alone, unnoticed, be toboggans pouring out readers in the midst of a universe without witnesses, in short that our books exist in the same manner as things, plants, and events, and not at first as the products of man" (SSII, 256). In Joyce the density of cultural allusions and intertextual references certainly does not allow one to forget the presence of the author. Sartre instead, aware that erudition and intellectualism are perhaps the most serious risks he runs as a novelist because of his formation as a

*Normalien*, is attracted by novels that appear to him as "natural phenomena." At a conference held at Yale University in 1946, he shared the unfounded stereotype with which many European readers have approached the American novels: the idea that the originality of the texts is the product of a spontaneous and brutal talent, possible in a nation free from the tradition and the culture that crush the European writers.[19]

Moreover, perhaps Sartre rejects the author's intrusion in the novel for deeper reasons. He shows in all his literary and philosophical work a fascinating repugnance for any form of "substance between two states"[20]—the "root" in *La Nausée*, the "viscous" in *L'Etre et le néant*. These realities are symbols of a contamination between consciousness and being (in its different forms: matter, nature, female sex, social determinations). Such a mixture is perceived by Sartre as dangerous and unbearable for the freedom and transparency of consciousness (cf. BS, 102, 266). Therefore, paradoxically, the most seductive representation that the writer can give of the world is, in the eyes of the philosopher of the subject, the most impersonal representation, one that seems to expel consciousness and bestow on human reality the same nature as plants, minerals, and objects.

The fact is that Sartre, like every authentic writer, is led to the choice of models by a spontaneous attraction for works in which he recognizes congenial directions of research, antidotes for faults to which he is prone, and solutions for which he feels the need. In particular, the techniques of the Americans seem to him extraordinarily matched to his own philosophical exigencies (cf. BF, 157-60; SSII, 255 f.). For the philosophy of consciousness there is not an absolute reality, there is no reality beyond that one seen by a particular consciousness. Focusing on a point of view allows one to mimic the conscious vision with all its limits or the enigmatic effect of a vision from the outside. It is true that research in this direction dates back to the nineteenth century, but Sartre sees in the American novel a particularly successful and radical solution that totally excludes the omniscient narrator and explicit logical-causal links and, in so doing, modifies art in the narration. Thus, the American novelists' way of dealing with temporality is consequent: "If we in fact plunge the reader without mediation into a consciousness, if we refuse him all means of remaining above it, then it is necessary to impose on him without shortcuts the time of that consciousness" (SSII, 327). Sartre, who discovered through Heidegger in 1939 the importance of temporality, is particularly sensitive to the transformations that temporality undergoes in the twentieth-century novel, so much so that he is undoubtedly among the first ones to recognize in this "a very general literary phenomenon," which is in common with "most great contemporary authors" (SSI, 71).

From this develops his attention to the techniques that the American novelists use to render the discontinuous time of consciousness, where perceptions, thoughts, and emotions follow each other without any link and have a highly variable stress, according to the importance that the subject assigns them.[21] Moreover, in practicing what Sartre eventually defines as "the hard realism of subjectivity without mediation or distance" (SSII, 327), all these novelists discover with an unprecedented harshness, "behind the sweetened ceremonies which camouflage the world, the tragic violence of need, of desire and of perversities which their inability to be satisfied brings about" (BF, 214). They show how one can treat social and sexual conditioning with a "materialistic depth." This indication would appear precious to Sartre when, starting from *L'Enfance d'un chef*, he faced the problem of showing how the singularity of an individual life can reconcile itself with collective determinations which, through family and environment, orient, since childhood, the individual's destiny.[22] Sartre admires in particular the way Dos Passos has resolved the problem, with a focus that swings from the character's point of view to the image that a "sententious and collusive" chorus could give of the same character (SSI, 19).

## THE LESSONS OF THE AMERICAN WRITERS

What are the effects of this admiration for American writers? "A great number of rules that we impose upon ourselves in our novels were inspired by Hemingway" (BF, 160). This and similar affirmations in *La Force de l'âge* allow the perception of a rather peculiar relationship with the models: a pair of writer-apprentices who reflect together on their common readings and, as they are accustomed by their philosophical formation to abstract and generalize, they derive from them a set of explicit principles to follow in writing. In such a way, they build a grammar of the novel that does not specifically correspond to any of their models but is a sort of monstrous synthesis of rules inspired by what, in each novel, struck them the most. In conclusion, their point of departure, more than specific novels or pages, is a sort of Vulgate of what is an abstraction: *the* American Novel. Sartre refers to this code when he speaks of "precise laws,"[23] and when in his critical articles he tells the French novelists, with such a peremptoriness, what *is* a novel. The American lesson is not therefore turned into an "influence," according to the Lansonian concept: a direct imitation or reminiscence in the style or in the plots; neither does it express itself through a transformation or a negative reference, as a parody or polemic counterpoint. Therefore we can understand that the majority of the exegetes do not take too seriously the repeated declarations with which Sartre and Simone de Beauvoir acknowledged their debt to the American novel. But these references appear of great importance if one admits that Sartre's work—especially in *Les Chemins de la liberté*—can be technically distinguished from the contemporary French production for the rigor with which he observes the rules of "subjective realism" derived from the Americans. Michel Contat recognizes this when he claims that *L'Age de raison* and *L'Invitée* owe to a common "confirmed romanesque code" their narrative structure: This represents something new in the French novel—even if at first it appears traditional, because it only radicalizes "a certain number of techniques of the realist novel of the nineteenth century . . . resumed and reinvented by the American novel."[24]

As Contat observes, the basic technique remains the same as well in the following volumes of *Les Chemins de la liberté*.[25] In addition, there is the exploration of other possibilities, which Sartre recognizes having conceived thanks especially to Dos Passos: "And as for me, it was after reading a book by Dos Passos that I thought for the first time of weaving a novel out of various, simultaneous lives, with characters who pass each other by without ever knowing one another and who all contribute to the atmosphere of a moment or of a historical period" (SA, 115). Also in his last conversations, his first answer to a question about what had influenced him was: "Dos Passos had an enormous influence on me," and Simone de Beauvoir even replicates: "There wouldn't have been *Le Sursis* without Dos Passos" (BC, 255). Geneviève Idt, who recognized in detail the models present in Sartre's fictional works, undervalues the importance of this statement: "The simultaneity of *Le Sursis* is less a copy of Dos Passos, moreover unfaithful, than the sign of that copy, destined to point out the eruption of history in the order of the Old Continent" (Idt, SO, xxviii n. 1). It is true that the ambition to realize a cycle of novels with a historical background and a multitude of characters could have been suggested by French examples such as Martin du Gard, Aragon, and especially Jules Romains. But only in Dos Passos does Sartre believe to have found a satisfying solution, on the esthetic level, to reconcile the story of a collective event like world war—in which "One Hundred million free consciousnesses" are simultaneously involved (SO, 1025)—and the uniqueness of one life, letting the reader feel at the same time the burden of historicity and the solitude of consciousness. It is also in reading Dos Passos that Sartre matures the conviction that it is possible to realize a form of political commitment through writing: he discovers that it suffices "only *to show,* without explanation or commentary," to push the reader to revolt (SSI, 14). It is true that Sartre freely transforms

Dos Passos's technique of simultaneity: he accelerates the orchestration of sequences and, rather than signaling the passage from one point of view to another, he underlines the continuity, using a routine of transition by analogy. If the importance of a model is derived not by faithfully copying it, but, instead, from the possibilities that, perhaps by contrast, the model allows one to discover, then Dos Passos himself confirms the fundamental reference in *Le Sursis*, on the conceptual level and on the technical level.

Sartre owes to the American writers other aspects of his writing style that, while no less important, are less visible at first sight. They can be recognized in the technique of *La Mort dans l'âme* and in *Drôle d'amitié*. Dos Passos inspired Sartre with his vertiginous collage of heterogeneous styles of discourse, borrowed from literature and from daily life: quotations, songs, newspaper articles, official speeches, and radio news. It is the journalistic tone so much admired in Dos Passos and in Hemingway that makes possible the purposely anonymous style—a "crude document," not a literary one—that is prevalent in the last volumes of the cycle. In short, one must not accept in a myopic way the role of a model to see that the lesson of the American masters was decisive, even though one would look in vain in Sartre's work for the "nuances which would permit one to distinguish the style of Faulkner from that of Dos Passos or of [John] Steinbeck" (IM, 81).

## SARTRE'S KEY ROLE IN THE "AGE OF THE AMERICAN NOVEL"

I do not care to discuss here the success of Sartre's attempt to surpass his masters. His novels that openly apply—albeit in a way sometimes monotonous and mechanical—some of the rules derived from American models were, however, events in the history of the French novel. They expressed a very effective popularization of American techniques, due to the fame that their author started to gain in 1945.[26] Sartre's novels have certainly had a key role in the affirmation of the American novel and in the attention to the technique that suddenly exploded in the French novel at the very end of the war. The phenomenon assumed such clamorous dimensions that Claude-Edmonde Magny, one of the most brilliant and influential representatives of the then-emerging new criticism, dedicated to it in 1948 a book with a meaningful title: *The Age of the American Novel*. Through Sartre's work, American "subjective realism" imposed itself on the new generation as "the zero degree of writing," the obvious technique of a modern novel, suddenly rendering Gide and Proust outdated in their taste for introspection, Malraux hasty, and the French novel an aged tradition needing renewal at the school on the other side of the Atlantic. In this invasion of American novels into France at the liberation, Sartre played an enabling and determining role, thanks to his critical essays, which he had published since 1938 in the N.R.F. and collected in the first volume of *Situations* in 1947, and also to some pages of *Qu'est-ce que la littérature?* and to the many lectures and interviews he gave during that period.

To understand the impact of Sartre's position as a critic and theorist of literature after the war, we must consider the extraordinary philosophical authority that he achieved with *L'Etre et le néant* and, at the same time, the situation of relative indigence of literary criticism and theory in France: there had not yet appeared in the twentieth century any position that had the air of a theory, and, on the other hand, nobody knew the interesting foreign contributions in this field. Russian formalists would only be discovered in 1965, thanks to Tzvetan Todorov's translation. The New Criticism that developed in the thirties in the United States was still unknown, too. In the French university, the literary historiography of Gustave Lanson, who renounced following contemporary production, still dominated. The most famous representatives of criticism between the two wars, such as Jacques Rivière, Albert Thibaudet, Ramon Fernandez, André Suarès and Charles Du Bos, even though they questioned the evolution of the "concept of literature," of the novel and poetry, and inspired Sartre much more than one might expect,[27] did not give the impression of having founded their analyses on a coherent and systematic conceptual elaboration.

One can say the same of the twentieth-century French novelists who preceded Sartre in reflecting on the transformation of the novel and on the techniques that translate these changes. From romanticism onward, writers and, in general, all categories of artists have been induced more and more to accompany their work with an effort to explicate and systematize their ideas on art: the search for originality, which has become the fundamental criterion of evaluation, pushes artists to question themselves on the specificity of their project and to fight to have it recognized. Therefore, artists must not only master the history of their field of production but must also be able to render explicit the differences among various positions. It is thus comprehensible that technique assumes a growing importance: by closely analyzing the functioning of their works, artists become aware that formal procedures are the decisive principle of distinction. First in poetry, then in other literary genres and other artistic fields, the interventions of authors multiply from simple statements of poetics to more ambitious operations that are proposed as true and proper theories on the criteria for the value and on the nature of art but that are, in reality (and understandably so), strategies of self-legitimation. Certain artists' capacity for conceptual elaboration is probably a decisive factor in explaining the strength with which they succeed in imposing their vision and making themselves recognized as leaders. One must recognize how important doctrines, manifestos, and public statements have been in affirming groups and individuals throughout literary history.[28] A very relevant precedent for Sartre was certainly Gide, who, not satisfied with including his ideas in the novel *Les Faux-monnayeurs*, also published a *Journal des Faux-monnayeurs*. But as Gide was not a philosopher, this reflection looks like the expression of a personal research. By contrast, Sartre appears credible in claiming to say what the novel is or is not and in offering universal keys to analyze and evaluate literary achievement. Because of his prestige and competence in philosophy, no other writer or contemporary critic can compete with him when it comes to giving an authoritative theoretical form to his convictions. At the same time, he is a great writer who appropriated the knowledge of a century of literary history and who could not only speak as an expert about technical problems of the novel, but could also shape an essayistic rhetoric, which is by itself an extraordinary accomplishment. When he coquettishly affirms, "There is a crisis of the essay. . . . The contemporary novel . . . has found its style. That of the essay remains to be found. And I say the same of criticism; for I am not unaware that in writing these lines, I am using an out-of-date instrument that university tradition has conserved up until now" (SSI, 133), he has already realized the desired revolution, a new model of essayistic writing and criticism, a fight with the object that from the first sentence strikes and captivates the reader with its absolutely new combination of passion and rhetorical experience, competence and irreverence.

It is also true that in reality Sartre expresses more than a general theory in his ideas about the novel. He articulates a particular position, the implicit "rules" of the "subjective realism" that he learned to practice on the tracks of the Americans. He is the first to attempt to give a coherent shape to this concept, showing how focus, temporality, and the implicit relationship with the reader are aspect-linked among themselves and with all the other choices of the novelist: the grammatical persons and tenses, syntax, the treatment of description, dialogue, and interior monologue.[29]

## THE STRATEGIC FUNCTIONS OF SARTRE'S THEORY

What mainly contributes to making Sartre's approach and verdicts convincing is an axiom, which, when peremptorily expressed like an indisputable truth, seems to give a philosophical foundation to his analysis and provide the literary critic with a new criterion of approach, both simple and enlightening: "A romanesque technique always refers to the metaphysics of the novelist. The task of the critic is to free the latter before appreciating the former" (SSI, 66). This principle is the most clearly ideological aspect of Sartre's formulation, because it actually favors him, bringing out his position. More than any other modern author, he can claim to have founded his novels on a perfectly coherent metaphysics, since he is also the author of an original system of thought. Moreover, he persuades himself that his philosophy is the only appropriate philosophy for a novelist. Creating an easy link between the ontological freedom of man and the freedom of the characters of a novel, Sartre came to think that only an author who believes in human freedom can create characters that are free, therefore unpredictable and thereby more interesting for the reader. And when in 1938-39 he formulated these ideas in his critical articles, he was preparing to write two works, *Les Chemins de la liberté* and *L'Etre et le néant*, which fundamentally propose, in the form of a fictionalized epic and in an ontological form, the same ambition: to show that man is radically free.

The ideological nature of such a conviction appears more evident if we consider the use that Sartre makes of it in his critical interventions before 1945, published in *Situations, I*. These texts are fundamentally inspired by the exigency of showing that no contemporary author, not even among the masters he admires, has fully reached that perfect coherence between technique and metaphysics that seems to him the condition of true greatness and that he feels he himself can realize. In fact he insists on the philosophical weakness of the analyzed writers: incompetence, contradictions, errors, or the inconsistency between metaphysics and technique.[30]

The way he treats Proust, in particular, is meaningful. Among the novelists of the preceding generation, perhaps Proust, more than anyone else, is the author that Sartre is anxious to rid himself of: the *Recherche* had been for Sartre and Nizan when they were adolescent writer-apprentices the first great discovery of the contemporary novel. Jacques Deguy shows that its presence in Sartre's work is very strong, as Sartre acknowledged much later in the film by Alexandre Astruc and Michel Contat: "Someone who had much influence on me, but not directly for it cannot be seen, was Proust. . . . Proust was most certainly one of the initiations to modern literature."[31] To become a great novelist meant therefore, first of all, to surpass Proust.

He did not confront him directly but mentioned him in three articles published in the N.R.F. between August 1938 and July 1939: it had become urgent to declare Proust surpassed at the moment that *La Nausée* was published, a book that, as Deguy says, could be entitled *La Recherche travestie*,[32] since the parodistic reference to the Proustian model is so important. The cry from the heart: "Finally we are delivered from Proust. Delivered at the same time from 'internal life'" is revealing (SSI, 32). Sartre released this statement in a context that at first sight seems incongruous, like the article on Husserl. We can actually better understand Sartre's almost lyric enthusiasm for the idea of intentionality: besides relegating to the past the masters of French philosophy, Léon Brunschwicg, André Lalande, and Emile Meyerson, it helps him on the literary front. It allows him to confute on the philosophical level Proustian psychology and its vision of the world, rejecting the notion of interior life that he, together with Nizan and the other "petits camarades," had abhorred since the time of the *Ecole normale* (BF, 28). The intention of "getting rid of Proust," attacking his vision of man as outdated and unacceptable, is evident in *L'Imaginaire*[33] and in part two of *L'Etre et le néant*, where Proustian psychology is labeled as being like one of those "mechanical interpretations" typical of the last century and untenable after Husserl and Heidegger.

But Sartre must also prove that Proust is surpassed on the technical level—the fundamental level for a novelist. Here the importance that the American masters have for him comes out: the models that he sets against Proust are in fact Dos Passos and Faulkner. In Dos Passos he extols the art of showing "a more flexible order . . . than the psychological mechanism of Proust"; in Dos Passos "the passions and gestures are also things. Proust analyzes them, attaches them to past states, and, by that, renders them necessary" (SSI, 17, 22).

The comparison between Proust and Faulkner is less summary. In fact, even Faulkner is not spared with regard to his implicit philosophy. It is on this level that Sartre considers himself superior to Faulkner and Dos Passos, even if they are the writers he most admires: their world is "impossible . . . because it is contradictory" (SSI, 24). It is meaningful that the fundamental intention we can recognize in both of Sartre's articles about Faulkner is to criticize his metaphysics, "so unromanesque and untrue" (SSI, 74). In his first article, Sartre claims that Faulkner's man is unacceptable: "Faulkner's creatures have a spell cast on them . . . these spells are not possible. Not even conceivable" (SSI, 12). In the second article he condemns the concept of time in Faulkner, and he reaches the conclusion: "I like his art, I don't believe in his metaphysics" (SSI, 74). He needs to point out what seems to be the only limitation of his masters, because it is on this very point that he believes he can surpass them, creating characters coherently inspired to a metaphysics of freedom, in which man "is hardly the sum of what he has, but the totality of what he does not yet have, of what he could have" (SSI, 74).[34]

The enormous admiration that he had for Faulkner, however, showed itself clearly in comparison with Proust. It is true that they are both guilty in Sartre's eyes of having mutilated time: "Proust and Faulkner simply decapitated it, took its future away; that is, the dimension of the actions and of freedom" (SSI, 71). In Proust, however, the technique was also wrong; it was not adequate to this metaphysics of time, unlike that of Faulkner: "To say the truth, Proust's romanesque technique *should have* been that of Faulkner; it was the logical result of his metaphysics. But Faulkner is a lost man and it is because he feels lost that he risks, that he goes to the limit of his thought. Proust is a classic and a Frenchman: the French lose themselves day-to-day and they always end up finding themselves. Eloquence, the taste for clear ideas, intellectualism required Proust to keep at least the appearances of chronology" (SSI, 71).

The counterposition of the American models versus the French regarding the technique is a constant motif. Thus Sartre follows Hemingway in criticizing François Mauriac: "Things in Hemingway's admirable *A Farewell to Arms* are time traps; it populates the story with innumerable resistances, tiny and stubborn, that the hero must break, one after another" (SSI, 48). Only Dos Passos seems to have resolved very adequately "the problem of passage to the typical stumbling block of the social novel," against which, in addition to Proust, Zola and Nizan also clashed (SSI, 22).

## A CONTAGIOUS ADMIRATION

Sartre's influential and contagious admiration for American writers contributed to spreading the vogue for them even outside of France, due to the international fame he enjoyed after the liberation. If Hemingway was already famous, the same could not be said of Faulkner and Dos Passos, who were more difficult writers and thus remained unknown for a long time outside the circle of connoisseurs. It is no doubt because of Sartre that "the glory of Faulkner was more quickly established in France than in the United States"[35] and also that Faulkner could more readily impose himself on the world's attention, so much so that he obtained the Nobel prize.

We must also bear in mind that Sartre's analyses and evaluations have been received and amplified by his disciples: teachers and high-school students, writers, critics. In *Temps et roman*, which develops and tries to systematize Sartre's reflections on point of view and temporality in the novel, Jean Pouillon gives much space to the study of the American models. Claude-Edmonde Magny is also clearly subjugated to Sartre; she quotes him continuously, faithfully taking his position in her essay, *L'Age du roman américain*,[36] which has been widely read because it corresponds to a well-diffused expectation.[37]

One could say that we are especially indebted to Sartre that Hemingway, Dos Passos, and especially Faulkner became essential references in the formation of the New Novelists. Butor has told how in the fall of 1944, when he was a young aspiring writer, attracted by Sartre's fame, he went to listen to the lecture, "A Social Technique of the Novel," at the Maison des Lettres of the rue Saint-Jacques, which was "the first time that I heard of Virginia Woolf, Dos Passos, Faulkner." He even affirmed: "It is absolutely certain that a good part of the problematic of my own novels developed from the reflections which came to me during that conference."[38] Even today Robbe-Grillet remembers having read certain articles by Sartre as a revelation, such as the one about Mauriac and the one about Husserl. These statements may come as a surprise, at a moment when Nathalie Sarraute, Claude Simon, and Marguerite Duras—in the years when, in order to affirm themselves, they in their turn needed to make it appear as if the models in force had been "surpassed"—helped lend credence to the idea of a radical counterposition between their position and that of Sartre, without mentioning what they owed to him and reducing "engagement" to a conversion to "socialist realism." In reality the first Sartre, the Sartre of *La Nausée* and *Le Mur* and especially of *Situations, I,* was a fundamental reference in the epoch of their apprenticeship, as it was unavoidable in a field where every newcomer had to start from the heritage of his or her predecessors. It suffices to consider a meaningful manifesto like *Pour un nouveau roman* to see how the major part of Robbe-Grillet's ideas derived, at that time, from Sartre. One can find here, in a radicalized way, principles of "subjective realism," as Sartre defined it, reading his American models under Husserl's and Heidegger's influence: it is a question of proposing the view of the world of a consciousness that remains on the surface of the objects, that does not want to explain them but rather to present them in their *être là*. Particularly, in his refusal of psychology, of interior life, Robbe-Grillet follows the position expressed by Sartre in the article on Husserl. The New Novelists, in their way of considering description, have recalled Sartre's considerations on Hemingway and his art of rendering the resistance of things and the time flow by pausing on the objects (SSI, 48).

Thus it is natural that they went straight from Sartre to his American masters. Bruno Vercier remarks: "the central silence of Robbe-Grillet's *Le Voyeur* reminds one of *Sanctuary,* and Butor studies 'the family's relationships in *The Bear*' a few years before writing *Degrés* where they occupy such a place" (700). Among the many other examples that we could quote, there is Perec, who certainly thought of the two stories juxtaposed and alternated in *The Wild Palms*, when he wrote *W ou le souvenir d'enfance*. To explain the evolution of Claude Simon with respect to his first novels, his encounter with Faulkner, in particular, is fundamental. It is not an accident that we find in Simon the "oddities of technique" that Sartre, and then, following his example, Jean Pouillon and Claude-Edmonde Magny, noticed in Faulkner, such as: the fragmentation of time, made by an addition of gestures and thoughts and then recomposed in a disordered fashion or according to "the order of the heart," sometimes stopped in a *tableau vivant* or in a repetition of suspended scenes; the propensity to tell in reverse, to leave in silence or just evoke in an eluding way those events that in a traditional novel would be the core of the action; the reticence to explain, making his stories similar to riddles; the monstrous proliferation of sentences and long parentheses and the accumulation of epithets. Both Simon and Faulkner like the great family sagas that incessantly overlap and transform into legends with inexhaustible variations, episodes, and characters distributed along several generations, like biblical genealogies. We could apply to Simon what Sartre says about Faulkner's style: "his abstract, superb, anthropomorphic preacher's style . . . [that] slows down daily gestures, renders them heavy, burdens them with an epic magnificence and makes them sink like a stone, like leaden dogs" (SSI, 9).[39]

It is as if Simon, departing from Proust, had accepted Sartre's judgment: Sartre recognized in Faulkner what, for him, was the Proustian technique, if Proust had dared to go "to the end of his thought" (SSI, 71). In this judgment, which dates back to the article on Faulkner of 1939, it is not audacious to recognize the expression of a personal fear on Sartre's part: he certainly realized that it would have been difficult for him to get rid of "the eloquence, the taste for clear ideas, the intellectualism" and that instead he would remain, in spite of his efforts, "a classic and a Frenchman." But he had pointed out the path to the new generations, and he had recognized that the European novel, to renew itself, had to go to school on the other side of the Ocean.

### ABBREVIATIONS

BC: Simone de Beauvoir, *La Cérémonie des adieux*.
BF: Simone de Beauvoir, *La Force de l'âge*.
BL: Claude Burgelin (ed.), *Lectures de Sartre*.
BR: Pierre Bourdieu, *Les Règles de l'art*.
BT: Anna Boschetti, *Sartre et "Les Temps Modernes."*
CR: Michel Contat, "Les Représentations de l'écrivain dans les écrits de jeunesse."

IC:   Geneviève Idt, "Les Chemins de la liberté, les toboggans du romanesque."
IM:   Geneviève Idt, "Les Modèles de l'écriture dans Les Chemins de la liberté."
SA:   Jean-Paul Sartre, "American Novelists in French Eyes."
SO:   Jean-Paul Sartre, Œuvres romanesques.
SSI:  Jean-Paul Sartre, Situations, I.
SSII: Jean-Paul Sartre, Situations, II.

## NOTES

1. On the American myth in Italian writers, see Dominique Fernandez, Il Mito dell'America negli intellettuali italiani (Caltanissetta-Roma: Sciascia, 1969).
2. For example, in the last "entretiens," in Simone de Beauvoir, La Cérémonie des adieux (Paris: Gallimard, 1981), 245, 248, 254 ff., 301, henceforth abbreviated BC.
3. Jean-Paul Sartre, Situations, III (Paris: Gallimard, 1949), 122 ff. In 1930, in addition to Morand's book, alluded to by Sartre (BC, 248), appeared Scènes de la vie future by Georges Duhamel, which shows in its very title how deeply rooted this idea was in an influential writer of the time.
4. Simone de Beauvoir, La Force de l'âge (Paris: Gallimard "Le Livre de Poche," 1960), 160-61, henceforth abbreviated BF.
5. Jean-Paul Sartre, Les Mots (Paris: Gallimard, 1964), 49.
6. Among the commentators who have given excessive credit to the idea of Sartre as an author who belongs fundamentally to the nineteenth century, and diffident toward the avant-garde, see in particular Geneviève Idt, "Préface," Œuvres romanesques, by Jean-Paul Sartre (Paris: Gallimard, 1981), xv-xxxiii (henceforth abbreviated SO) and Michel Contat, "Les Représentations de l'écrivain dans les écrits de jeunesse: une forme gaie de la haine de soi," in Gli scritti postumi di Sartre, ed. Giovanni Invitto and Aniello Montano (Genova: Marietti, 1993), 309-19, henceforth abbreviated CR. In reality, to receive from the family and from school a traditional literary culture is what normally happens, and precocious familiarization with books is an advantage with respect to the situation of a first-generation intellectual. Moreover, as we saw, Sartre had the opportunity to learn about contemporary literary research from adolescence and possessed an exceptional precocity in comparison to other students of the same age.
7. Régis Michaud, Le Roman américain d'aujourd'hui (Paris: Boivin, 1926).
8. Cf. Pierre Bourdieu, Les Règles de l'art (Paris: Seuil, 1992), 337 f., henceforth abbreviated BR.
9. Not in the sense according to which Sartre used this expression (Les Carnets de la drôle de guerre [Paris: Gallimard, 1983], 105 ff.), but in Bourdieu's sense ("L'Illusion biographique," Actes de la Recherche en Sciences Sociales 62-63.6 [1986]: 69-72). On the artistic course as trajectory in social space, see also BR, 356-71.
10. To explain the exigency that leads Sartre to put in question all the images of the

writer, Michel Contat invokes the "delay" in formation and a presumed "self-hatred." But the first hypothesis, as we saw, is very disputable. The second seems to me even unsustainable: on the contrary, one could easily show that in Sartre the critique of literature and self-critique are in fact one form of self-love, as these allow him to put himself always above and beyond any position.

11. As to the relationship with Proust, see Jacques Deguy, "Sartre lecteur de Proust," *Lectures de Sartre,* ed. Claude Burgelin (Lyon: Presses Universitaires de Lyon, 1986), 199-216, and following notes, henceforth abbreviated BL. About the reference to Gide, see Pierre Masson, "Sartre lecteur de Gide: authenticité et engagement," BL, 217-40. On the relationship with Maupassant, see Jacques Lecarme, "Sartre lecteur de Maupassant?" BL, 185-98. On the models in *Les Chemins de la liberté,* in particular Malraux, see Geneviève Idt, "*Les Chemins de la liberté:* les toboggans du romanesque," *Sartre,* special issue of *Obliques* 18-19 (1979): 75-94 (henceforth abbreviated IC) and "Les Modèles de l'écriture dans *Les Chemins de la liberté,*" *Etudes sartriennes, I,* Cahiers de Sémiotique Textuelle 2 (1984): 75-92, henceforth abbreviated IM.

12. Anna Boschetti, *Sartre et "Les Temps Modernes,"* (Paris: Minuit, 1985), henceforth abbreviated BT; translated as *The Intellectual Enterprise* by Richard C. McCleary (Evanston, IL: Northwestern University Press, 1988).

13. Jean-Paul Sartre, *Situations, IX* (Paris: Gallimard, 1972), 12.

14. "On the whole," Simone de Beauvoir writes in *La Force de l'âge,* "we found that the technique of French novelists was quite rudimentary, compared to that of the great Americans" (157).

15. The confrontation with them remains mainly implicit, in the form of a parody of the models. Céline and Proust are very present in *La Nausée* (cf. Geneviève Idt, *"La Nausée": Sartre, analyse critique par Geneviève Idt* [Paris: Hatier, 1971] and Michel Contat and Michel Rybalka, "Notice," *La Nausée,* SO, 1663-66). Gide, Romains, Aragon, and Malraux are present in *Les Chemins de la liberté* (cf. IC; Idt, "Préface," SO; IM). But there are some explicit references that confirm how strong the need to surpass them is in Sartre. For instance, some sentences about Malraux in *Les Carnets de la drôle de guerre* are meaningful: "Began to reread *La Condition humaine.* Irritated by a fraternal resemblance between the literary processes of Malraux and my own. . . . I was never influenced by him but we have undergone the same common influences—influences which were not literary. . . . I am epoch-making with Malraux (same intellectualism). I must say that nothing is brought to perfection with him. The syntax is weak, the words are often ugly and ambiguous. I have the impression of rereading my first draft" (429-30). See also note 7.

16. Jean-Paul Sartre, "Prière d'insérer," *L'Age de raison* and *Le Sursis,* SO, 1912.

17. In the last interviews (BC), Sartre fluctuates between uncertainty (254) and the admission that he did not read it until war time (281). So Sartre is not very precise about himself when he says: "thus we have learned from Joyce to search for a second type of realism: the unrefined realism of subjectivity without mediation or distance" (*Situations, II* [Paris: Gallimard, 1948], 327,

henceforth abbreviated SSII). But in this text he speaks on behalf of his generation, and therefore it is natural that he recognizes Joyce as the master of all, including the Americans.
18. Jean-Paul Sartre, *Situations, I* (Paris: Gallimard, 1947), 7, henceforth abbreviated SSI.
19. Jean-Paul Sartre, "American Novelists in French Eyes," *The Atlantic Monthly* 178.2 (August 1946): 115, henceforth abbreviated SA.
20. Jean-Paul Sartre, *L'Etre et le néant* (Paris: Gallimard, 1943), 699.
21. Read, for example, Sartre on Dos Passos (SSI, 16), on Hemingway (48), on Faulkner (66), and Beauvoir on Hemingway (BF, 159 ff.), and on Faulkner (272 ff.).
22. The problems posed by Marxism and psychoanalysis were topical subjects in the literary world during the thirties, as the surrealists helped stir up interest. Freud's thought was a very important reference for Céline's *Voyage au bout de la nuit* or *Antoine Bloyé* by Nizan. These books counted for Sartre and certainly stimulated his decision to portray the evolution of characters marked by history and society (see BT, 72).
23. Claudine Chonez, "Jean-Paul Sartre, romancier philosophe," *Marianne* (23 November 1938), SO, 1696.
24. Michel Contat, "Notice," *L'Age de raison,* SO, 1892. Which are these rules? Speaking of *L'Invitée,* Simone de Beauvoir has evoked some of them: "I observed the rule that we held, Sartre and I, as fundamental and that he exposed a little later in an article on Mauriac and the French novel: in each chapter, I coincided with one of my heroes, I forbade myself to know more or to think more than he" (BF, 389). "Refusing to take in at a glance the multiple consciences of my heroes, I . . . forbade myself from intervening in the unfolding of time; I carve from it certain moments from chapter to chapter: but I present each one in its integrality, without ever summarizing a conversation or an event." Then she adds: "There is one rule, less rigorous, but of which the reading of Dashiell Hammett as well as that of Dostoevski had taught me the effectiveness, and that I tried to apply: every conversation must be in action, that is, must modify the relationship of the characters and the whole of the situation. Moreover, while it is unfurling, something else of importance must happen elsewhere: thus leaning toward an event that the thickness of the printed pages separates from him, the reader feels, as do the characters themselves, the resistance and the passage of time" (396).

It is evident that de Beauvoir is talking about the same principles that Sartre had formulated in an extremely assertive tone in the 1939 article on Mauriac. For him as well the fundamental rule is rigor in focusing:

A novel is an action told from different points of view. . . . But each of these interpretations must be in movement, that is, carried along by the very action that it interprets. In a word, it is the testimony of an actor and it must reveal the man who witnesses as well as the event that is witnessed; it must evoke our impatience (will it be confirmed, or contradicted by events?) and from there make us feel the resistance of time: each point of view is therefore relative and the best will be such that time offers to the reader the greatest resistance. The interpretations, the explanations given by the actors will all be conjectural: perhaps the reader, beyond these conjectures, will have a foreboding of the absolute reality of the event, but it is for him alone to recover it, if he has the taste for this exercise, and, if he tries it, he will never leave the domain of likelihoods and probabilities. In any case, the introduction of the absolute truth, or God's point of view, in a novel is a double technical error: first of all, it supposes a commentator removed from the action and purely contemplative, which would not agree with that esthetic law formulated by Valéry, according to which a given element of a work of art must always maintain a plurality of relations with the other elements. Secondly, the absolute is atemporal. If you carry the story to the absolute, the ribbon of duration breaks clean; the novel fades before your eyes: only a languishing *sub specie aeternitatis* truth remains. (SSI, 42 f.)

Another rule, as a corollary of the first one, is the elimination of comments and explanations to maintain the unpredictability of the characters: "Do you want your characters to live? Make them free. It is not a question of defining, even less of explaining (in a novel the best psychological analyses smell of death), but only of presenting unforeseeable passions and acts" (33 ff.).

Sartre has also explained, in a suggestive way, his preference for narration in the third person:

It also happens that this pronoun leads us into an intimacy which should logically express itself in the first person. . . . In fact novelists use this conventional mode of expression by a sort of discretion, in order not to ask of the reader a complicity without recourse, to cover with a glaze the vertiginous intimacy of the "I." The conscience of the heroine represents the opera glasses by means of which the reader can get a glance of the romanesque world, and the word "she" gives the illusion of a recoiling of the glasses; it recalls that this revealing conscience is also the creature of a novel, a point of view on the privileged point of view, and accomplishes for the reader the vow so dear to lovers: to be at the same time oneself and another than oneself. (38 f.)

Finally, he expressed himself on how to deal with objects and dialogues: "The true novelist is passionate for everything that resists, for a door, because it must be opened, for an envelope, because it must be unsealed. . . . In a novel one must be quiet or say all, and especially not omit anything, not skip anything" (48).

25. Michel Contat, "Notice," *Le Sursis,* SO, 1967.
26. For instance Gerald Prince says: "By refusing to mutilate the conversations of his characters, Sartre renewed the traditional dialogue of the French novel" (*Métaphysique et technique dans l'oeuvre romanesque de Sartre* [Geneva: Droz, 1968], 39), and he quotes Jean-Bertrand Barrère, according to whom, after Sartre, the dialogue of the novels tends toward "parlerie" (*La Cure d'amaigrissement du roman* [Paris: Albin Michel, 1964]).

27. For instance, in Jacques Rivière's essay, "La Crise du concept de littérature," *La Nouvelle Revue Française* (1 February 1924), it is possible to recognize the embryo of the problems expressed in *Qu'est-ce que la littérature?* The Bergsonian concept of the novel as "duration" is introduced by Albert Thibaudet in "Réflexions sur le roman," *La Nouvelle Revue Française* (1 August 1912), 9 f., and it is commonly used since the twenties. Sartre himself quoted Ramon Fernandez, *Messages*, first series (Paris: Gallimard, 1926), on the distinction between the "novel [which] unfolds in the present" and the "story [which] is written in the past [and] explains" (SSI, 15 ff.). It is Maurice Coindreau who introduces the expression "subjective realism," using it to define Faulkner's vision of the world in the preface to the translation of *The Sound and the Fury*.
28. Pierre Bourdieu shows how this ever more accented inclination toward reflexivity correlates with the evolution of a cultural field toward autonomy (BR, 334 ff.).
29. Narratology will, twenty years later, assimilate and develop these directions of research and some of the indications about the method, through the mediation of *Temps et roman* (Paris: Gallimard, 1946), the book published by Sartre's disciple, Jean Pouillon. In particular, it seems that Gérard Genette owes much to Sartre: if we look closely at the approach that he uses in *Figures III* (Paris: Seuil, 1972), we can see that it is already sketched, in its main categories, in the articles about Faulkner, Dos Passos, and Mauriac published in *Situations, I* (1947). Sartre already expresses enlightening considerations about the order, the speed, and the frequency of time in the story, and he distinguishes time of narration from that in the plot and in the story (SSI, 72). The Sartrean analysis on point of view and the modalities of discourse are also considered in the fourth part of *Figures III*, which is dedicated to the "mode" of narration. Sartre also dwells on aspects that Genette includes in the fifth section, "Voice"—on the use of pronouns (SSI, 38), for instance, or on narrative levels (43). Moreover, on a page about the fantastic, apropos of "Aminadab," we find precious hints for the history of genre transformations. On the other hand, commenting on Dos Passos (15-16) and Albert Camus (109), Sartre makes some observations about the implications of verbal tenses, which, although not totally original (Sartre himself mentions Fernandez), indicate a line of research that Weinrich will examine more closely. Also, some considerations on syntax are worthy of certain analyses of Spitzer (for example, 109, apropos of Camus's *L'Etranger*).
30. He rebukes Mauriac for not giving his characters the freedom that he should give them, as a Christian novelist. He says that in Giraudoux "we discover Aristotle's world, a world buried for four hundred years" (90). Regarding *L'Etranger* he declares quite openly: "Mr. Camus uses some coquettishness in citing texts by Jaspers, Heidegger, and Kierkegaard, which he moreover does not seem to understand well" (94). Bataille "has evidently not understood Heidegger, of whom he speaks often and in an unfitting manner" (145), and he is put down as a thinker. On Parain: "his knowledge is that of his genera-

tion: he does not know about today's psychologists and German philosophers, or he does not understand them. He knows Hegel very badly; he is not up to date on Kant's writing; the recent works on aphasia have escaped him (Gelb and Goldstein). Therefore he debates, without realizing it, in the midst of out-of-date problems. He arrives at conclusions from that French philosophical movement which goes from Ribot to Brunschwicg through Bergson. He liquidates, tabulates the results. For us, all of these names are quite dead" (222-23). About Ponge he says: "his art appears to us as of a rule, going farther than his thought" (270).

31. *Sartre: texte du film*, ed. Michel Contat (Paris: Gallimard, 1977), 30.
32. Jacques Deguy, "Sartre lecteur de Proust," BL, 212.
33. Jean-Paul Sartre, *L'Imaginaire: psychologie phénoménologique de l'imagination* (Paris: Gallimard "Idées," 1940; reprint 1966), 136-37.
34. From this comes the persistence with which he presents this intention, both in his declarations about his projects released to Claudine Chonez after the publication of *La Nausée* ("Jean-Paul Sartre, romancier philosophe," *Marianne* [23 November 1938], SO, 1697), and in the title itself of *Les Chemins de la liberté* and in the "Prière d'insérer" that accompanies the first two volumes (SO, 1911). One of the main reasons that led him to abandon *Les Chemins de la liberté* and also literature is certainly, as Michel Contat recognizes (see the "Notice" to *Les Chemins de la liberté*, SO, 1869 f. and CR, 318-19), the awareness that he will not succeed in "surpassing" the Americans, that he will not be able to make of his characters the embodiment of freedom and heroism in the resistance movement. Paradoxically, the very fact of having claimed this intention since the beginning causes him to fall into the same error for which he had rebuked Mauriac: his characters are too predictable for the reader. Other reasons converge into this, as Contat himself indicates ("Notice" to *Les Chemins de la liberté*). For me it is also important to recall that around 1950-52, Sartre ends up resigning to the psychological pressure of the French communists, who put in question the writer's social utility. Then he loses interest in the novel even as a reader: after the Americans, the only contemporary writers who attract his attention are Melville, Genet, and later Gombrovitch (see, for example, BC, 278-80).
35. Bruno Vercier, "Traduit de l'étranger," *La Littérature en France depuis 1945* (Paris: Bordas, 1974), 698.
36. Claude-Edmonde Magny, *L'Age du roman américain* (Paris: Seuil, 1948).
37. Magny quotes Sartre to point out that French writers consider the Americans masters of the contemporary novel (46). The attention to technique, which is already taken for granted, derives from Sartre (chapter 2), in particular the attention to point of view, the different ways of expressing temporality, and the journalistic style in the novel (on Steinbeck, 187 f.). The idea of a link between technique and metaphysics is received, especially regarding Dos Passos (72), and Sartre's statement, according to which in Dos Passos "the technique is pregnant with metaphysics" (137), is quoted. Moreover, one can

find already in Sartre (SSI, 52), who resumes in his turn an argument spread throughout France since the twenties (cf. Michel Raimond, *La Crise du roman: des lendemains du naturalisme aux années vingt* [Paris: Corti, 1966], 325), Magny's thesis (111 f.) that the adoption of a particular point of view corresponds to an unavoidable exigency, in an epoch of "generalized relativity." Magny also inherits one of the newest and most important aspects of Sartre's reflections on literature, that is, the importance given to the role of the reader. But it would take a long time to list all of Sartre's quotations and the cues of analysis deriving from him. This does not take into account—and this is important—the fact that Magny considers Sartre's preferences her own, helping to spread them: the models that she presents with greater admiration are Dos Passos and Faulkner. Especially in regard to Dos Passos, one wonders if there would be such an admiration if Sartre had not written: "I consider Dos Passos the greatest writer of our time" (SSI, 24).

38. Michel Butor, "Une Technique sociale du roman," *Sartre et les Arts*, special issue of *Obliques* 24-25 (1981): 67.

39. The reference to Faulkner on behalf of the New Novelists—in particular Claude Simon—has been pointed out and analyzed many times. See, for instance, André Bleikasten, "Faulkner et le nouveau roman," *Langues Modernes* 60 (1966): 422-32; Alastair B. Duncan, "Claude Simon and William Faulkner," *Forum for Modern Language Studies* 9 (1973): 235-52; J. de Labriolle, "De Faulkner à Simon," *Revue de Littérature Comparée* 53 (1979): 358-88; Stuart Sykes, *Les Romans de Claude Simon* (Paris: Minuit, 1979); and Vercier, "Traduit de l'étranger."

# 6

# The Narrative of Return in "Orphée noir"

## Marie-Paule Ha

Sartre's celebrated and celebratory essay on negritude, "Orphée noir," which served as the preface to L. S. Senghor's *Anthologie de la nouvelle poésie nègre et malgache de langue française*, has inspired a great many critical commentaries ever since its first appearance in 1948.[1] Whatever merits or demerits can be seen in Sartre's understanding of the predicament of the colonized Africans, critics invariably credit him as being one of the rare European intellectuals of his generation to promote actively the negritude movement: "Sartre speaks of black poetry with a prophetic fervor, a sensibility, a simplicity and a sincerity that were quite rarely displayed by Europeans up to that time."[2] While recognizing these highly laudable efforts at advancing the cause of the colonized, I propose here another rereading of this justly famous essay by focusing on the narrative of return that frames Sartre's discussion of the negritude movement. My reading will show that the Sartrean narrative, which relies heavily on a manichean positioning of colonizer/colonized relations,[3] fails to account for the highly and necessarily complex character of the colonial and postcolonial situations.

### I

At the most obvious level, the chief textual strategy deployed in "Orphée noir" is to present the worlds of the colonizer and the colonized in terms that are posited (at least in Sartrean discourse) as diametrically opposite. Hence, while the colonizer is referred to as "the white man," the colonized is reduced to the color synecdoche of "black." This black/white opposition is later relayed in the text by pairs such as poetry/prose and agriculturist/engineer, which are again presented as antinomic: "We would say that a poetry of agriculturists poetry is *opposed* here to a prose of engineers" (ON, 265, my emphasis). Sartre's deployment of these series of binary terms in his discussion of the colonial condition proves to be quite problematic. While devoting three pages of the essay to demonstrating how "the objective features" (238) of the situation of the white proletariat, "oppressed by the technical" (234), necessitate for their liberation the mastery of a "professional, economic and scientific know-how" (234), which in turn requires the use of prose as a means of self-expression, Sartre has not explained why the most efficient way for blacks to resist exploitation is to construct "a more accurate view of black subjectivity" (238), a subjectivity best expressed by poetic language.[4] Without denying that there are differences between the condition of the white proletariat and that of the colonized, I find that Sartre, by insisting on the racial aspect of colonial exploitation, seems to overlook the double alienation of the colonized, as René Depestre has pointed out: "the black proletarian is doubly alienated: on the one hand, alienated (like the white proletarian) as a source of labor . . . ; on the other hand, alienated as a being with black pigmentation."[5] Indeed, at the time of Sartre's essay, far from being that ethereal romantic figure of the hellenic poetic god, "Black Orpheus," Depestre reminds us, "was mainly a sugar cane cutter, a cook, a scavenger, a coal-trimmer, a shoe-shine boy, a groom, a nightman, a jack-of-all-trades, a do-all, cleaning and smoothing everything out for the well-being of the white colonists" (DR, 86).

Sartre's use of antithesis in "Orphée noir" as a textual device to produce a certain rhetorical effect aims primarily at dramatizing for a metropolitan audience the plight of the world of the colonized, which is constructed in all aspects as contrary and inimical to the colonizer's world. Yet this strategy is itself subverted by other discursive practices within the text, which in turn problematize its manichean representation of the colonial condition. The first inconsistency concerns Sartre's own positioning, which is constantly shifting throughout the essay. The tactic that consists of presenting the colonial world in antithetical terms of black/white, poetic/prosaic, subjective/objective, and synthetic/analytic also comes to structure the locutionary stand of the essay, which rests on an us/them binarism. Sartre starts the essay by addressing himself directly through the use of the second-person plural pronoun "you" to a group of implied readers whom he presumes to be solely both whites and males. In a few sentences later, this "you" group apparently merges with the authorial voice to become a "we" that is in turn pitted against the group of the colonized referred to in the third-person pronoun, thus making them into a discursive object qua the Other of the "we" group.

Yet even within the first section, Sartre moves from "we" to the authorial first person "I," a move that would enable him, as pointed out by Stuart Z. Charmé,[6] to displace himself from the collective "we" and to confer upon himself the role of the interpreter of the blacks to his fellow white readers: "In a word, I am addressing myself here to whites and I would like to explain to them what blacks already know" (ON, 233). The resulting effect is the blurring of the initial oppositional groupings, since Sartre, a member of the white male community, not only presents himself as their mediator, but also assumes the role of the prophet predicting on behalf of the blacks the future orientation of the negritude movement, when he claims toward the end of the essay that "He [the man of color] is the one who walks on the crest between past particularism which he has just surmounted and the future universalism which will be the twilight of his negritude" (283). Yet at other times Sartre seems to display a momentary about-face as he admits, after devoting many pages to explaining to the metropolitan readers the characteristics of "the black soul" or "the black Essence," that the latter is a subject about which "a white would not know how to speak appropriately because he has no interior experience of it" (261). In this reversal, Sartre, by virtue of his whiteness, repositions himself as an outsider to the inner world of the black experience. In fact, the whole essay bears witness to this constant shifting of Sartre between the two polarized black/white communities as he moves in and out of what he believes to be the consciousness of the two groups, thereby undermining the very segregation the text elaborates.

Similar contradictions also underlie Sartre's formulations of negritude, which, while aiming to bring out what he calls "black Essence," are paradoxically framed in the archetypal Christian narrative of Eden-Fall-Redemption. The very language he uses in the description of the negritude poets' enterprise is loaded with biblical expressions and images such as: "Negro poetry is evangelical, it announces the good news" (ON, 239); "the quest for the black Grail" (261); "the black race is a chosen race"; "to call negritude a Passion" (270). Hence, one of the most profound contradictions in Sartre's essay is that, on the one hand, as Charmé points out, the black is represented as the "perpetual negation" of the white culture (CV, 201); on the other hand, the author of "Orphée noir" could find no better way of envisioning the situation of the colonized than in Western mythical schemes. His use of the Orphic myth to describe the negritude poets' enterprise is a case in point, for is not Sartre here doing exactly what he later accuses the imperialists of doing, when he criticizes Europe for having "hellenized the Asians, created a new breed, the Greco-Latin Negroes" (168)?[7] Besides the Orphic myth, another Greek myth is later introduced in the essay when Sartre formulates the relations between the colonized, Mother Africa, and the white patriarchal culture in terms of the Oedipean triangle:

> Negritude, present and hidden, haunts him [the Negro], brushes him; he brushes against its silky wing; it flutters, all spread out across him like his deep memory and his highest exigency, like his buried and betrayed childhood, and the childhood of his race and the call of the earth. . . . But if he turns around to look at it face to face, it will disappear in smoke; the walls of white culture with their science, their words and their mores, stand between it and him. (241)

Following the Oedipean logic, the frustrated black sons should destroy the white Father so as to reunite with Mother Africa: "It will nevertheless be necessary to tear down the walls of the prison-culture, it will be necessary to return to Africa one day" (242). Such a reading of the colonial situation in Oedipean terms can be troublesome on different grounds. On the political level, it can be construed as reinforcing the stereotypical imaginary colonial relation of paternalism in which the colonized are traditionally assigned the infantile qua primitive role; hence the danger of the call so persistent in "Orphée noir" for a return to a past associated with the land of childhood: ". . . comes the dazzling circle of the Islands and of childhood which dance in a ring around Africa" (ON, 240). This stubbornness on Sartre's part to see precolonial Africa as the pristine prelapsarian childhood paradise to which the alienated blacks should seek to return stems from his manichean perception of the colonial relations in which the colonizers' world is represented as fallen and corrupted to the core by barbaric capitalist values. Moreover, the Sartrean narrative of return seems to overlook the ironical fact that the negritude theory draws in important ways its inspiration from the works of a great number of Western thinkers. Abiola Irele establishes such a genealogy in his discussion of Senghorian negritude:

> The terms in which Senghor formulates his theory of Negritude resound with distinct echoes of the work of a whole group of writers, thinkers and scholars in the West who can be situated within a single perspective—that of the anti-intellectual current in European thought. . . . his notion of "vital force" . . . can be attributed to Father Placide Tempels' now classic study of Bantu philosophy, while that of "participation," as well as his distinction between the traditional forms of the collective mentality in Europe and Africa respectively, owes much to the work of Lucien Lévy-Bruhl. . . . To Bergson, Senghor owes the concept of "intuition" on which revolves his explication of the African mind and consciousness.[8]

## The Narrative of Return in "Orphée noir"

This rhetoric of return to a fantasized precolonial space as a means of "disalienation" of the colonized results in two contradictory understandings of the negritude movement in "Orphée noir." On the one hand, negritude is seen as part of a historical process, namely "the minor moment of a dialectical progression: the theoretical and practical affirmation of the supremacy of the white man is the thesis; the position of negritude as an antithetical value is the moment of negativity" (280). In this dialectical movement, negritude "in order to destroy itself . . . is a transition and not a conclusion, a means and not an ultimate end" (280).[9] Framed in this narrative, the blacks' oppression is linked to Western capitalist exploitation as their condition is compared to that of the white proletariat. Yet while admitting that both groups are victims of capitalism, Sartre emphasizes the fact that the black is first and foremost victim "as a black" (236). His next move is to equate color with race without further defining the two terms, a move that brings him to conclude that "since he [the black] is oppressed in and because of his race, he must first of all take cognizance of his race" (236). It is this "prise de conscience de la race" that constitutes one of the main goals of negritude. What Sartre seems to imply here is that color/race is the cause of the Africans' oppression by Europeans who "for centuries tried in vain to reduce him, *because he was a Negro,* to the state of an animal . . ." (236, my emphasis); yet one could very well argue that color/race has been used by the colonizers as a pretext to justify their inhuman exploitation of the colonized.

Such a use of the notion of "race" without a critical examination of the historical development of this term[10] leads Sartre into the trap of essentialist nativism that runs counter to the understanding of negritude as a historical process. Indeed, it is highly perplexing that Sartre, the existentialist philosopher, who, in his famous motto "existence precedes essence," taught a whole generation of Europeans that "if man . . . is not definable, it is because to begin with he is nothing. He will not be anything until later, and then he will be what he makes of himself,"[11] has not the slightest hesitation to assign to the colonized what he calls "black soul," "black Essence." What is even more disturbing, as many critics have pointed out, is that this so-called "old black being" as fantasized by Sartre is made up of all the nineteenth-century European clichés about the Africans. Buried deep within them, we are told, are those "primitive rhythms" or "immemorial instincts" (ON, 253) that can be awakened to the sounds of the tam-tam as our black brothers throw themselves "in trances, rolling on the ground like a possessed person falling prey to himself" (242).

By thus preaching a return to their "essence," which is presented as a kind of imagined natural state *à la Rousseau,* Sartre encloses the colonized in a timeless primitive and archaic space, as seen in this passage in which the black is described in the atemporal anthropological present as essentially "the natural man," who

> grows at the same pace as his wheat; minute by minute, he exceeds himself and turns golden; on the watch in this gentle breeze which blows stronger, he intervenes only to protect.... Technology has contaminated the white farmer, but the black remains the great male of the earth, the sperm of the world. His existence is the great vegetal patience; his labor is the repetition from year to year of the sacred coitus. (266)

Here again Sartre sets up the worlds of the blacks and the whites in contrasting terms. If the whites have incurred the misfortune of living in the fallen state of technological progress, their black brothers find themselves confined in a "natural" state (on a par with plants and animals) totally immune to and untouched by historical changes the most important of which is, of course, colonization. It is no surprise then that later on in the essay, when Sartre has to find a comparative model to negritude poetry in the West for his European readers, he has to reach back to the archaic past of Western antiquity: "Thus the black bears witness to natural Eros; he is both its manifestation and incarnation; to find a comparative term [to negritude poetry] in European poetry, one would have to go back to Lucretius, the peasant poet who celebrated Venus, mother-goddess, at the time when Rome was nothing more than a big farmers' market" (269).

This essentializing of the condition of the colonized leads Sartre into reducing and simplifying the complexity of African cultures and histories into a monolithic figure known as "the Negro" or "the black" in the essay. One wonders to what historical realities this generic "black" corresponds. Is Sartre justified in assuming that the negritude poets who belong to the elite class of the Westernized, male, African or Carribean intellectuals can adequately represent the aspirations and sentiments of all African and Carribean men and women who might not share their fortune or misfortune of belonging to the bourgeois class? Such a skepticism has been voiced by Stanilas Adotevi in his discussion of negritude:

> One might well wonder whether this tireless descent of the Negro (of negritude) into himself (itself) reveals, as Sartre claims, the old black being.... Do these exhibited "wounds," this feeling of being torn between "civilization" and the black land mean anything to those who remain in the homeland? ... does this great collective poetry which Sartrean lyricism institutes partake of the

black totality? Does it speak for all the Negroes as stated in "Orphée noir"?[12]

The nostalgia for a return to a precolonial past fantasized as some uncorrupted Edenic site may very well be an expression of the specific historical situation of the negritude poets in view of their deep immersion in the French metropolitan culture. One such influence is their link with surrealism.[13] It is indeed significant that in the surrealist movement one also finds this same fascination with a kind of "natural state" associated with the child and the primitive,[14] who are endowed, according to André Breton, with the unique ability to reconcile the dualisms that tear asunder modern Western men:

> For surrealism—and I think that one day this will be its glory—everything has been put to good use to overcome those oppositions wrongly presented as insurmountable and gouged deeply in time; these are the true refiners of suffering: the opposition between insanity and so-called "reason" which refuses to take irrationality into consideration, the opposition between mental representation and physical perception, both of them products of the dissociation of *a unique original faculty whose trace remains in the primitive and the child*. . . . (my emphasis)[15]

The surrealist remedy that would enable men to retrieve the lost original state, the author of the "Second manifeste" claims, is to undertake a descent into our innermost being, a metaphor that echoes that of the Orphic descent that Sartre ascribes to negritude poetry: "Let us recall that the idea of surrealism is directed simply to the total regaining of our psychic power by that means which is none other than the dizzying descent into ourselves, the systematic illumination of the hidden places and the progressive darkening of others . . ." (CB, 20). These parallels lead us to wonder whether the negritude movement could not be read as a form of "recycled primitivism," as the negritude poets engage in an act of poetic reappropriation and "detour"[16] rather than a *retour* or return. Through these strategies, the colonial or postcolonial subject comes to a *prise de conscience* of his/her identity through the mediation of the Other, which means that the identity in question necessarily results from a reconstruction rather than a recovery from an "original" state.

The contradictions and difficulties that underly Sartre's reflections on negritude have a certain usefulness in that they illustrate the extreme complexity of the post/colonial conditions, which requires a rethinking of the traditional strategy of "reversing the hierarchy" (ON, 249) as practiced in

"Orphée noir." First of all, such an inverting of the hierarchical order of the terms as defined by the existing power structure has very limited subversive effect if the validity of the hegemonic discourse has not been questioned. An instance of this failure to challenge truly the premises of colonial discourse in Sartre's essay is his uncritical use of notions such as "culture," "race," "language" or "nègre," which he inherits directly from the nineteenth-century European imperialist ideology. In his discussion of postcolonial nationalisms in his book *In My Father's House*, Anthony Appiah warns us precisely of the danger of adopting these concepts without first replacing them in their former historical context:

> Indeed . . . the very invention of Africa (as something more than a geographical entity) must be understood, ultimately, as an outgrowth of European racialism; the notion of Pan-Africanism was founded on the notion of the African, which was, in turn, founded not on any genuine cultural commonality but, as we have seen, on the very European concept of the negro. "The negro," Fanon writes, is "never so much a negro as since he has been dominated by whites." But the reality is that the very category of the negro is at root a European product: for the "whites" invented the negroes in order to dominate them. Simply put, the course of cultural nationalism in Africa has been to make real the imaginary identities to which Europe has subjected us. (62)

Appiah's argument is highly reminiscent of what Sartre himself said about the anti-Semitic invention of the Jews: "Far from experience producing his idea of the Jew, it was the latter which explained his experience. If the Jew did not exist, the anti-Semite would invent him."[17] Yet in "Orphée noir," Sartre seems to find unproblematic the concept of "le nègre" as instituted in Western colonial discourse.

Likewise, Sartre's discussion of negritude poetry is framed within the nineteenth-century narrative of European nationalisms whose relevance to or validity for the peoples of Africa and the Carribean has never been seen as an issue. At one point in the essay, to illustrate the language dilemma confronting the negritude poets, Sartre quotes the cases of the Hungarian and Irish nationalist movements as comparative models: "The majority of ethnic minorities, in the nineteenth century, passionately tried to revive their national languages while fighting for their independence" (ON, 243). The chief manifestation of the tragic plight of the colonized is, Sartre believes, their alienation from themselves, the result of the colonizers' imposing onto them an alien culture and language: "The herald of the black soul passed through white schools. . . . Due to the shock of white culture, his negritude has passed from immediate existence to a state of reflection" (240). The means for the blacks to attain their disalienation is to undergo a second birth or a rebirth that is no less than a return to their roots: "For the black it is a question of dying in white culture in order to be reborn with a black soul. This dialectical and mystical return to origins necessarily implies a method" (252). The method for this return to origins takes the form of the "Orphic descent": "this tireless descent of the Negro into himself" through "a continuous effort of deepening" (242).

The narrative of the quest of the colonized to recover their authenticity is also based on an organic view of culture widely popularized by German romanticism through the influence of Johann Herder; its dominant metaphor is, as Abiola Irele points out, a vegetal image: "The life of societies is likened to that of a tree, growing slowly and imperceptibly, *sending firm and strong roots,* producing with time the ripe fruits of a settled way of life."[18] In both the "Orphic" and "organic" views, the major metaphor is that of depth as the site of origin to be recaptured through a vertical descending movement. The organic conception of culture has been criticized for fostering a "static" (IP, 209) view of the life of societies, thereby concealing their "constructed and disputed historicities," which are "sites of displacement, interference, and interaction."[19] Discussions in current cultural studies show that any one culture, far from being a product of what Sartre believes to be a recuperable "original purity" (ON, 252), comes into being out of the interaction between at least two groups. For as Fredric Jameson argues, "no group 'has' a culture all by itself: culture is the nimbus perceived by one group when it comes into contact with and observes another one. It is the objectification of everything alien and strange about the contact group."[20] In other words, not only is a cultural group formed through a mediation by the Other, its formation is always, as James Clifford shows, actively contested even by its own members: "If 'culture' is not an object to be described, neither is it a unified corpus of symbols and meanings that can be definitively interpreted. Culture is contested, temporal, and emergent. Representation and explanation—both by insiders and outsiders—is implicated in this emergence."[21] Hence the illusion of claiming a return to what Sartre calls "this original simplicity of existence" (ON, 252).

Ironically, this yearning for an unproblematic return to a precolonial origin—constructed as both the antithesis to a less than ideal postcolonial present and an expression of our freeing ourselves from the colonial past—is itself a legacy of the Western influence from which we want to escape in our quest for cultural "authenticity." In his critique of what he calls the "nativist" stand, which sees a reembracing of "traditional qua indigenous" cultures as a means to reestablish our links with our ancestral world that has been disrupted by colonial violence, Appiah points out the extent to which such "reverse discourse" is itself a product of the Western cultural hegemony it sets out to contest:

> Railing against the cultural hegemony of the West, the nativists are of its party without knowing it. Indeed, the very arguments, the rhetoric of defiance, that our nationalists muster are, in a sense, canonical, time-tested . . . defiance is determined less by "indigenous" notions of resistance than by the dictates of the West's own Herderian legacy—its highly elaborated ideologies of national autonomy, of language and literature as their cultural substrate. (AH, 59)

It is my contention, moreover, as I now intend to argue, that the narrative of return in the form of an about-face reversal of the hierarchy as proposed by Sartre will not help us, the postcolonial subjects, to deal successfully with our colonial heritage.

## II

As shown in the foregoing discussion of "Orphée noir," the narrative of return is based on the myth of origin fantasized as a site where the black could finally achieve, in Sartre's own words, "coincidence with oneself" (ON, 252). In other words, what has been posited in the figure of return is the presence of a fixed, immutable self that transcends all historical vicissitudes and can therefore be recovered in its plenitude and purity. Such a presumption is neither credible nor useful as a strategy. For unless we believe in the absurd possibility of bringing about a tabula rasa of history (or, even more dangerously, historical amnesia), how could postcolonial subjects eradicate a century of colonial history that for better or for worse has shaped our lives and cultures? The belief that we could at will rid ourselves of the impact of foreign culture on us and our ancestors ensues from a notion of culture (usually associated with the notion of "civilization"[22]) as something "external," "superficial," or "artificial." This sense of culture stands in opposition to the organic view of culture seen as a process of "inner" development and "the deepest record, the deepest impulse, and the deepest resource" (WM, 15) of a particular group of people. In "Orphée noir," these two contrasting notions of culture exist side by side. It is highly significant that Sartre would apply the organic view to the indigenous culture of the colonized as suggested by the numerous vegetal images (ON, 265) in his descriptions of the black world while keeping the "external" view to "white culture." The color term "white" is moreover associated in the essay with images of clothing such as "pallid veneer" or "white vest" (ON, 230). The application of these two different sets of metaphors to the two cultural groups constructed as antithetical implies that the influence of Western culture on the indigenous peoples is really skin-deep. This superficiality of the Western impact on Africans leads Sartre to suggest to the latter that they reject Western culture in the same way as they remove their European garb: "rip off the white rags which masked his black armor" (282). While Sartre's intention may be a laudable one to rescue the Africans' "authenticity," such a strategy has also been used in colonial racist discourse to prove the inherently "savage" and therefore "inferior" nature of the colonized who can never be truly "civilized." One of the most infamous examples of such a representation of the Africans is that of Mister Johnson in Joyce Cary's book of the same name. The narration shows that Western civilization is nothing but a mere veneer to Mr. Johnson who remains an incorrigible wild man at heart.

A further problem with such a representation of the relationships of two cultural groups is its oversimplification and its one-sidedness. Notwithstanding the imbalance of power that structures colonial relations, when two persons, let alone two groups of peoples, are brought into the presence of one another, they are bound to influence each other mutually and bring about changes in their respective lives. Such a reciprocity has not been acknowledged in the traditional representations of colonial relations, which tend to assign a totally passive and receptive role to the colonized as opposed to the active and commanding position of the colonizers. Consequently, following the rhetoric of "civilizing mission," the colonized are seen always at the receiving end of the relationship, having little if anything to give to the other side. Even Sartre, for all his sympathy and admiration for the negritude poets, can see no significant contribution from them to the French language except "the rather ugly term of 'negritude'" which "is one of the only black contributions to our dictionary" (244-45).[23]

The idea of language as one of the most material expressions of a culture can be used to illustrate the complexity of cultural relations in the post/colonial context. Our use of the colonizers' languages, whether perceived as a choice or a necessity, has been lived as one of the most deeply felt dilemmas that never ceases to haunt yesteryear's colonial as well as our latter-day postcolonial writers and intellectuals. In "Orphée noir," Sartre also devotes many pages to the discussion of the unhappy linguistic plight of the negritude poets. In the absence of a common language by which they could communicate with one another, the blacks are forced to borrow that of their oppressors, hence their tragic dilemma:

> Blacks only find themselves on a terrain filled with traps that the white prepared for them: between the colonized, the colonizer contrived to be the eternal mediator; he is there, always there, even when absent, as far as the most secret confabulations. And since words are ideas, when the Negro declares in French that he repudiates French culture, he takes with one hand what he rejects with the other, he installs in himself, like a grinder, the enemy's thinking-machine. (244)

Besides the contradictions of having to use a language whose culture they want to reject, the colonized also face another problem, no less thorny, namely the inadequacy of a foreign language to express their thoughts and needs: "This syntax and vocabulary formed at other times and thousands of miles away, in order to respond to other needs and designate other objects, are unfit to provide him with the means to speak of himself, his concerns and his hopes" (244).

These same concerns seem to continue to plague today's postcolonial subjects who see the problems in almost similar terms as they still find themselves divided in "a dispute between a sentimental Herderian conception of Africa's languages and traditions as expressive of the collective essence of a pristine traditional community, on the one hand, and, on the other, a positivistic conception of European languages and disciplines as mere tools" (AH, 56). While not denying that, as postcolonial subjects, our relation to the colonizers' languages is bound to be problematic, could there be a truly non-problematic relation to language be it "our own" or a foreign one? For as Mikhail Bakhtin has shown, since the word is the ideological phenomenon par excellence, the way a language (whether native to the speaker or not) functions always carries within itself multiple contesting voices. The yearning for a totally unproblematic relation to language free from any mediation as suggested by Sartre's comments is as much a phantasm as the myth of the return to a prelapsarian origin. Indeed, in the postcolonial context, our relation to our "native" tongues is no less complicated than our relation to the colonizers'. For if we expected that our native tongues could recover for us "the collective essence of a pristine traditional community," we would be in for bitter disappointment. Language, whose existence is totally informed by social and political changes, undergoes constant transformations. If for us the postcolonial world we live in is different (read: more complex and unsettling) from that of our forebears, then our mother tongues, assuming they have survived as living languages, have also experienced those changes. We, as postcolonial subjects, whether by choice or not, all grew up having to learn at least one foreign language (usually a European one). In language pedagogy, we often focus on how our mother tongue can interfere with our acquisition of the other language. What has been overlooked or at least seldom discussed is that interference also goes the other way, meaning that our native tongue is likewise transformed as a result of our knowledge and use of the foreign language.

If we accept the view that the languages in which we express ourselves shape our vision of the world and ourselves, then, as speakers of multiple tongues, it is inevitable that postcolonial subjects would have more than one cultural identity or an identity that is multicultural. Yet due to the history of colonial oppression, it is very hard for us not to feel the part of violence that enters into the make-up of our multicultural heritage, which in another context, for example white middle-class America, would be celebrated as an enviable form of cosmopolitanism. Hence the poignancy of the postcolonial condition: characterized by highly ambivalent relations to the two cultures that in different ways contribute to shape it and lived by many of us as alienating.[24] Besides the history of colonial violence, this ambivalence is due to the fact that the colonizers' culture has also been presented to us by both sides as diametrically opposed to our "home" culture, which has been shown as inadequate, backward, and inferior. Consequently, one common response to the dilemma is to make it a question of choice: the postcolonial subject is confronted with the decision as to whether he/she should return to his/her original culture by rejecting what is perceived as the imposed Western culture, hence the decision of a number of African writers such as Ousmane Sembene to switch from writing in the colonizers' language to their African national languages. One problem in formulating the solution in terms of an either/or choice is to perpetuate the dualist schema that the colonizers used to dictate the form of their relations to the colonized. Even by reversing the hierarchical order of the terms, we still would find ourselves enslaved in the hegemonic order as shown in Sartre's strategy in "Orphée noir." More importantly, can we really choose sides if we are in fact made of both? Indeed, the different parts of our multiple cultural identity are so intricately intertwined that we ourselves cannot tell the West from the rest in us. I think the challenge in the postcolonial era is precisely to undo those binarisms of black/white or East/West that were construed to justify the domination of the one by the other. Our task is to rethink differences in terms of strategies and not in terms of essences. For more often than not, differences are constructed for a certain purpose. Why are some differences valorized and others devalorized? Do differences have to be thought of in hierarchical or antithetical terms? Should we let ourselves be enclosed and defined by some preestablished inclusionary or exclusionary categories?[25]

In the foregoing discussion, when I talked about "postcolonial subjects" I was thinking basically of all the peoples who have known Western colonization.[26] Yet I am also aware of the risk of reductiveness in the use of an all-inclusive concept of postcoloniality.[27] For not only are the histories of these peoples extremely diverse, even members of the "same" community would live their postcolonial condition differently depending on their social, economic, and personal situations. Some groups may find what is known in the Francophone context as *métissage* or in the Anglophone context as "hybridity" a most liberating experience. There, *métissage* is viewed, to quote Françoise Lionnet, as a "concept of solidarity which demystifies all essential glorifications of unitary origins," a strategy that would enable "the creation of a plural self, one that thrives on ambiguity and multiplicity, on affirmation of differences, not on polarized and polarizing notions of identity, culture, race, or gender."[28] Yet other postcolonial groups may experience this hybrid predicament as a source of deep anguish and confusion. The situation of certain groups of Chinese intellectuals in Hong Kong—a British Crown colony until 1997 when the island reverts back to China—illustrates the complexity of hybrid cultures. Leung Ping-Kwan, a contemporary Hong Kong Chinese writer, describes the more problematic side of hybridity: "our generation experienced tremendous influences from various foreign cultures, and could be said to have grown up in a hybrid culture, with all the confusion of values and with the anguish of constantly being misunderstood when one moves across borders."[29] For in Hong Kong, the problem is not a question of having to negotiate between two different cultures, but of growing up in "fragmented" cultures that are rejected, and debased as being "impure," by both Britain and China (whether Mainland or Taiwan, which both claim legitimacy to "true" Chinese culture). Indeed, the case of Hong Kong serves as another good example of the impossibility of a simple "return" to the "mother country" or of a straightforward reverting back to some original identity. For as the Hong Kong critic, Ackbar Abbas, explains, the end of the British colonial rule in Hong Kong does not signify "a simple return of a Chinese territory to the Chinese. Whatever Hong Kong used to be like in the nineteenth century, it has since become a very different entity. It is not true, as some may wish to think, that if you scratch the surface of a Hong Kong person you will find a Chinese identity waiting to be reborn: history has seen to that."[30] The relation between Hong Kong and China, her "mother country," turns out to be much more complex than a simple case of family reunion, as a large number of middle-class Hong Kong Chinese are desperately seeking to emigrate elsewhere or secure at enormous cost a foreign nationality before 1997. Given the specificity and complexity of each postcolonial society, it is neither possible nor useful to invent a narrative of the kind Sartre did in "Orphée noir" to account for all post/colonial situations, since each group has to devise its own form of resistance to domination on the basis of its own particular history.

## ABBREVIATIONS

AH: Anthony Kwane Appiah, *In My Father's House: Africa in the Philosophy of Culture.*
CB: Michel Carrouges, *André Breton et les données fondamentales du surréalisme.*
CV: Stuart Zane Charmé, *Vulgarity and Authenticity: Dimensions of Otherness in the World of Jean-Paul Sartre.*
DR: René Depestre, *Pour la révolution pour la poésie.*
IP: Abiola Irele, "In Praise of Alienation."
LC: Leung Ping-Kwan, *City at the End of Time.*
ON: Jean-Paul Sartre, "Orphée noir," *Situations, III.*
WM: Raymond Williams, *Marxism and Literature.*

## NOTES

1. All quotations of "Orphée noir" ["Black Orpheus"] are taken from the collection of essays in which it appears: Jean-Paul Sartre, *Situations, III* (Paris: Gallimard, 1949), 229-86; the essay will henceforth be abbreviated ON. English translations of this and other works in French (unless otherwise noted) are my own.
2. Jean Metellus, "Sartre et la négritude," *Sartre,* special issue of *Obliques* 18-19 (1979): 289.
3. In *Peau noire, masques blancs* (Paris: Seuil, 1953), trans. Charles Mackmann under the title *Black Skin White Masks* (New York: Grove Press, 1967), Frantz Fanon analyzes in detail the manichean discourse colonizers elaborated to legitimate their domination of the colonized.
4. The idea that poetry is the best medium for the expression of African subjectivity has also been widely promoted by Léopold Senghor. See his *Liberté I: négritude et humanisme* (Paris: Seuil, 1964).
5. René Depestre, *Pour la révolution pour la poésie* (Ottawa: Editions Lemeac, 1974), 77, henceforth abbreviated DR.
6. Stuart Zane Charmé, *Vulgarity and Authenticity: Dimensions of Otherness in the World of Jean-Paul Sartre* (Amherst: University of Massachusetts Press, 1991), henceforth abbreviated CV.

7. Jean-Paul Sartre, "Préface," *Les Damnés de la terre,* by Frantz Fanon, *Situations, V* (Paris: Gallimard, 1964), 168.
8. Abiola Irele, *The African Experience in Literature and Ideology* (Bloomington: Indiana University Press, 1990), 80.
9. In *Black Skin White Masks,* Frantz Fanon is highly critical of such a formulation of negritude: "And, when I tried, on the level of ideas and intellectual activity, to reclaim my negritude, it was snatched away from me. Proof was presented that my effort was only a term in the dialectic. . . . When I read that page, I felt that I had been robbed of my last chance. . . . What is certain is that, at the very moment when I was trying to grasp my own being, Sartre, who remained The Other, gave me a name and thus shattered my last illusion" (132-37). For a discussion of the complex Sartre-Fanon relationship, see Ronnie Scharfman, *Engagement and the Language of the Subject in the Poetry of Aimé Césaire* (Gainesville: University of Florida Monographs, 1980), 18-21.
10. For an excellent analysis of the history of the concept of race, especially in the nineteenth-century European context, see Anthony Kwane Appiah, *In My Father's House: Africa in the Philosophy of Culture* (Oxford: Oxford University Press, 1992), henceforth abbreviated AH, and *Anatomy of Racism,* ed. David Goldberg (Minneapolis: University of Minnesota Press, 1990).
11. Jean-Paul Sartre, *L'Existentialisme est un humanisme* (Paris: Nagel, 1946), trans. Philip Mairet under the title *Existentialism and Humanism* (New York: Haskell House Publishers, 1977), 22.
12. Stanilas Adotevi, *Négritude et négrologues* (Paris: Union Générale d'Editions, 1972), 68.
13. A large amount of critical work has been devoted to an analysis of the complex relationship between surrealism and negritude. See for example Jean-Claude Michel, *Les Ecrivains noirs et le surréalisme* (Québec: Editions Naaman, 1982). In his *Modernism and Negritude: The Poetry and Poetics of Aimé Césaire* (Cambridge: Harvard University Press, 1981), James Arnold discusses in detail the relation between André Breton and Aimé Césaire.
14. For a discussion of the surrealist fascination with the primitive, see James Clifford's *The Predicament of Culture: Twentieth-Century Ethnography, Literature, and Art* (Cambridge: Harvard University Press, 1988), in particular the chapter "On Ethnographic Surrealism."
15. Michel Carrouges, *André Breton et les données fondamentales du surréalisme* (Paris: Gallimard, 1950), trans. Maura Prendergast under the title *André Breton and the Basic Concepts of Surrealism* (University, AL: University of Alabama Press, 1974), 25-26, henceforth abbreviated CB.
16. The notion of "detour" is borrowed from Edouard Glissant's work, in particular his *Discours antillais* (Paris: Seuil, 1981).
17. Jean-Paul Sartre, *Réflexions sur la question juive* (Paris: Gallimard, 1954), trans. George J. Becker under the title *Anti-Semite and Jew* (New York: Schocken Books, 1974), 13.
18. Abiola Irele, "In Praise of Alienation," *The Surreptitious Speech: Presence Africaine and the Politics of Otherness 1947-1987,* ed. V. Y. Mudimbe (Chicago:

Chicago University Press, 1992), 208-9, henceforth abbreviated IP. This organic view of culture is linked to the other concept of culture as cultivation. For a discussion of the historical evolution of the term "culture," see Raymond Williams, *Marxism and Literature* (Oxford: Oxford University Press, 1977), henceforth abbreviated WM.
19. James Clifford, "Traveling Cultures" *Cultural Studies,* ed. Lawrence Grossberg, Carry Nelson, and Paula Treichler (New York: Routledge, 1992), 101.
20. Fredric Jameson, "On 'Cultural Studies,'" *Social Text* 34 (1993): 33.
21. James Clifford, "Partial Truths," introduction to *Writing Cultures: The Poetics and Politics of Ethnography,* ed. James Clifford and George E. Marcus (Berkeley: University of California Press, 1986), 19.
22. In *Marxism and Literature,* Raymond Williams gives a very clear history of the evolution of these two contrasting notions.
23. Besides the material wealth in the form of primary resources as well as cheap human labor that was taken from the colonies to enrich the colonizing nations, there are also important cultural contributions such as the borrowing of African art by European modernist artists or the concept of cultural capital in Pierre Bourdieu's work, which is taken from the model of Arab society. See Pierre Bourdieu, *Outline of a Theory of Practice,* trans. Richard Nice (Cambridge: Cambridge University Press, 1977).
24. For a discussion of the problem of alienation in the postcolonial context, see IP.
25. For a literary illustration of this refusal of categorization, see Mireille Rosello's analysis of Andre Schwarz-Bart's *La Mulâtresse Solitude* in her *Littérature et identité créole aux Antilles* (Paris: Karthala, 1992).
26. I am aware that this term can be and has been used to include other oppressed groups such as women and national minorities. For a good critical discussion of the use of the term "colonization," see Chandra Talpade Mohanty, "Under Western Eyes: Feminist Scholarship and Colonial Discourse," *Boundary 2* 12.3-13.1 (spring-fall 1984): 333-58, and Edward Said, "Representing the Colonized: Anthropology's Interlocutors," *Critical Inquiry* 15.2 (winter 1989): 205-25.
27. There is a great deal of debate on the many different meanings of postcolonial. For discussions of the term, see Patrick Williams and Laura Chrisman, eds., *Colonial Discourse and Post-colonial Theory* (New York: Columbia University Press, 1994), and Bill Ashcroft, Gareth Griffiths, and Helen Tiffin, eds., *The Post-colonial Studies Reader* (London: Routledge, 1995).
28. Françoise Lionnet, *Autobiographical Voices: Race, Gender, Self-Portraiture* (Ithaca: Cornell University Press, 1989), 9, 16.
29. Leung Ping-Kwan, *City at the End of Time* (Hong Kong: Twilight Books, 1992), 161, henceforth abbreviated LC.
30. Ackbar Abbas, "The Last Emporium: Verse and Cultural Space," introduction to LC, 5-6.

7

# Freedom and Flirtation: Bad Faith in Sartre and Beauvoir

## Toril Moi

> "I have never been able to follow the rules of flirting," she was saying. "I can't bear being touched: it's morbid."
> In another corner, a young woman with green and blue feathers in her hair was looking uncertainly at a man's huge hand that had just pounced on hers. . . . She had decided to leave her bare arm on the table and as it lay there, forgotten, ignored, the man's hand was stroking a piece of flesh that no longer belonged to anyone.
> —SIMONE DE BEAUVOIR, L'Invitée

### SEXUAL COMPARISONS

Traditional philosophers often take Beauvoir to task for deviating from Sartre's philosophical premises, for instance in *The Second Sex*.[1] Others claim that since her philosophical perspective exactly matches his, there is no point in devoting a separate chapter (or section, or paragraph) to *her* work. Unfortunately, the perfectly reasonable feminist wish to explore Beauvoir's works on her own terms is often taken by patriarchs to indicate a fanatical desire once and for all to "prove" her superiority to Sartre: it is as if the very fact of being interested in Beauvoir necessarily means slighting Sartre.

In spite of my own impatience with the comparison topos, I have to recognize its persistence and dominance in Beauvoir and Sartre criticism. Instead of dwelling in generalities, however, I want to compare the two writers through a detailed reading of two central and very similar passages, written roughly at the same time. In this essay I want to explore the question of women's freedom in heterosexual relations as discussed by Sartre in *Being and Nothingness* and by Beauvoir in *L'Invitée*, both published in 1943. My subjects, specifically, are the discussion in *Being and Nothingness* of the woman who has gone off to a first rendezvous in a Parisian cafe and the scene in *L'Invitée* where Françoise seduces Gerbert.

## A RENDEZVOUS IN A PARISIAN CAFE

Sartre's discussion of bad faith in a woman can be found in the chapter of *Being and Nothingness* entitled "Patterns of Bad Faith," where he is trying to show that it is possible to lie to oneself.[2] Sitting at the cafe table, the woman involved in a first rendezvous knows perfectly well, according to Sartre, what the man's intentions are. "She knows also that it will be necessary sooner or later for her to make a decision. But she does not want to realize [*sentir*] the urgency," Sartre continues, "she concerns herself only with what is respectful and discreet in the attitude of her companion" (BN, 96; EN, 91).[3] Refusing to see his conversation as an attempt to carry out "what we call [*ce qu'on nomme*] 'the first approach'" (BN, 96; EN, 91), she refuses to acknowledge the possible temporal developments of his behavior, Sartre complains. When the man declares "I admire you so much,"[4] he continues, the woman more or less perversely persists in taking it literally: she actually pretends to *believe* him. Depriving the sentence of its "sexual background," Sartre writes, she takes his discourse at face value. Or in other words: it does not even occur to Sartre that the woman may genuinely be taken in by the man's declarations of esteem and admiration. According to Sartre, every one of these aspects of her behavior demonstrates the woman's bad faith. In the end, he argues, her problem is that "she does not quite know what she wants. She is profoundly aware of the desire which she inspires, but crude and naked desire would humiliate and horrify her" (BN, 97; EN, 91; TA).[5] It is hard to judge from this sentence whether Sartre believes that the woman's bad faith consists in not knowing what she wants, or whether, on the contrary, it consists in most certainly knowing that the expression of *le désir cru et nu*—crude and naked desire—would be humiliating. Summarizing her initial behavior, Sartre sees it as a refusal to "apprehend the desire for what it is; she does not even give it a name; she recognizes it only to the extent that it transcends itself towards admiration, esteem, respect" (BN, 97; EN, 91).

This, then, is Sartre's analysis of the initial stages of the rendezvous. Trying to make sense of his account, I come up against a series of difficulties. First there is the fact that Sartre relies entirely on his readers' tacit recognition of the man's motives. While I think I understand what he is saying, I can hardly believe my own conclusions. The reference to the "sexual background" and "crude and naked desire" makes it clear that Sartre is thinking about sex. But is he really implying that *no* man ever meets a woman in a cafe without consciously and deliberately perceiving it as nothing but a prelude to sexual intercourse? And that every woman, whether she admits it or not, knows this to be the case? Ought I to know this every time I arrange to meet a man in a cafe? Is this really what men are like? The thought of having been in bad faith for most of my adult life is staggering.

Contemplating this problem, I am struck by the casual reference to "what we call 'the first approach.'" The rhetorical move here is obvious: gesturing toward a real world of shared conventions, Sartre attempts to establish a tacit community of values between himself and the reader. Masquerading as a general dictionary definition—we all call this the "first approach," don't we?—the phrase in fact reveals that Sartre imagines himself to be addressing men, not women. In French, *approches* in the plural *(les premières approches)* carries certain military connotations, referring to the efforts of an assailant to penetrate a fortress or to covert underground attempts to undermine the enemy. According to the dictionary, *Le Petit Robert,* this rather ancient military connotation has carried over in its more general and figural sense, which is "self-interested advances, manoeuvres to achieve a goal." Carrying an unmistakable flavor of male camaraderie, the phrase may well have been—and remained—current in conversations between men. I cannot believe that any woman at the time—or today—would use the phrase about her own attempts at flirtation. Unless she found him wickedly cynical and repulsive, I also doubt that she would use it about a man's attempt to flirt with her. But the fact that she would not dream of saying such a thing is precisely Sartre's point: refusing to take the different social conventions applying to the two protagonists into account, Sartre can only see her refusal as a sign of her will to self-deception. The full implications of his casual turn of phrase now become evident: *As long as the woman refuses to speak as if she were a man she is in bad faith.*

This unfortunate conclusion emerges in spite of the fact that Sartre's basic philosophical premise is supposed to be sexually neutral. To his mind, sexual difference has nothing to do with bad faith; every thinking subject has the same capacity for good or bad faith. Yet here he argues as if every thinking subject were a man: in his rush to produce a totalizing ontological analysis, he has overlooked the social and sexual differences that shape the discourse and behavior of the agents involved in this scene. The result is patriarchal philosophy, not the truly universal analysis he sets out to produce.

Sartre does not stop, either, to consider the problem involved in defining the activity engaged in in this scene. Using the word "flirt" to describe the cafe scene (BN, 97; EN, 91), he nevertheless insists on its goal-oriented nature: the man knows what he wants, the woman is to blame at once for pretending not to know what he wants and for truly not knowing what she wants. But if this is supposed to be a case of flirtation, his assumption runs counter to my own experience of social reality: surely, not every flirtation posits a clear sexual goal as the necessary outcome of the activity? Perhaps Sartre is not talking about flirtation at all? Perhaps this scene ought rather to be read as a seduction scene? But what difference would it make?

According to *Le Petit Robert*, a flirt designates "more or less chaste amorous relations *[relations amoureuses]*, generally devoid of deep feelings."[6] The word has no specific epistemological dimension: while perfectly superficial, a flirtation does not necessarily involve deceit. Given its rather open-ended, playful character, it is not supposed to be an authentic expression of deep feelings either. One may very well flirt without "meaning" it. My point is that if one "meant" it, flirtation would no longer be the appropriate word. Flirtation, then, is based on ambiguity: it is a game in which one does not declare one's hand. To have to "come clean," to confess what was "really" the case, is to destroy the very possibility of flirtation. In this sense, flirtation is not a goal-oriented activity. Because it does not promise anything, it does not commit its participants to anything either. Flirtation is a game from which one can always escape without damage. The point of the game is on the one hand to make all participants feel good: you make me feel attractive, I make you feel desirable; I brighten your day, you brighten mine. On the other hand, this agreeable game can, if desired, also be considered a pleasant space in which to figure out whether flirtation is all one wants to engage in.[7] A structurally ambiguous, playful activity with no clearly defined sexual aim, flirtation is eminently useful for women subjected to strict patriarchal control of their sexuality, since it provides them with an opportunity to test out the opposition, to play with the thought of involvement without actually getting involved and thus without risking the loss of their virginity, honor, reputation, or entire future at a stroke.[8]

To seduce, on the other hand, in its restricted and strong meaning, is etymologically to "lead astray" *[se-ducere]*, to make somebody take a wrong turn. According to *Le Petit Robert*, to seduce is to "turn away from good, to make somebody misbehave"; its synonyms are verbs like "corrupt," "dishonor," "debauch," "misuse," "mislead," "deceive," and so on. Always projecting a clear sexual goal as the end result of its activities, seduction also involves false appearances, lies, and pretexts of one kind or another. In seduction one person is taken cynically to manipulate the other, as for instance in the case of Valmont and Cécile de Volanges in *Les Liaisons dangereuses*. The person who is seduced is seduced precisely because she is ignorant of the real circumstances. According to Sartre, one may add, a liar is not in bad faith (see BN, 87-88; EN, 83-84); neither, one must assume, is the victim of the lie.[9]

Sartre and his male protagonist would seem to be firmly convinced that what is going on is a scene of seduction. According to Sartre, the man is not in bad faith: knowing what he wants, *he* would presumably not find it difficult to talk about the "first approach," nor to acknowledge that all his talk about his admiration and respect for the young woman amounts to not much more than a means to an end. He is, in other words, a seducer. But Sartre does not say this. On the contrary, according to him, the woman is a *coquette* (BN, 99; EN, 93) precisely because she pretends not to know that the man is a seducer. But given that at this stage nothing but pleasant conversation has transpired between the protagonists, it is hard to see how she could tell. After all, even men flirt. For Sartre, the woman is in bad faith because she refuses to cast herself as transcendence and posit a desiring project of her own. But what is a project? There is no space here to discuss this in detail. I will simply have to claim that Sartre tends to describe the project in fairly phallic terms. It represents an active, transcendent, and teleological "throwing forward": the project hurls itself forward into time and space until it strikes home. Metaphorically, both Sartre and Beauvoir cast the transcendent project as violent, penetrative, and phallic. No wonder, then, that Sartre automatically takes seduction and not flirtation to be the paradigmatic example of authentic sexual behavior. But if one disengages oneself from the Sartrean equation of male seduction with transcendence, there is no reason why one should not argue that the woman may be involved in a perfectly transcendent project of her own and that that project is flirtation. In this sense, her aim may well be to produce a space in which she can take some pleasure without too much risk, a space in which she can observe the man at leisure and decide what kind of involvement she may or may not wish to have with him. Sartre, in fact, is perfectly aware of this: "The point is," he writes, "to postpone the moment of decision as long as possible" (BN, 97; EN, 91; TA). It is obvious that such a project may be extremely irritating to a male hell-bent on rapid seduction; it is equally obvious that it *is* a project and as such in no way ontologically inferior to the man's. At this point, it may be worth remembering that France in 1943 was a country in which a woman—Marie-Jeanne Latour—was sent to the guillotine for performing illegal abortions.[10] It was also a country in which contraception was outlawed and where the main method of birth control was withdrawal or the bidet. Under such circumstances, the woman would have to trust the man considerably before deciding to have sex with him. No wonder she wanted to take her time. Based on the unargued assumption that she has no project of her own, Sartre's analysis casts the woman as an absence, a negative, a zero: she becomes at one and the same time the blank screen on which the man is expected to inscribe his project and a mindless and opaque obstacle to his transcendence.[11]

Against Sartre, then, I hold that the initial stage of this rendezvous may be read as a confrontation between two conflicting projects, the woman's flirtation and the man's seduction. The situation is strictly symmetrical, in so far as both parties believe that the other person's project coincides with or ought to coincide with their own. This stalemate is finally broken by the man: "But then suppose he takes her hand," Sartre writes (BN, 97; EN, 91). Quite rightly stressing the difficult position in which the woman now suddenly finds herself, Sartre shrewdly analyzes her dilemma: if she withdraws her hand, she breaks the "charm" of the evening; if she does not she may be taken to express consent and engagement. While all this is true, this account still presupposes that the woman has no project of her own. In Sartre's view, her behavior simply represents a desire not to engage herself: she is cast as utterly passive. At the end of his phenomenological description of the woman in bad faith, Sartre's prose is remarkably perceptive but still fails to capture the logic of the woman's position:

> We know what happens next; the young woman leaves her hand there, but she *does not notice* that she is leaving it. She does not notice because it happens by chance that she is at this moment all intellect [*tout esprit*]. . . . She shows herself in her essential aspect—a personality, a consciousness. And during this time the divorce of the body from the soul is accomplished; the hand rests inert between the warm hands of her companion—neither consenting nor resisting—a thing.
> We shall say that this woman is in bad faith. (BN, 97; EN, 91-92)

For Sartre, the man's grabbing of the woman's hand highlights the essential logic of the whole scene. For me, it introduces a dramatic change in relation to the initial situation. Acting from a position of social power, the man is free to seize the woman's hand. Seizing the initiative, imposing his hand on the woman, the man now defines the stakes: he is free to move his hand any time, under any pretext, without necessarily breaking the "charm" of the hour. Were she to withdraw her hand, however, she would most certainly, as Sartre puts it, "break the troubled and unstable harmony which gives the hour its charm" (BN, 97; EN, 91), presumably because the man would get angry or start to sulk. Yet, I would argue, the man, by making his move, has already broken the ambiguous charm of the moment. Revealing his project of seduction, his act literally forces the woman's hand: she is now obliged to choose her line of action on his terms, not on her own.[12]

No wonder that Simone de Beauvoir, when describing the same scene in *L'Invitée,* has the woman "looking uncertainly at a man's huge hand that had just pounced on hers" (SC, 52; I, 72). Her vocabulary here represents a considerable shift in perspective: where Sartre has the man's "warm" hand "taking" the woman's, Beauvoir sees the "fat" or "huge" *[grosse]* hand of the man "pouncing on" *[s'abattre sur]* the woman's. Once one perceives the violence of the man's move, the woman's abandonment of her hand represents a desperate but doomed attempt to cling to her own original project.[13] But on this point, of course, Sartre is right. Once things have gone this far, the woman can no longer maintain the ambiguous space of flirtation: the man's grabbing of her hand most certainly forces her to take his project into account. Whatever she decides to do now will be nothing but a response to a situation defined by the man. But to define oneself simply as the negation or affirmation of somebody else's project is precisely not to assume one's existential freedom. It is astonishing to discover that this is precisely the "decision" Sartre apparently sees as the only course of authenticity for the woman in the cafe. But this is more than a little illogical: if each individual defines herself by freely recognizing responsibility for her own projects, the woman can only be defined by her own project, not by anybody else's.

On Sartre's own philosophical terms, then, there is no authentic mode of behavior for a woman in this position. Abandoning her hand like a thing, she seeks refuge in facticity and the *en-soi* and is obviously in bad faith. But were she to make a forceful decision then and there, she would still not be positing a project of her own. In this cafe scene, the "freedom" to choose whatever project one likes is sorely circumscribed in one case and not in the other. Or to put it differently: here the man represents what Sartre would call the woman's *situation,* whereas she is not his. The lack of reciprocity in this situation flies in the face of the existentialist belief in the necessity of respecting the fundamental freedom of every consciousness: "As soon as there is engagement," Sartre writes in *L'Existentialisme est un humanisme,* "I am obliged to want the freedom of others along with my own; I cannot take my freedom as my aim unless I also take that of others as my aim."[14] On this definition, the hand-grabbing man's understanding of freedom and good faith leaves rather a lot to be desired.[15]

## AN ENCOUNTER IN A MOUNTAIN BARN

Is there, then, any conceivable way in which women can successfully flirt or seduce and still remain in good faith? Toward the end of *L'Invitée*, in the chapter describing Françoise's seduction of Gerbert as seen from Françoise's point of view (Part II, chapter 8), Simone de Beauvoir sets out to answer precisely that question.[16] Dwelling on a sexual encounter somewhere in the French mountains, it is the only chapter in *L'Invitée* in which there is not a single cafe. In terms of the plot of the novel, the chapter is intended to demonstrate Françoise's complete sexual victory over her rival Xavière. From a structural point of view, the "seduction chapter" reads as a rather awkward interlude in the densely melodramatic closing stretches of *L'Invitée*: one may well wonder why Beauvoir feels the need to produce so many pages simply to send Gerbert into Françoise's arms. It is as if Beauvoir decided that the thematic concerns of her only non-Parisian chapter—the questions of freedom, desire, and discourse—were too important to be sacrificed in the name of structure or plot.

In the novel, the social relationship between the two protagonists appears to be strikingly unequal. Endowed with more social, intellectual, and cultural capital than Gerbert, Françoise is in every way his social superior. She is thirty, he is twenty; she is the consort of the prestigious actor-director Pierre Labrousse and a successful dramaturge and aspiring novelist in her own right, whereas he is just a young, unknown actor who idolizes Pierre.

By the time Françoise and Gerbert arrive at a lonely mountain inn, the former is consumed by desire: "The vague yearning that had been hanging over her all these days . . . had become choking desire" (SC, 362; I, 446). Sitting down by the fire at the inn, she dreams of touching Gerbert: "If only she had been able to touch Gerbert's hand, to smile at him with affection" (SC, 363; I, 448), but such behavior is clearly out of the question. Françoise is left feeling that the whole situation is meaningless. The idea of touching Gerbert nevertheless continues to haunt her: "Was he really beyond reach? Or was it just that she had never dared to reach out her hand to him? Who was holding her back?" (SC, 364; I, 449). The palms of her non-touching hands are moist with desire and anxiety: "Why did she not make up her mind to will what she hoped for?" (SC, 364; I, 449).

In the light of what is not being said in this scene, the inane dialogue between the two becomes both witty and poignant. Unlike Sartre's Casanova, Gerbert truly respects Françoise: in this scene there will be no sudden pouncing on hands. If Françoise's social superiority makes the traditional discourse of female flirtation unavailable to her, Gerbert's inferiority makes him incapable of making the first move: "She was distressed [*angoissée*] now. He was there, facing her, alone, unattached, absolutely free. Owing to his youth and the respect he had always shown Pierre and herself, she could hardly expect him to take any initiative. If she wanted something to happen, Françoise could count only on herself" (SC, 366; I, 451). By the time the meal nears an end, Françoise would seem to be on the verge of a nervous breakdown. At this point Gerbert starts complaining about how difficult it is to be relaxed and easy with women, referred to in the third person plural, as if Françoise had nothing to do with the species: "you always have to make a fuss of them or you always feel you're in the wrong" (SC, 366; I, 451). What he likes, he says, are relationships where one can be oneself, without the "fuss" [*manières*]:

> "Don't stand on any ceremony with me," said Françoise. Gerbert burst out laughing.
> "Oh you! You're like a man! [*Vous êtes comme un type!*]" he said warmly.
> "That's right, you've never regarded me as a woman," said Françoise. She felt a queer smile on her lips. Gerbert looked at her inquisitively. She looked away and emptied her glass. She had made a bad start; she would be ashamed to treat Gerbert with clumsy flirtatiousness [*coquetterie maladroite*], she would have done better to proceed openly [*franchement*]: "Would it surprise you if I were to suggest that you sleep with me?" or something of that sort. But her lips refused to form the words. (SC, 366; I, 452)

Françoise's dilemma is here made graphically evident. Her exceptional position as a woman who can deal with men on an equal footing, that is to say, without making them feel ill at ease, is confirmed when Gerbert compares her to one of the boys. Here at least, she is being acknowledged as an equal. Given her evident social superiority to Gerbert, however, there is more than a touch of irony in such an accolade. And the price she pays is steep: she can only accede to a position of equality at the cost of her femininity. The sexism of Gerbert's description of the "fuss" required by the women he knows is obvious and remains unquestioned by the text: there is little doubt that the narrator concurs in the idea of Françoise's exceptional status.

Françoise's riposte—an effort to reclaim her femininity through coquetry—misfires entirely. Spoken by the young woman at the Sartrean cafe table, these lines ("you've never regarded me as a woman") would produce an instantaneous rejoinder of the "oh but to me you are very much a woman" kind. But Gerbert says nothing. Traditional female flirtation presupposes the subservient status of the woman: for the superior Françoise the discourse of flirtation simply does not work. Her alternative, she concludes, would be plain speech ("she would have done better to proceed openly"), but at this point she discovers, much to her dismay, that she cannot even bring herself to open her mouth: the literal expression of her desire is physically impossible. As Sartre puts it in *Being and Nothingness,* "crude and naked desire would humiliate and horrify her" (BN, 97; EN, 91; TA).

Cued to take up a position as Gerbert's equal, Françoise automatically finds herself cast as an honorary male ("you're like a man"). Such a discursive position puts her in a double bind, preventing her at once from flirting like a female and from speaking (or grabbing hands) like a man. From her position as honorary male, she could hardly start telling Gerbert—one of the boys, after all—how much she admires and respects him, as Sartre suggests a would-be male seducer might. "To say it straight," then, represents Françoise's dream of escaping from what she herself perceives as the bad faith or dishonesty of traditional female flirtation, without falling into the cynical stance of male seduction and without foundering on the reef of *le désir cru et nu.* For Beauvoir, what is at stake in this scene is Françoise's status as a free consciousness. Perceiving Gerbert as another freedom, Françoise wants to be perceived as a freedom by him. The existentialist ideal explored by Françoise here is that of *reciprocity,* where each freedom recognizes that of the other. Behaving like Sartre's male seducer, Françoise would simply negate Gerbert's freedom. So what is she to do? Desperately looking for an acceptable female model for her enterprise, the only thing that comes to her mind is the wholly negative example of Pierre's sister Elisabeth, who describes herself as a "woman who takes." The very thought of Elisabeth, however, makes Françoise blush: "a woman who takes . . . she loathed the thought" (SC, 368; I, 454).

In Françoise's vision of Elisabeth's sexuality we glimpse her horror of becoming a woman who is not truly desired by the men she sleeps with: Elisabeth's lovers screw her for convenience, not for passion. But Françoise's distaste for such relations is not simply an effect of social conventions; it expresses her deep-seated philosophical commitment to her own freedom. If she wants Gerbert freely to choose her, it is not only because this will make her feel desirable, but because it is only by appealing to his freedom that she can avoid being reduced to a simple object in his eyes. Or in other words: only by offering one's freedom to the freedom of the other can one hope to have one's own freedom respected in return. On this logic of reciprocity it follows that it is only by having Gerbert choose her in the same movement as she is choosing him that Françoise can hope to escape having their sexual relationship reduced to no more than a casual sexual encounter.

No wonder, then, that Françoise finds that she cannot make herself utter the crucial words: deprived of discourse and caught in the double binds of sexual politics, she has not the slightest idea of what "the words to say it with" might be. Her silence, however, is only a temporary retreat. Spurred on as much by self-respect as by desire, Françoise refuses to abandon her project: "She did not want this trip to end in regrets that would soon turn into remorse and into self-hatred: she would speak" (SC, 368; I, 454; TA). Unlike Sartre's female flirt, then, Françoise knows exactly what she is doing. Moreover, unlike Sartre's male seducer, Françoise is suddenly seized by doubt about her own capacity to produce pleasure in Gerbert: "But did she even know whether Gerbert would find pleasure in kissing her?" (SC, 368; I, 454). Hanging on to her self-respect, she decides that the only honest course is to go ahead, while making sure that he has every opportunity to make a "frank refusal" (SC, 368; I, 454). By the time the two of them are getting into their sleeping bags in the barn, Françoise remains determined, but speechless: "She had absolutely no idea how to approach the question" (SC, 369; I, 455; TA). After an increasingly desultory dialogue, Françoise reaches a stage of acute distress: "Suddenly, tears rose to her eyes. She was at her nerves' end: now she had gone too far. It was Gerbert himself who would force her to speak, and perhaps this delightful friendship between them would be ruined forever" (SC, 371; I, 458). Here Françoise does not simply worry about losing the initiative of the conversation, but about losing her freedom: if she were to speak simply because Gerbert forced her to, she would lose her sense of independence in relation to his projects. In that case, one may add, she would be in exactly the same position as Sartre's *coquette* after the seizing of her hand. Speaking out, Françoise risks it all: her metaphysical freedom, her self-respect as an acting subject, her sense of her own femininity and Gerbert's friendship:

> Françoise emptied herself of all thought *[fit le vide en elle]* and finally the words crossed her lips.
> "I was smiling because I was wondering how you would look—you who loathe complications—if I suggested that you should sleep with me." *[Je riais en me demandant quelle tête vous feriez, vous qui n'aimez pas les complications, si je vous proposais de coucher avec moi.]*
> "I thought you were thinking that I wanted to kiss you and didn't dare," said Gerbert. (SC, 371-72; I, 458; TA)

A masterpiece of syntactical and grammatical circumlocution, Françoise's attempt to "tell it straight" would seem to imply that the most direct expression possible of female desire takes place in the past and conditional tenses.

After another page of hesitations, Gerbert at last expresses his desire. Finally, then, we have arrived at the crucial moment in which the two bodies are about to touch for the first time, the moment in which Françoise's project is about to be crowned by success. At this point, something strange seems to happen to Beauvoir's—and Françoise's—style: "'I'd love to kiss you,'" Gerbert says. Françoise's reply is astonishing, to say the least: "'Well, kiss me, you silly little Gerbert,' she said offering him her mouth *[Eh bien, faites-le, stupide petit Gerbert, dit-elle en lui tendant sa bouche]*" (SC, 373; I, 460).

Supposedly playful and inviting, Françoise's reply is in fact dismayingly condescending and clumsily unerotic. Producing the wholly unintended ideological effect of casting Françoise as a maternal figure in relation to the "little" and "stupid" Gerbert, this highly embarrassed and embarrassing textual moment drains Françoise's discourse of its sexuality and unwittingly castrates Gerbert in the process. Yet the whole point was to represent Françoise as a mature, autonomous, *sexual* woman. Fleeing from the body in the very moment Françoise's erotic project succeeds, Beauvoir's own discourse loses its power.

From this point on, the chapter throws itself into an orgy of saccharine sweetness and ends up reading like pure Harlequin romance.[17] How are we to explain such a radical shift of discursive register? In my view, Beauvoir's sudden change of tone indicates the moment in which the discursive and the philosophical projects of the text suddenly and dramatically start to diverge. Françoise's autonomous exploit succeeds, but it is no longer carried forward by an equally autonomous discourse: instead of originality we get clichés. The fact that this *décalage* occurs exactly at the moment when the two lovers' bodies are about to meet for the first time reveals the anxiety produced by the appearance of the body in Beauvoir's works. The most physical passage in *L'Invitée* remains the description of Elisabeth's wholly negative sexual experience with Guimiot. As for Françoise and Pierre, they undress behind screens and turn the lights off before quietly sliding into bed.

Beauvoir's modesty may of course have much to do with the sexual repression of the Vichy regime, but this cannot fully explain the logic of this scene. Her sudden change of register represents a flight away from the body and into the romantic soul. Until the moment of sexual convergence, Beauvoir succeeds reasonably well in representing free consciousness in a desiring woman. It is when the very project of that free consciousness is on the point of materializing in a desiring female body that the trouble starts. "Desire," Sartre writes, "is defined as *trouble*" (BN, 503; EN, 437). Beauvoir's stylistic switch to romantic clichés at this point unconsciously signals the difficulty she experiences in writing about the desiring female body in general. What I have registered as an astonishing shift in tone and style, then, points to a fundamental philosophical problem in Beauvoir's works: the problem of how the body, and particularly the desiring female body, relates to the projects of consciousness. Neither a thing in the world nor free consciousness, neither transcendence nor brute facticity, the body, as Sartre says, spells trouble.[18]

## FREE WOMEN OR GENDERLESS SUBJECTS?

Displaying the same preoccupation with consciousness, freedom, responsibility, and transcendence as *Being and Nothingness*, Beauvoir's seduction scene would seem to be absolutely faithful to Sartre's original concepts. Yet her own brief cafe scenes already provide a gentle reminder of the violence that may be involved in a man's sudden pouncing on a woman's hand. In the seduction scene, the difference between her and Sartre emerges more starkly: having reversed the gender roles, Beauvoir is forced to display a much greater awareness of the social pressures on her protagonists than Sartre. Beauvoir poses the question of reciprocity and respect for the other's freedom; Sartre does not. She registers the impact of social roles; he does not. Furthermore, Françoise's physical inability to speak her desire vividly dramatizes the situation of women under patriarchy.

Precisely because of this swerve away from Sartre, Beauvoir's account is no longer a "seduction scene" in the traditional sense. Nor is it an example of flirtation: Beauvoir's effort to represent free female desire in fact ends up questioning the very categories of flirtation and seduction. The remarkable shift in tone at the moment of the successful seduction suggests that in 1943 Simone de Beauvoir failed to grasp fully the implications of her own discourse. One reason for this failure is the fact that, in spite of the considerable differences between these two texts, Beauvoir's is not a conscious critique of Sartre. I have claimed elsewhere that Beauvoir must be understood as investigating her own marginality from a position of centrality. The consequence of this structural ambiguity is a noticeable uncertainty about whether her theme is "women" or the "free (genderless) subject." By her own admission, by 1943, Beauvoir had given no thought at all to matters of sexual politics: she thinks of Françoise as a free consciousness, not as a free woman. Writing about Françoise, Beauvoir firmly believes that she is doing the same thing as Sartre writing about Mathieu. The paradox is that, in the very act of imitating Sartre, she ends up criticizing and transforming his categories.

This transformation, however, does not go far enough. Beauvoir's relative lack of awareness of the gender of her heroine, for instance, is to a large extent responsible for the desexualization of Françoise. In Beauvoir's fiction, women struggle with what they take to be universal philosophical problems as if it were their obvious duty and right. By contrast, Sartre's fiction does not portray a single thinking woman. Compared to Sartre, Beauvoir's absolute faith in women's moral and philosophical capacities is refreshingly non-sexist. This positive result is the direct consequence of the fact that it never occurs to her to label thought or philosophy "male." Yet the price she pays is high: in autobiography as well as essays and fiction, what one might call the problem of the incipient masculinization of the free woman returns to haunt her texts.

If the ostensibly genderless free subject of existentialism is in fact marked as masculine in Sartre's and Beauvoir's discourse, any attempt to cast women as free subjects must have the effect of marking them as somewhat masculine as well. This is clearly what happens to Françoise, caught up as she is in the contradictions created by her role as "one of the boys." In my view, this is a theoretical and not a psychological problem: it does not follow that Beauvoir wants women to become like men. On this point, her own earnest protestations to the contrary should be taken at face value: Beauvoir does not expect women to take on any particular identity at all, she simply wants them to be free. This must not be taken to mean that Beauvoir is against identity. Unlike many present-day feminists, however, she sees identity as a consequence and not as a cause of freedom. For her, women do not have a secret, long-oppressed identity that must be liberated if the struggle for freedom is to be won. On the contrary, the struggle for freedom is what will enable women to forge freely their own identity, unencumbered by patriarchal myths of femininity.

Beauvoir's blindness to the sexual politics of existentialism is rooted in her own personal and historical situation. Her later development amply confirms her capacity to transform her own analytic categories. Even *The Second Sex,* however, does not display the sophisticated understanding of rhetoric and ideology required to develop a sustained feminist critique of her own philosophical categories. In this sense, I would argue, the real cause of Beauvoir's problems is above all the fact that she relies on Sartre's disastrously simplistic theory of language as a transparent instrument for action (see *What Is Literature?*) and that her only approximation to a concept of ideology is the schematic and limited notion of "mystification." What she fails to see is the way in which patriarchal power relations sometimes worm their way into the very core of philosophical concepts.[19] This blindness is largely responsible for the contradictions and difficulties of her attempt to represent Françoise as a free woman. Given the logic of her own problematics of freedom and domination, however, it does not follow that such power relations cannot be overthrown: on the contrary, the very fact of exposing them is already a first step toward change.

To return, finally, to the question of comparisons. On my reading of the two seduction scenes, Beauvoir's analysis of heterosexual seduction is more powerful, more complex, and more alert to the contradictory interests at stake in such a situation than Sartre's discussion of flirtation in *Being and Nothingness*. Were I to argue with the acumen of the average patriarchal critic, I would now conclude that Beauvoir turns out to be superior to Sartre after all. Such a claim would of course be absurd: one cannot ground a claim for general superiority on one example alone. The fact that patriarchs regularly get away with the practice does not make it any better. What matters, clearly, is what one is reading *for*. My own deliberate strategy has been to shift the ground of the debate. Given that every other critic seeks to compare Beauvoir to Sartre on *his* terrain by raising questions belonging to the repertoire of classical philosophy, I think it is only fair for once to compare Sartre to Beauvoir on *her* terrain: the subject of women's—and particularly intellectual women's—position in patriarchal society. By reading one of her literary texts, I also decided to take seriously Beauvoir's claim to be a novelist rather than a philosopher. What I have shown is that when it comes to the question of women's freedom in general and their sexual freedom in particular, Sartre—not surprisingly—does not have much to offer. My reading does not prove that Beauvoir is "superior" to Sartre: what it does demonstrate is that there is at least one significant field of inquiry—that concerning women's freedom—in which Beauvoir's analyses are more subtle than Sartre's. That fact alone ought to make it harder to return to further mindless rounds of the comparison game.

## ABBREVIATIONS

BN: Jean-Paul Sartre, *Being and Nothingness*.
EN: Jean-Paul Sartre, *L'Etre et le néant*.
I: Simone de Beauvoir, *L'Invitée*.
SC: Simone de Beauvoir, *She Came to Stay*.
TA: "Translation amended."

## NOTES

1. Simone de Beauvoir, *The Second Sex*, trans. H. M. Parshley (Harmondsworth, UK: Penguin, 1984); *Le Deuxième Sexe* (Paris: Gallimard "Folio," 1949). This essay is an edited and abbreviated excerpt from chapter 5 of my *Simone de*

Beauvoir: *The Making of an Intellectual Woman* (Oxford, UK and Cambridge, MA: Blackwell, 1993). In my book the chapter has a somewhat different title: "Freedom and Flirtation: The Personal and the Philosophical in Sartre and Beauvoir." The quotation in the epigraph is taken from Simone de Beauvoir's *She Came to Stay,* trans. Yvonne Moyse and Roger Senhouse (London: Fontana, 1984), 52-54. Readers should note that although the published English translation of *L'Invitée* (Paris: Gallimard "Folio," 1943) is entitled *She Came to Stay,* I use the original French title throughout my own text. References to this novel are given in parentheses in my text, first to the English translation (abbreviated SC), then to the French original (abbreviated I).
2. In *Hipparchia's Choice: An Essay Concerning Women, Philosophy, etc.*, (trans. Trista Selous [Oxford: Blackwell, 1991]; translation of *L'Etude et le rouet: des femmes, de la philosophie, etc.* [Paris: Seuil, 1989]), Michèle Le Doeuff was the first to draw attention to the curious politics of Sartre's accounts of bad faith. According to Le Doeuff, there is in Sartre's writings a tendency to attribute bad faith primarily to women and subordinate or marginal males such as waiters, students, and homosexuals (see 70-74).
3. References to Jean-Paul Sartre's *Being and Nothingness* (trans. Hazel E. Barnes [New York: Washington Square Press, 1966]) are given in parentheses in the text, first to the English translation (abbreviated BN) and then to the original French *L'Etre et le néant: essai d'ontologie phénoménologique* (Paris: Gallimard "Tel," 1943) (abbreviated EN).
4. In French: *Je vous admire tant.* The English translation here has "I find you so attractive," which is already an interpretation, precisely of the kind Sartre would want the woman to have.
5. Here and henceforth, TA means "translation amended." Hazel Barnes's translation of *le désir cru et nu* is, strangely enough, "the desire cruel and naked." While there may well be some cruelty in "crude" male desire, I doubt that Sartre intended to say so.
6. The dictionary actually claims that these relations take place "between persons of different sex," but I can see no reason why persons of the same sex should not engage in flirtation, or seduction for that matter.
7. Or in other words: every flirtation contains an element of danger. This is surely why apparently "innocent" flirtations may provoke strong feelings of jealousy in the flirtatious person's partner and why, in many historical periods, "true" decency in a woman has been considered incompatible with even the mildest flirtation.
8. The very ambiguity of the idea of flirtation guarantees that there will be all sorts of intermediate positions between flirtation and seduction. My aim here is not to provide a general analysis of such activities but simply to sketch out some definitions that would seem to be operative in Sartre's text.
9. Perhaps the relationship between flirtation and seduction may be conceived of as a continuum, in which the extreme positions are represented by an exchange of smiles in the grocer's shop, on the one hand, and Valmont's cyn-

ical debauching of Cécile de Volanges on the other. In the middle of this sliding scale there will be a large grey area in which subtle shades of seduction and flirtation will be acted out. This area will certainly allow abundant misunderstandings to take place.

10. See Claude Chabrol's film *Une Affaire de femmes* [*A Story of Women*] (MK2 Productions, Films A2, Films du Camelia and La Sept, 1988) for an unsettling reconstruction of Marie-Jeanne Latour's life.
11. I am not, of course, arguing that I, unlike Sartre, know that the woman has a project of her own. After all, this "woman" is nothing but a philosophical illustration intended to prove Sartre's point. My intention is rather to point to the limitations of Sartre's philosophical imagination: the scandal is that Sartre never even stops to consider alternative explanations of the woman's behavior.
12. In *What Is Literature? and Other Essays* (ed. Steven Ungar [Cambridge: Harvard University Press, 1988]; *Qu'est-ce que la littérature?* [Paris: Gallimard, 1948]), Sartre explicitly opposes the freedom and generosity of the acts of reading and writing to the idea of being *obliged* to do something. When it comes to readers and writers, to be free is to act generously and with confidence in the other's freedom; when it comes to men and women, apparently, it is not quite that simple (see 61-62).
13. In a brief discussion of this scene, Lorna Sage notes interestingly that "Beauvoir's woman . . . is a lot sadder than Sartre's." *Women in the House of Fiction: Post-War Women Novelists* (London: Macmillan, 1992), 6.
14. Jean-Paul Sartre, *L'Existentialisme est un humanisme* (Paris: Nagel, 1946), 83.
15. In a footnote in *The Literature of Possibility: A Study in Humanist Existentialism* (Lincoln: University of Nebraska Press, 1959), Hazel Barnes also draws attention to the man's bad faith: "What strikes me as odd," she writes, "is that neither Sartre nor de Beauvoir points out that there is some bad faith on the man's side as well. His choice of ambiguous words is explicitly designed to allow him to retreat rapidly to the plane of polite friendship in case he has misjudged the situation" (52).
16. I will return to the question of whether this *is* a scene of seduction.
17. It is interesting to note that Beauvoir herself admits to a certain penchant for sentimental and vaguely romantic texts. In 1930 she started work on a novel inspired by Alain-Fournier's *Le Grand Meaulnes* (1913) (Paris: Livre de Poche, 1967) and Rosamond Lehmann's *Dusty Answer* (1927) (Harmondsworth, UK: Penguin, 1991). (Translated into French under the title *Poussière,* Lehmann's novel remained one of Beauvoir's favorite texts: there is an interesting study to be done on the implications of Beauvoir's lifelong admiration for the British writer.) "I became vaguely aware that enchantment *[le merveilleux]* didn't do much for me, though this didn't prevent me from chasing it stubbornly, and for a long time. I still have a touch of 'Delly' about me; it is very noticeable in the first drafts of my novels" (*The Prime of Life,* trans. Peter Green [Harmondsworth, UK: Penguin, 1988], 60; *La Force de l'âge* [Paris: Gallimard "Folio," 1960], 71; TA). "Delly" was the pseudonym of Jeanne and

Frédéric Petitjean de la Rosière, whose sentimental novels long dominated the market for popular romances in France. When it comes to the end of the seduction chapter in *L'Invitée,* one has to conclude that the "Delly" side of her imagination remained evident even in the final version.

18. Because it represents such a large and complex topic in Beauvoir's work, I will not discuss it any further here. Body trouble is the central preoccupation of chapter 6 of *Simone de Beauvoir: The Making of an Intellectual Woman.*
19. I discuss the way in which this works in *The Second Sex* in chapter 6 of my book.

# 8

## Snails and Oysters:
## Sartre and His Homosexualities

### George H. Bauer

> *It's food crammed deep inside an object that has to be pried out. More than anything it's the idea of extirpation that disgusts me. The fact that the flesh of the creature is so snug in its shell that you have to use tools to get it to come out instead of cutting it off.*
>
> —JEAN-PAUL SARTRE quoted in *La Cérémonie des adieux*

> *The oyster, the size of an average pebble, looks rougher, its color less uniform, brilliantly whitish. It is a world stubbornly closed. Still, it can be opened. . . . Curious fingers cut themselves on it, nails break: it's a dirty job. . . .*
> *Inside, you find a whole world, to be drunk, to be eaten.*
>
> —FRANCIS PONGE, *Le Parti pris des choses*

Letters to the Editor in the pages of the *New Yorker* are rare, so it was with some surprise that Craig Claiborne's signature in capital letters caught my attention. The error in terminology he was discussing was one concerning culinary matters—in this instance a question of something fishy. In a short story written by Katherine Weber ("Friend of the Family"), the recipe identified as *truite au bleu* is mistaken and is thus corrected and placed in perspective by the master writer-chef who gave us the remarkable *New York Times Cookbook*. It is not a question of a trout with its tail in its mouth boiled alive. The dish she has used to express her contempt for the gentleman with whom she dined is the French *merlan en colère*—a whiting in anger, he translates. "It is prepared by twisting the fish into a circle and tying or otherwise securing the tail in its mouth. It is then deep-fried (not boiled) and served with parsley, lemon, and tartar sauce. When it is served hot, it has a distinctly choleric, or irascible, appearance."[1] A little vinegar is the secret to being blue. Claiborne underscores the unfortunate error. His fish is fresh. "It does not have its tail in its mouth. The dish is prepared by eviscerating, or cleaning, the fish the moment it is tossed into a kettle of boiling water, plus a trace of vinegar. When it is tossed in the kettle, the water destroys its nervous system, and it curls naturally. The vinegar gives the fish its blue color."

Katherine Weber's unfortunate error could have been avoided if she had stuck to lobster and the French *rouge comme une écrevisse* [red like a crayfish][2] or to vegetables without turning "red as a beet." Apollinaire's own bestiary dips into aquatic solution for crayfish, octopuses, medusas, and carp for poetic inspiration:

| La Carpe | The Carp |
|---|---|
| Dans vos viviers, dans vos étangs, | In your fishponds, in your pools, |
| Carpes que vous vivez, longtemps! | You carps live so long! |
| Est-ce que la mort vous oublie, | Is it that death forgets you, |
| Poissons de la mélancolie. | Fishes of melancholy.[3] |

If in Sartre's own Dürer-inspired *Melancholia* there is no carp except in the *carpe diem* of writing as a remedy for nausea, he dishes up and serves out in menu detail the truth he discovered in Naples: "the filthy relationship between love and Food."[4] It is in his love letters to Olga Iaroslaw that he details his Naples—a "city with a belly"—experience of the summer of 1936; food and sex come to a head, however, on a Tuesday in April 1937 when he is writing, not to Olga, but to his "charmant Castor." "There. I have been writing you since seven. It is now nine-thirty—just a half-hour off for dinner (*soupe aux pois* [pea soup]; *filet de barbue Bercy* [fillet of brill Bercy],[5] smelling so *femme* that I got half a hard-on but only barely like a dog that raises his head and goes back to his nap on seeing that it isn't his master, that he was mistaken; *hachis parmentier* [shepherd's pie], and dessert) my hand is damp, trembling. I just have the strength to say I love you with all my heart, my charming, my tender Castor, and that I think of you intensely."[6] There is something fishy here in this bearded lady, this brill of Bercy. One whiff is enough to arouse the culinary curiosity.

Sartre's *Nausea* is literary. The crab as metaphor, as philosophical or psychological object, has been extirpated masterfully. The flesh pried from its snug shell ends up this way. In Marie-Denise Boros's words, "It [the crab] in effect embodies one of the fundamental ideas of Sartrean ontology, reality fallen into the trap of the En-Soi."[7] But here and in other readings of his texts the taste and smell of food and sex seem *de trop* [too much]. Castor, *charmant Castor,* attempts to rectify the situation. "We are going to talk about a theme that has been little discussed, that is your relationships with food."[8] Her culinary investigation follows hard on a discussion of dreams. "Do you sometimes have dreams?" "No," he answers. "Sometime around the age of thirty I completely lost the ability to remember my dreams" (CA, 419). He still remembers the nightmares—the lobsters and the crabs—but dreams, not for years. The crustaceans are gone. His sleep is sound. His digestive organs are in good shape. It is that old nausea, only once, that provokes the slip to the questions of tastes, of appetites, of food in all of its ambiguity. His unique experience of being sick to his stomach, he insists, occurred the night before an awarding of prizes. "First I had dinner on the beach with some students, then I ended up the night in a bordel *où je n'avais pas consommé* [where I had not consumed]" (CA, 421). No question of a gut reaction. Not *La Barbue.* Not *La Morue.*[9] One other time. Castor oils his memory machine, orients him. In Japan. Remember the raw fish. She insists, there it wasn't a physical reaction. He couldn't understand what was happening to him. She suggests that his psychosomatic side ought to be discussed, because on the whole he is "very much in control, very organized, very cerebral, very conscious of what goes on. There are, however, instances when your body reacted almost without your knowing it, as in that case, for example" (CA, 421). Lived nausea. Nausea written up. Nausea written out.

Real food? *Nourritures terrestres* [earthly nourishments]? "Basically there are very few things that I like to eat. Some things I absolutely refuse to eat. Tomatoes, for example, which throughout my life I have practically never eaten. I don't find them so bad and the taste is not that disgusting, but because they give me no pleasure I made a decision not to eat them and, generally, people around me go along" (CA, 421). All food is a symbol, he explains. Yes, it nourishes, it's edible, but its taste, its appearance evoke other things. He reminds her that he discussed this in *L'Etre et le néant.*[10] There it was chocolate and pink—cookies and crustaceans—not the metaphorical, philosophical crab. "It is not a matter of indifference whether we like oysters or clams, snails or shrimp, if only we know how to bring out the existential significance of these foods. Speaking in general there is no irreducible taste or inclination. They all represent a certain appropriative choice of being" (EN, 707). She probes. "Other than the tomato, what foods do you find the most repugnant?" *Les crustacées, les huîtres, les coquillages* [crustaceans, oysters, shellfood]. He explains: "That white flesh is not made for us; it is stealing from another universe" (CA, 422). She reminds him of the link between them and his thoughts on *le glaireux* [the slimy], on *le visqueux* [the viscous], but he insists that it is as well "that repugnant aspect of lymphatic flesh, strange in color, of a gaping hole in flesh" (CA, 423). That's it in a shell. Going on. "Do you find anything else repugnant?" The *pomme d'amour*, the tomato bobs up again in these auto-interdicted *nourritures terrestres*. Maybe, it's the acidity, he offers. Going on, permit me to back up. Before going on with Sartre's crabs and *coquilles Saint Antoine,* disgust and nausea, let me insert here Apollinaire's "The Crayfish":

| L'Ecrevisse | The Crayfish |
|---|---|
| Incertitude, ô mes délices | Uncertainty, how delicious, |
| Vous et moi nous nous en allons | You and I, forward go, |
| Comme s'en vont les écrevisses, | Going like the crayfishes |
| A reculons, à reculons. | Backwards, backwards, O. |

(AO, 24)

From *la barbue* and the scent of a woman, let's slip to *le barbu,* Adam's apple, and the scent of a man. Sniffing around, Castor asks him about the smell of the adult male that draws other males to him. Gide is the pretext. "Couldn't it also be said that in a certain way the adult male is a little your 'mauvaise odeur,' as Genet would say?" . . . "Yes, perhaps. . . . I don't like *ça* [that] at all, and I don't like being called one. . . . if I'm still male, it's only slightly" (CA, 363-64). Sartre hates what she suggests is his pheromone attraction as an adult male, because he can't stand adult males. "The adult male to me is deeply disgusting; what I really like is a young man to the extent that a young man is not completely different from a young woman. Not that I'm a pederast, but the fact is, especially now, young men and young women are not so different in costume, in the way they talk, in the way they carry themselves. For me they have never been all that different *[tellement distincts]*" (CA, 364).

*Reculons. Reculons.* The scent and the taste of a man are at the center of Sartre's reflections on loving. Men are an acquired taste—even for women, he insists in *Les Carnets de la drôle de guerre.*[11] He draws a situation map in this other *drôle de guerre* [phoney war]. "Quite obviously, if the other is a man, the ruggedness of his physique is an invincible obstacle in the establishment of this situation" (CG, 335). He well understands the resistance a young woman must overcome "avant de désirer un homme *pour de bon* [before desiring a man for good]." Men are too spicy, too rich. They taste too strong. "I have always felt that the body of man was too spicy, too rich, too strong a taste to be desired *tout de suite* [immediately]. Certainly an apprenticeship is needed" (CG, 335). Jean-Paul's thoughts on the matter were confirmed to him by Olga. He agrees with her that "the charm of a woman or a young man is discovered immediately, whereas lengthy familiarity and particular attention are needed to discover a man's charm." He adds his own worries about his manly taste. "As I was enjoying the charm of kissing a fresh and tender mouth, I always wondered about the singular impression that my own was making—rough, smelling of tobacco" (CG, 335-36). The idea that the woman desires a man *because she is a woman* doesn't make sense to him. Woman is the object of desire for both a man and a woman. "In order for a man to become desirable in turn, some kind of '*report*' must be effected." But here isn't the place to deal with that, he notes.

Instead, he turns to his relation with *hommes-femmes* curiously rendered by his English translator as "women-men." What he has a taste for is tenderness between men and, for him, that is inconceivable.

> For my part, I cannot conceive of tenderness in my relations with men. So I've only had friendships with what I will term *hommes-femmes*, a very rare species, separated from the others by their physical charm, sometimes by their beauty and by a thousand intimate riches that the average man knows nothing of. Guille, in his splendor, could waste hours talking to me about a face, a fleeting nuance of light or his mood, about some trivial scene that passed before our eyes. So I am an *homme-femme* myself, I feel, despite my ugliness, at least in my main preoccupations. (CG, 336)

All of these *drôle de guerre* reflections are written in a *Foyer du Soldat* [Soldier's Quarters]. The men around him disgust him. "There isn't one among them that I'd like to get to know. *Je n'aime pas les hommes* [I don't like men], by that I mean the males of the species" (CG, 338). Yet, in retrospect *(reculons, reculons)*, there was the camaraderie of Paul Nizan, the simultaneity. Reading and writing together, the dream of the double desk, *le pupitre double.* "In short, have I ever really strictly speaking loved a man of my own age—except Nizan once? I don't think so. Nor ever wanted one to love me." Women are his thing. He has cut himself off from males. "In short, for me there is one half of the human race that hardly exists. The other—and it has to be said—the other is my unique, my constant concern." In the words of his pal, Bost, "On my knees, I'd go!" (CG, 341). But the next day, Thursday, February 29th, he returns to his taste for handsome men, his appetite for things beautiful. "I should have liked to eat beauty and incorporate it. I imagine that to a certain extent I suffered from an identification complex, and that explains why I have always chosen handsome men to be my friends—or ones I deemed to be so" (CG, 342). His appetite for beauty is not sensual but magical he insists.

From our consideration of mollusks and muscled men that are too disgusting, too repugnant to his taste, let's return to the *Cérémonie des adieux* to see if there is anything at all tempting on the menu. "I don't much care for vegetables." They, too, come from another universe. Raw, no, but the cooked is different. "When it is cooked a vegetable ceases to be a vegetable to become a purée or a cooked salad. It is the raw that distances it from us" (CA, 422). As we have seen, the tomato, even cooked, has been crossed off the list. Fruit, too, is something he practically never eats. If the status of the tomato as fruit or vegetable is something incomprehensible, its place is probably on the fruit side. "Fruit has a dicey taste—*un goût de hasard*: chancy; it is on the tree, it is on the ground in the grass. It's not for me, it doesn't come from me, I'm the one to decide to make it edible" (CA, 423). The pineapple, miraculously, receives a reprieve. Bananas? They have to be consumed on the spot, like "I discovered jazz in America" jazz. "Pineapples, because the pineapple looks like something cooked. I was familiar with canned pineapple, but when I ate some raw for the first time in South America, I had the impression that it was a big cooked object" (CA, 424). *Le jazz hot*. Ah, the ambiguities of the cooked and the raw. Which brings up meat. No, even cooked, he doesn't like meat. "There was a time when I liked a fine piece of rumpsteak, a *chateaubriand*, a leg of lamb, but I gave it up because it made me conjure up the idea of eating *la bête* [the beast]" (CA, 424). Curiously his piscatorial preferences are never pursued. Perhaps Castor remembers the long letter and *la barbue* and simply avoids *La Halle aux morues* of *Nausea* and *les maquereaux*[12] of *Saint Genet* and its codpieces. Cheese, too—all the fragrant 400 French varieties of it—remains untouched like Antoine Roquentin's problematical camembert.

His real appetite—other than for beauty—is for the products of the *boulanger* [baker], the *pâtissier* [pastry chef], and the *charcutier* [pork butcher]. Despite the counsel of diet for *le petit gros* [the fat little man] and his own self-imposed dietary restrictions, he has his passions: bread, pastries, and *charcuterie* [pork meats]. "From time to time, when I was told not to eat that [*il ne faut pas manger ça*], I went along for a while, then I went back to eating it because I have very special tastes . . ." (CA, 403). Castor queries: "But eating was something that gave you great pleasure?" "Oh yes, a great deal! Relatively speaking, I ate quite a lot" (CA, 403). In other places I have discussed his "Just Desserts," "Faces and Food," and his reflections on "The Sweets of History." Here, now thanks to Castor, I add these food-notes on Sartre's sweet tooth. "I prefer to eat things made by men, a *gâteau* [cake], a *tarte*. There, in the making, the taste itself, was intended, rethought by man. . . . A *gâteau* . . . has a regular shape like, for example, that of an *éclair au chocolat* or *au café;* pastry cooks make them, in ovens, etc. So an entirely human thing . . . food must be the result of men's actions. Bread is like that. I always thought of bread as a relation with men" (CA, 423). Bread. O.K. But his passion for *charcuterie?* Could that be explained by his Alsatian origins? Not quite. "In any case, obviously, that's its origin; but does that explain it? It's something else *[C'est une autre affaire]"* (CA, 424). Innovative packaging of meat products counts. Can knotted string tie up the unravelled ends of culinary dénouements?

In an attempt to wrap it up, Simone de Beauvoir asks and summarily rephrases: "To put it another way you are fond of *charcuterie* because the flesh is less immediately present than in red meat?" (CA, 424). He strings her along. "It seemed to me that men were using meat to make something new, for example, an *andouille* [sausage made of chitterlings], an *andouillette* [small sausage made of chitterlings], a *saucisson* [sausage]. They only existed through men. Blood was caught in a quite specific way, invented by man. They gave this *saucisson* a form that was for me quite tempting, tied at the end by bits of twine!" (CA, 424). For him it's something to eat but it's no longer meat. Wienies are wienies. Meat is meat. "Red meat, even cooked, is still meat. It has the same consistency, blood oozing, it has the same quality; there is too much of it to eat. A *saucisson*, an *andouille, ça n'est pas comme ça* [that's not like that]. A *saucisson* with its white flecks and its pink flesh, round, *c'est autre chose* [it's something else]" (CA, 424).

Eerie, eely, magically it comes from but is not meat. The *andouille,* and the *andouillette* are man-made; the *saucisson's* flecked, rose flesh distances itself through an act of prestidigitation; man frees himself from red meat and "lymphatic flesh, strange in color." Incredibly edible, it is not from an alien universe, not mineral or vegetable ("vegetables have no consciousness," Castor has noted earlier); it is flesh but it is a long way from the disgusting worm flesh of *L'Idiot de la famille* ("What is a whore except a long, white worm?)"[13] and the limp hand of *Nausea's* self-taught man ("This great white worm in my hand. I dropped it quickly and the wrist fell limp").[14] This is something else—*autre chose*. Castor calls it a wrap. She ends on an anthropological note, concluding philosophically: "To sum it up you are resolutely on the side of the cooked against the raw?" "Absolutely. Obviously I can eat almonds or walnuts, although they hurt my tongue" (CA, 424). Nuts are exceptional, the pineapple, too. Delicious, prickly ambiguity. The pineapple is the raw seen cooked; the fruit is the center of Brunet's Vicarios-Schneider dream brought on by hunger in the unfinished *Les Chemins de la liberté* [*The Roads to Freedom*].

*Reculons. Reculons.* It was with a certain apprehension that I accepted the invitation to revisit Sartre: homotextualities, alimentarities, culinary aspects. The recently released uncut version of the film *Spartacus* seduced me. The focus here is different: homosexualities; Sartre in the flesh; Sartre and the flesh: Sartre and the *homme-femme*. Censorship, dream censorship, real and imagined censoring brought me to mollusks and men,[15] to oysters and snails, to the homoerotics of seduction and the question of freedom. What I thought to be a filmed version of Sartre's reflections on snails and oysters picked up from the cutting room floor had nothing to do with Howard Fast's reading of *La Nausée* or *L'Etre et le néant* ("It is not a matter of indifference if we like oysters or clams, snails or shrimp . . ."). The scene is not in the book. *Spartacus*,[16] as novel, is homophobic, but ironically the source of revolt and the discovery of freedom is repugnant, deadly homosexual desire. "So when he [Spartacus] was chosen as one of four gladiators to satisfy the caprice of two perfumed homosexuals from Rome, to fight in two pairs to the death, he was torn by such a struggle and unholy contradiction as he had never experienced before. It was a new struggle, and when he conquered in that struggle, he made the first real penetration of the protective covering with which he had encased himself" (S, 230).

By contrast, Sartre's struggle with and discovery of freedom came from an act, a gratuitous act fleshed out—unlike the textuality of Gide's Lafcadio's self-inflicted wound, a fictional *coup dans la cuisse,* a stab in the thigh. If existentialism had its phenomenal origin in café-drunk apricot cocktail or beer (Sartre's version differs from de Beauvoir's), freedom was revealed to Sartre by that other *homme-femme,* Paul Nizan. The subject of long discussions and fruitless conflict between Sartre (abstract man) and Nizan (historical materialism) fell by the wayside when Nizan embodied freedom and made it real—an *acte gratuit* [gratuitous act]. "I was taken by surprise. Nizan was Catholic, the son of a very Catholic mother, and I did not understand his reasons. I asked him what they were. He said it was cleaner *[plus propre],* without further explaining himself. The event seemed to me *sans cause* [without cause]. He had decided to have himself circumcised—a stupid decision because nothing militated in its favor. He had gone to see a doctor; he circumcised him, he stayed two or three days in a hotel with a bandage around the end of his penis" (CA, 445). *Je pense donc je suis. Je suis pansé donc. Tu me suis? On est pansé.*[17] The shift is from Descartes to Rimbaud to Gide. Castor's question makes the Gide connection specific. "At that point in time freedom and the gratuitous act were for you alike, weren't they?" Sartre answers. "For the most part. Still the gratuitous act as it is defined and described in Gide's *Les Faux-Monnayeurs* [sic] didn't tempt me. When I read the book I didn't find freedom as I understood it. But Nizan's circumcision was in my eyes certainly a gratuitous act which was in fact done for motives he hid from me" (CA, 445). The knot that bound the two as one—as Nitre-Sarzan—began to loosen and eventually is undone.

*Spartacus* not only has freedom as its subject, but the revolt it inscribes, as I have noted above, was unleashed by a private "performance" of naked men. "Never in a thousand years would he have had the courage to demand that the gladiators fight naked; yet that was one of the reasons why they were having a show for their own amusement at Capua instead of going to the arena in Rome" (S, 87). Spartacus, before Howard Fast, had been relegated to a footnote in history. Fast had been jailed for his association with the Communist Party and redeemed himself with all-American books on Tom Paine and on the father of the country, George Washington. His Marxist, chaste dream of fraternity exploits homophobia while glorifying wholesome male camaraderie and the splendors of male flesh in hand to hand combat to the death. Disgust at this "entertaining" experience was momentous and historical: "a moment of changed motion in history, a beginning, a stirring, a wordless whisper, a portent, a flash of light which signifies earth-shaking thunder and blinding lightning" (S, 237). Cleverly, Fast deals with the improbability and gratuitousness of this event he uses as the origin of the slave's revolt. Unlike many, his Lentulus Batiatus "could not accept the fact that what happened afterwards happened because two Roman Fops desired to see a private combat to the death" (S, 99). Roman tastes in food, amusements, and sex share the responsibility for the revolt against Fast's Roman decadence. "One does not fight well on a heavy stomach. In any case, Spartacus was not hungry. They [the four gladiators] sat apart from the others, the four of them, and they shared a distaste for food" (S, 98). Spartacus, however, receives a fraternal kiss before dying from the man he must kill. "Gannicus went over to Spartacus and embraced him and kissed his lips; it was a strange thing to do, and the price was high, thirty lashes, but there were very few among the gladiators who did not have a sense of why he had done it" (S, 99).

The other flight to freedom is Hollywood politics at its best. That's where the snails slip into the existential movie. I leave aside the lengthy story of the making of the movie. Kirk Douglas, Spartacus himself, recounts "The Wars of Spartacus" in his autobiography, *The Ragman's Son*.[18] Tony Curtis, a buddy and *homme-femme* in his youthful beauty, needed a part:

I didn't think there was anything for him, or that he was right for this kind of picture. Since *The Vikings*, he had done *The Defiant Ones*, playing a runaway from a chain gang, shackled to Sidney Poitier. Then *Operation Petticoat* and *Some Like It Hot*, in drag. But Tony was insistent. We made a role for him, a poetic young man named Antoninus who becomes like a son to Spartacus. In the end, the Romans force the two of us to fight to the death. The survivor will be crucified. Neither of us wants the other to have to undergo that agony, so we try to kill each other. I kill Tony. (R, 286)

How Tony as Antoninus came to join Spartacus's camp is a snippet picked up from the cutting room floor. There lies the motivation for the poet as runaway slave from the colossal appetites of decadent Rome embodied by gay Laurence Olivier.

Now, the uncut version restores the attempted culinary seduction; the scene, written by blacklisted Dalton Trumbo, restores the taste for snails and menu seduction. Here it is not a restaurant, not the Roman arena, but a private bath.

"Do you steal, Antoninus?"
"No."
"No, *Master.*"
"No, Master. . . ."
"Do you eat oysters?"
"When I have them."
"Do you eat snails?"
"No, Master."
*Crassus laughs softly.*
"Do you consider the eating of oysters to be moral, and the eating of snails to be immoral?"
"I don't think so."
"Of *course* not. It's a matter of appetite, isn't it?"
"Yes, Master."
"An appetite has nothing to do with morals, has it?"
"No, Master. . . ."
"Therefore no appetite is immoral, is it? It's merely different."
"Yes, Master. . . ."
"My robe, Antoninus. . . ."
*"My appetite includes both snails and oysters."*
(R, 293-94, emphasis added to last line)

Sir Laurence is a colossus. He is Rome. "You must grovel at her feet. You must love her." The revolt now is against the censors. A brilliant seduction scene, Douglas calls it, but unlike the violent, bloody combat and the origin of that other revolt, this runaway's reason for the escape to freedom was simply revolting. "It was very subtle; nothing explicit. The censors weren't even sure it was about homosexuality, but just in case, they wanted it out. We argued, hoping to keep it in" (R, 292). A question of taste? "We argued and argued, and finally the censors hemmed and hawed and said the scene *might* work if we changed 'snails and oysters' to 'artichokes and truffles.' They were also uncomfortable with the word 'appetite.' We shot it, hoping to convince them. They looked at it, stood firm. We had to cut it out of the picture" (R, 294). Tony's loss. Dalton Trumbo's gain. In an act of defiance, Kirk Douglas a.k.a. Spartacus, credits Dalton Trumbo for the screenplay. "All my friends told me it was being stupid, throwing my career away. It was a tremendous risk" (R, 295-96). Sexual politics. Like Sartre, Douglas speaking of his sexual attractions in relation to Rock Hudson, "a tall, dark, husky actor," the son of a ragpicker tells us: "I don't think that way. I don't draw a sharp line between masculine and feminine. We all have both sides. And we need them, especially artists" (R, 300).

Snails and oysters then; in light of other moving appetites we are led back to alimentary seduction and *Nausea*'s La Maison Bottanet, to "homo/textuality."[19] Tony Curtis as Antoninus fled from the Roman Crassus and his taste for snails into the arms of freedom and was embraced not only by Spartacus, who had no appetite, but a whole army fleeing from Roman amusements, Roman tastes in sex and food—Sartrean existentialists at heart. Let's do lunch. But it is over lunch that the fictional Antoine, not Antoninus, does battle with and cuts up those humanists, those lovers of men, the *hommes-femmes*. Pierre Guille (the Left), Paul Nizan (the materialist/Communist), Ogier P . . . (self-taught), all *hommes-femmes* are threatened by the just-desserts knife. It began with a reading *à l'envers* [backwards] of the violet Frequent Diners Discount Card. "One does not fight well on a heavy stomach." Not at any price. Clearly Flaubert's hand is behind all of this, but it is not the seduction of Emma at the Fair. "To kiss is to eat." Emma, like Spartacus, will not eat. Her appetite is elsewhere. Antoine will not be seduced anymore than Antoninus. The appetizer is existential choice. *Hors-d'œuvre au choix.* "I am allowed one *hors-d'œuvre:* either slices of *saucisson* or radishes or shrimps or a dish of stuffed celery. Snails are extra." *Saucisson.* "Isn't there anything better?" "Here, *escargots de Bourgogne.*" "The fact is I don't much care for snails." The Autodidact, the library-man who eats books and tenderly caresses the hands of *hommes-femmes*, tempts him with oysters. "They're four francs more. . . ." "All right, oysters, Mademoiselle—and radishes for me" (OR, 124-25). The Pléiade editors interject, append: "When you know the horror Sartre had of shellfish and crustaceans, one can gauge the sacrifice his character faced with the weighty generosity of the Autodidact" (OR, 1778). Maybe. Maybe Antoine, unlike Antoninus and like the budding poet Poulou of Les Mots,[20] could be seduced like Lucien Fleurier—seduced, despite his taste for *saucisson* and *andouillettes*—with those *menhirs,* those *mein herrs,* oyster-books that enclose pages cut and uncut, enclose the pale flesh of their guts, their interior organs. In that other library to be ingested, Poulou looks at Grandpa's collection (Grandma's books are *confiseries de Nouvel An* [New Year's sweets], feminine pink and sweetly suckable); "Sometimes I would go up to them to look at those casings that split open like oysters, and I discovered the nudity of their inner organs, pale, musty leaves, slightly puffy, covered with little black veins which drank ink and smelled of mushroom" (LM, 30). "This little fellow has a thirst for knowledge; he devours the Larousse!" (LM, 56). But Roquentin is not Poulou, he is not Lucien Fleurier. He is losing his appetite. Oysters to open. "I glance over the meat list. The *boeuf en daube* [beef stew] would tempt me. But I know already that I will have the *poulet chasseur* [chicken in mushroom sauce], the only extra meat." "Give the gentleman the chicken. Spiced beef for me" (OR, 125). The lunch seduction begins with a carafe of Anjou Rosé. "I usually come here with a book, even though my doctor has advised against it: one eats too fast and doesn't chew. But I have a stomach like an ostrich, I can swallow anything" (OR, 125). The radishes ready before the oysters are quickly gone leaving behind an inedible "packet of green tails *[queues vertes]* and a little damp salt. Oysters. The "pale flesh of their guts, their interior organs" disappear leaving their *coquillages* [shells] and slimy traces to be replaced with the rage-provoking "Sale bête! Sale bête! [Filthy beast!]" of Proust's Françoise: chicken, the barely covered leg swimming in brown sauce. "You must eat that." The gravy slowly congeals around the capon. Culinary seduction does not lead to dessert. Instead "the waitress puts a plate of chalky Camembert in front of me. I look around the room and a violent disgust invades me" (OR, 144). The runny, ripe Camembert stands in as a solution at hand, providing a blunt-edged dessert knife and the heavy scent of sex. "The taste of cheese in my mouth. . . ." Does he regret the meal uneaten? Sliced *saucisson,* displaced viscera, emptied and refilled, desired, denied, string-tied *charcuterie;* the taste of *boeuf en daube;* the sweetness of a choice pastry—man-made.

The taste and smell of bovine-produced viscosity. He chews a piece of bread but is unable to swallow. The hand as crab displaces Lafcadio's thigh, the wounded thing that binds; the self-inflicted wound as gratuitous act haunts the scene. He can't cut it. The dessert knife doesn't cut it. "The knife falls on the plate." Again. "I pick up the knife, I support it with the table and bend it" (OR, 145). Why not stick the knife, not in myself, but into the eye of the other, "a taste of blood in the mouth instead of the taste of cheese." All eyes are on him. The young lovers. A shift from uneaten *poulet* to *poule.* "The woman's mouth seems to be a chicken's ass *[cul de poule]*." Knife in hand, he exits. "They saw a crab running backwards running out of the place" (OR, 146). The Self-Taught Man's last question to him remains unanswered: ". . . de la Rome antique, monsieur?" (OR, 145).

Despite the American censors, artichokes and truffles are no substitute for oysters and snails in culinary seduction. What is missing from the *Nausea* prescription of *Manger et dormir* [Eat and sleep] as it takes a Neapolitan twist in *Manger, caresser ou vomir* [Eat, caress or vomit] is the caress. Like Roquentin, Sartre has no taste for oysters. What he has is a certain *saucisson* regret for shared tastes, shared conversation. The oyster is difficult to open, but in the *immonde parenté* [disgusting kinship] of comestibles and sex, we should remember that for him "sexual relations with women" were required because the classical relationship implied these relations (CA, 385). He consumed. Yes. "But, properly speaking, *ça* didn't interest me as much as caresses. To put it another way, I was more a masturbator of women than a copulator." Go on. Go on. "For me, the essential and affective relation involved my embracing, my caressing, my running my lips all over a body. But the sexual act—that existed too—I did it, even often—but with a certain indifference" (CA, 385). In *Les Mots,* Sartre writes of Poulou, his other—"I performed my alimentary obligations, and God sometimes—rarely—blessed me with the grace that enables one to eat without disgust, namely appetite. Breathing, digesting, defecating unconcernedly. I lived because I had begun to live. I was unaware of the violent and savage demands of that gorged companion, my body, which made itself known by a series of mild upsets" (LM, 71). "I wasn't even sure of preferring a *filet de boeuf* [beef fillet] to *rôti de veau* [roast veal]" (LM, 72).

After Nizan's circumcision, a real *Kaiser-schnitt*, Nitre-Sarzan as twins from Siam were no longer joined in the playfully hip games of Rastignac, of Lafcadio, of Charlus and Morel. With the birth of liberty born of male flesh and gratuitous act, Sartre became not a *merlan en colère* but a raging crab. He tied his tongue to his tail. Sartre did it in print with all *hommes-femmes,* with himself. They became *traîtres en puissance* [potential traitors]. The menu is long: Baudelaire, Mallarmé, Daniel, Lucien, Genet, Nizan, Guille, both in textuality and reality, his receipts, his cooked books, more Proustian than Gidean—serve us up the unappetizing dishes. In turn his received ideas of homo/textuality, critiqued by Lawrence Schehr,[21]

Oreste Pucciani, and others,[22] should not turn us away from Sartre's *homme-femme* living and writing despite his "ugliness." He and his *hommes-femmes* exist *en daube*, smothered in the cooking, *étouffé*. *Daubeur* [jeerer] to the end, his jibes reveal his continuing fascination for *hommes-femmes* art and beauty. In his posthumously published *La Reine Albemarle ou le dernier touriste*,[23] snippets attest to uneasy attraction. Carpaccio's *Saint Ursula*. Probably "the two young personages on the far left, one of whom holds a falcon," Arlette Elkaïm-Sartre notes. "What happiness he has in painting the well-formed thighs, the golden hair of these companions and their ravishing little buns. Hatred of women. It is that love of men that makes the beauty of his paintings. It's like the *Outlaw* where Jane Russell's breasts hide *une histoire de pédés* [a history of queers]" (RA, 102). In this tattered, patchwork text, Sartor's painful needling gives way to real, remembered pain. "What I regret, is *amitié* [friendship], but it is a certain *amitié italienne,* that I have observed a hundred times, that tenderness of a man for a man that is almost sensual and so little pederastic" (RA, 151).

*Reculons. Reculons.* The insistent opposition between the sensual and the pederastic blues. Eros rides the lobster at Pompei where pineapples lie among the fruit. In extirpation, in excavation, in dream, the desired object counts. I have a taste for Craig Claiborne's *Truite au bleu* and James Beard's Blue Trout[24] caught by Whitman and his pals, a trout curling naturally and not to be mistaken for a *Merlan en colère* or the suspect *Barbue de Bercy*. I am intrigued by Sartre's—and the Self-Taught Man's—hunger for tenderness and caresses. Sartre's taste is stifled, shelved in tainted oyster books; hermaphroditic snails leave their slippery trace transformed as sticky sweetness of pineapple juiciness in a tale of men at war: *Les Chemins de la liberté.* Sartre's version of Kirk Douglas's *Spartacus* (freedom and fraternity in defeat) is his *La Mort dans l'âme* (translated as *Troubled Sleep* by Gerard Hopkins) originally announced as *Drôle d'amitié,* a naming deferred for later. In this "strange friendship," the disgust Antoine felt at Ogier P...'s snails proposed and his repugnance for his experience as a prisoner of war ("I loved these men like brothers. I wanted to embrace them all" [OR, 135]), regurgitated between the oysters and *poulet chasseur,* is displaced in and tailored otherwise in a last stab at fiction. There, tins of monkey meat (*boîte de singe*—rations of canned beef) uneaten give rise to pineapple dream. The *amitié* is not ancient Roman, not *à l'italienne,* but uniquely Alsatian French, harking angelically back to Nitre-Sarzan resurrected as Brunet-Schneider/Vicarios. Schneider shares his name with Sartre's own *sartor;* tailor, now seen as well as *cutter,* is not simply Alsatian in original nominalism. Like Sartre's taste for *saucisson, andouille,* and *andouillette,* "c'est une autre affaire."[25]

The Italian *manger, caresser, vomir* of *Nourritures* and the extracts of *Nausea*'s *manger et dormir, dormir et manger* give way to the sleep of dreams: to sleep, to caress in dream, to eat dreamily—not oysters, not snails, but problematic Sartrean fruit; the dream is brought on by a strange hunger and the proximity to the other Paul, the Nizan-inspired, resurrection—Vicarios/Schneider—and the security of their shared blanket and tastes. "I would have been very content to be in a bed naked with a naked woman, to caress, to kiss, but without going on to the sexual act" (CA, 400). "My chief desire in love is bodily nearness, or contact, to sleep naked with a naked friend"[26] was the dream of Edward Carpenter, not unlike Gide's own Edouard's tender watch of slumbering Olivier in *Les Faux-Monnayeurs*. Brunet's sleep of reason brings not monsters but caged simians and the prickly pineapple that Louis XIV cut his lip on and banned from France.

> It is the cool delicious taste of pineapples, a young taste, a little gay, childish; he is chewing pineapple, he munches its sweet fibrous resilience; when was the last time I ate pineapple? I loved pineapple, it was a defenseless wood, stripped of its peel; he chews. The youthful yellow taste of tender wood comes softly again from the back of his throat; like a tentative sunrise it spreads over his tongue, it means something, it wants to say something, what does it mean, what does it want to say, this sunny syrup [*sirop de soleil*]. (OR, 1388)

Groggily, he stirs. *L'Age de raison* [*The Age of Reason*]. *Le Sursis* [*The Reprieve*]. The roads ahead call to him in this troubling alimentary dream. He gives in to the incubus. "Fragile. What have I done with my loves: they said to me: You do not love us enough. They had me, they stripped me, *a young tender strippling,* sticky with sap [Sartre's italics]; when I get out of here I'll eat a whole pineapple. . . . I have no desires, I am the peel, the sap is dead, the monkeys gripping the bars of their cages stare. . . . He falls back into the stickiness. The monkeys guffaw and slap their thighs" (OR, 1388-89). These are not Lafcadio's thighs. These monkeys are not the hamadryad of the Hamburg Zoo with pricks so long Sartre feared they would step on them (LC, 66). Bathed in the sound of music ("Some evening I'll whisper sweet nothings, some evening I'll tell you I love you") he is aroused to hear nothing. Delirious he calls out to the sleeping form beside him. "Ho! Schneider." Brunet finally wakes, *pour de bon*, brought back to life by the taste of spoonfuls of Barley soup tendered by the nurturing Vicarios. *Orgie/Orgeat/Orge.* "Qu'est-ce que c'est? Une soupe d'orge [What is it? A barley soup]." *Orgie/Orgeat/Orge.* "To taste man, that is what is best," Sartre writes in his *roman vrai* [true novel]: "love devours; to kiss is to eat—Hegel said it first" (IF, 708 n).

Uniquely here, it is the taste of a man that makes the beauty of the tale of *Troubled Sleep, drôle d'amitié* in a *drôle de guerre*. There is no end to *Drôle d'amitié,* no end to *Les Chemins de la liberté.* Sartre deserts the novel. But in a brief, critical moment, before awkwardly rising to defend Jean Genet as he had come to the aid of Ogier, that other P..., he shared that pineapple taste of prickly, wounding *amitié (si peu pédérastique?* [not very queer?]) salvaged from the tailor's cutting room floor. *Sartor Resartus* is Gide's Edouard's dandy, tailor point of departure, an outlaw, (lawless) origin of blanket shared friction. Thanks to Sartre and other tailors, Brunet and Schneider/Vicarios replace their prison garb with mufti to play out a touching scene in the darkness of the escape tunnel of love. "Brunet is happy because Vicarios is near him. From time to time, he reaches his hand out and touches him, from time to time he feels touched by a hand" (OR, 1530). Coming out on the other end, there is a playful poke in the ribs. "He takes his hand, walking into the wind, they suddenly feel jostled on the flank, they grow wings, they fly" (OR, 1530). Somebody squealed ["On nous a donnés"]. Vicarios/Schneider is cut down, mortally wounded. The other Paul dies in his arms. Brunet is left with his dream. He will never really munch and savor the whole pineapple. He is left with the bitter taste and sticky trace of bloodstained ends of butcher twine.

Castor's *Farewell* inscribes and reinscribes Sartre's tastes. *Charcuterie,* the auto-interdicted tomato, pineapple, and the bitter taste of raw nuts are now part of the enigmatic mix (not a Barthes compote recipe), a mix of hermaphroditic angels in flight, of the raw and the cooked, of the dreamt and the tasted, of a consideration of oysters, of "snippets and snails and puppy dog tails." AD HOMINEM. CARPE DIEM.

## ABBREVIATIONS

AO:  Guillaume Apollinaire, *Œuvres poétiques.*
CA:  Simone de Beauvoir, *La Cérémonie des adieux.*
CG:  Jean-Paul Sartre, *Les Carnets de la drôle de guerre.*
EN:  Jean-Paul Sartre, *L'Etre et le néant.*
IF:  Jean-Paul Sartre, *L'Idiot de la famille,* vol. 1.
LC:  Jean-Paul Sartre, *Lettres au Castor et à quelques autres,* vol. 1.
LM:  Jean-Paul Sartre, *Les Mots.*
OR:  Jean-Paul Sartre, *Œuvres romanesques.*
R:  Kirk Douglas, *The Ragman's Son: An Autobiography.*
RA:  Jean-Paul Sartre, *La Reine Albemarle ou le dernier touriste.*
S:  Howard Fast, *Spartacus.*

## NOTES

1. Craig Claiborne, letter to the *New Yorker* (14 February 1993): 72.
2. English translations in brackets, unless otherwise indicated, are by the editors.
3. Guillaume Apollinaire, *Œuvres poétiques,* ed. Marcel Adéma and Michel Décaudin (Paris: Gallimard "Pléiade," 1959), 25, henceforth abbreviated AO; translations by the author.
4. Jean-Paul Sartre, *Nourritures suivi d'extraits de La Nausée* (Paris: Jacques Damase, 1949), 13, translations by the author.
5. *Barbue:* "brill" and/or the feminine form of "bearded" (editors' note).
6. Jean-Paul Sartre, *Lettres au Castor et à quelques autres,* vol. 1, ed. Simone de Beauvoir (Paris: Gallimard, 1983), 104, henceforth abbreviated LC; translations by the author.
7. Marie-Denise Boros, "La Métaphore du crabe dans l'oeuvre littéraire de Jean-Paul Sartre," *PMLA* 81.5 (October 1966): 450; translation by the author.
8. Simone de Beauvoir, *La Cérémonie des adieux, suivi de Entretiens avec Jean-Paul Sartre: août-septembre 1974* (Paris: Gallimard, 1981), 421, henceforth abbreviated CA; translations by the author.
9. *La Morue:* "cod" and/or "tart, whore" (editors' note).
10. Jean-Paul Sartre, *L'Etre et le néant: essai d'ontologie phénoménologique* (Paris: Gallimard, 1943), henceforth abbreviated EN; translations by the author.
11. Jean-Paul Sartre, *Les Carnets de la drôle de guerre* (Paris: Gallimard, 1983), henceforth abbreviated CG; translations by the author.
12. *La Halle:* "market"; *maquereaux:* "mackerels" and/or "pimps" (editors' note).
13. Jean-Paul Sartre, *L'Idiot de la famille,* vol. 1 (Paris: Gallimard, 1971), 1009, henceforth abbreviated IF; translations by the author.
14. Jean-Paul Sartre, *Œuvres romanesques,* ed. Michel Contat and Michel Rybalka, with the collaboration of Geneviève Idt and George H. Bauer (Paris: Gallimard "Pléiade," 1981), 9, henceforth abbreviated OR; translations by the author.
15. Cf. Tom Junod, "On Men and Mollusks," *GQ* (May 1992): 170-73.
16. Howard Fast, *Spartacus* (New York: Dell, 1951), henceforth abbreviated S.
17. *Penser:* "to think"; *panser:* "to bandage"; *suis:* (I/you) "am"/"are" and/or "follow" (editors' note).
18. Kirk Douglas, *The Ragman's Son: An Autobiography* (New York: Simon and Schuster "pocket edition," 1989), henceforth abbreviated R.
19. A term I coined for the paper "Homo/Textuality: Eating/The Other," that I read for the First International Sartre Colloquium in Los Angeles in May 1978. For the published version, see George H. Bauer, "Homo/textuality: Eating/The Other," *Homosexualities and French Literature: Contexts and Criticisms,* ed. George Stambolian and Elaine Marks (Ithaca, NY: Cornell University Press, 1979), 312-79.
20. Jean-Paul Sartre, *Les Mots* (Paris: Gallimard, 1964), henceforth abbreviated LM; translations by the author. "Poulou" was Sartre's childhood nickname.
21. Lawrence R. Schehr, "Sartre as Midwife," *Alcibiades at the Door: Gay Discourses in French Literature* (Stanford: Stanford University Press, 1995), 68-112.

22. Oreste Pucciani, "Sartre, Genet et l'homosexualité: ébauche d'une lecture homosexuelle du *Saint Genet*," *Les Temps Modernes* 46 (1990): 638-57.
23. Jean-Paul Sartre, *La Reine Albemarle ou le dernier touriste: fragments,* ed. Arlette-Elkaïm Sartre (Paris: Gallimard, 1991), henceforth abbreviated RA; translations by the author.
24. James Beard, *James Beard's American Cookery* (Boston: Little, Brown, 1972), 137.
25. Cf. Rybalka's splendid introduction to *La Mort dans l'âme* (OR, 2011-12), and the Nitre-Sarzan *Tailleur* in "La Semence et le scaphandre," written at the time of the original quarrel of 1923.
26. Edward Carpenter, *Selected Writings: Volume I: Sex* (London: G.M.P., 1984), 290.

# 9

## Adrift in the Realm of the Senses: Sartre and Fusional Being

### Robert Harvey

*Aux Le Goïc qui demeurent
sur l'estuaire du Gouet.*

What figuration and (inevitable) disfiguration will a current immersion in Marguerite Duras's literary *imaginaire* bring to this return to Sartre: this ritual of repaying a visit? In order to visit, there must be a *site* other than the here and the now. The site that comes to mind when I think of Sartre is the one where he meditated upon relations among nature, our sexed beings, and, be it ontological (as "being-for-itself") or ethical (as "responsibility in freedom"), our essence. That place is not the Bouville Public Gardens (though they are never far away), but the sea. Whenever the theory of being was his self-imposed order of the day, Sartre's vision drifted to oceans, with their hidden perils, or else to those regions of the salty expanses that meet and mingle with fresh water delivered from far uphill, from within the land masses left behind by the sea's prehistoric retreat.

In affirming that the sea constitutes a privileged Sartrean site, it must be recognized that Sartre remains a resolutely land-bound thinker. While life-giving and life-taking waters may often have been the unspoken background for his deepest meditations, fear kept his imagination safely stationed on the shore. Of necessity, the sea is to be seen only from a vantage that is its contrary: the sea is a sight to be seen, not a site to be visited.

Hence the currents I would like to follow (or invent) running from archaic myths about the oceans through Marcel Proust and Jules Verne to

Duras and Sartre. If I insist on the unlikely pairing of Sartre and Duras, it is because I believe that what everyone knows a priori about Duras can elucidate Sartre's predilection for the site of the sea.[1] Through every Duras text blows the sea air. The sea is always within her characters' sight or pounds away at them in the form of desire. For the sea *is* desire. Madeleine de Scudéry cautioned that, in love, a lady is safe only if she and her beloved dare not to venture beyond "Tender," via the mouth of its river, into "Dangerous Sea": a caution sign one also often reads in Sartre; it is a realm into which the desiring subject passes only at great risk. If Duras too can write that "heterosexuality is dangerous [because] it is *there [là]* that one is tempted to reach the perfect duality of desire" (DV, 40), then why do so many of her "adorable" characters—mostly women, but some men—choose to sail out to the limits of desire?

Let us start in another way, with a cue provided by Michel Butor in "The Cerebral Grotto," one of the "Little Liturgies" in *Illustrations III*,[2] and imagine some time- and space-altering process by which we could enter the confines of geological matter in the process of transformation of mountain into boulders, pebbles, sand, and mud. Split away from the mother mass, cracked and strewn by glaciers, before a majestic peak, our capsule would lie in a tumbled sea of granite awaiting further impetus toward the ocean. Dropped into a stream by some earthquake, we would be rolled downward, our vehicle split into smaller bits, rounded by millions of cycles of snow, thaw, rain, rushed by torrents toward a river's mouth. Encountering the tidal ebb and flow, let us suppose that our stony bathyscaphe escapes the fate of silt or mud and, as pebble or sand, is pulled away from the river's mouth by currents and washed up on the shore to form, along with millions of other similar units, a beach.

At the apparent term of our voyage, we would have arrived at the site where a listless Marcel suddenly saw and began to study the evolution of a scene that came to emblematize his amorous convalescence.[3] Suffering from a worsening respiratory congestion, he had just recently left Paris for a healthier environment. Having recovered from his first exogamic erotic disappointment two years earlier at the hands of Gilberte, the bright vista of Balbec-Plage and the sea beyond enticed the sickly observer, who had been "hanging about in front of the Grand Hotel" (PW, 503), to venture forth where the rebirth of desire would hypostasize around the band of rowdy and robust young girls espied frolicking against the horizon. From Balbec hence, Proust was to dissect the psychological effects wrought upon a physically weak and neurasthenic male of having committed his gaze and his underlying "desire for possession" (503) to hardy, sexually untamable females.

## FROM BALBEC TO BERCK

An approximate measurement of a certain debt Sartre owed Proust can be obtained by recalling that as a young philosophy student, he lent the title, "A l'ombre des vieilles billes en fleur," to a sophomoric theatrical production staged in 1925 at the *Ecole normale supérieure* that lambasted "old nincompoops" like Gustave Lanson and, less directly, Proust's novel. Although he would later often acknowledge in print Proust's influence on his literary development, Sartre, a member of "the anti-Proustian generation,"[4] was also a relentless critic of artifices to which he claimed Proust had recourse in order to render human psychology through the novel. In a typical formulation, Sartre accuses Proust of "perpetually trying to find bonds of rational causality between psychic states," then having to resort to "magic" in order to make the bonds work within his system.[5] But while the parodic distancing revealed in "A l'ombre des vieilles billes en fleur" may be one of the most characteristic moves of Sartre's discursive practices, denial, as psychoanalysis has shown, always hides strong affirmation.

Years later, with World War II behind him, Sartre chose Berck-Plage—a setting altogether analogous to Balbec—for a scenic sequence with strikingly similar elements and comparable purposes to those of Proust. For *The Reprieve*,[6] the second volume of his saga novel, set on the eve of the war, Sartre composed and arranged a rash of events, of both grand and lesser import, breaking out all over Europe during the week of September 23-30, 1938. The novel's successive tableaux involve a cast of personalities crucial to the impending conflagration, identifiable by their real names, as well as everyday men and women, invented by Sartre, whose activities during this "reprieve" history would ignore. Not surprisingly, Sartre's tone expresses more empathy with the insignificant lives of the latter. The elaborate construction of *The Reprieve* delivers the events of that single important week in a kaleidoscoping and sometimes telescoping succession. Transitions from one tableau to another often occur in mid-sentence: from one character's direct or indirect discourse to another's; from one character's subconscious metaphor to the same metaphor occurring in the utterance of another. Because Sartre is concerned both with leveling the hierarchy that places fame above anonymity and with collapsing narrative time through a semblance of simultaneity, these transitions are founded on pure linguistic coincidence regardless of the locutor's social status. Sartre's attempt to emulate cinematic syntax is obvious: *The Reprieve* takes shape within a framework of thematic match-cutting or montage by association.

One such shift wrenches the reader in mid-paragraph from the beach at Juan-les-Pins to Berck-Plage as two characters experience simultaneous reflections inspired by the sea before them. So dazzling is Sartre's montage that reading several more sentences is necessary before one becomes aware that while Odette gazes out onto the Mediterranean, Charles is contemplating the Strait of Dover at its opening onto the Channel.

Among a small group of intimates including her husband, Jacques, and brother-in-law, Mathieu, Odette is vacationing in that early September of 1939. Instead of Albertine,[7] Sartre places his Odette at the seaside. Instead of a carefree blossoming girl, he creates a fretful woman probably in her thirties. But the onomastic wink at Proust is patent and signals Sartre's rethinking of what a psychologically troubled individual might imagine when moved by a vision from the beach. Bored with Jacques, Odette has been playing a game of mutual flirtation with Mathieu, whom she has come to perceive as the incarnation of a self-assured free spirit. Neither of them make a move toward fulfilling their sexual fantasies involving each other. A resilient and robust woman (at least in Mathieu's eyes), Odette has just listened to the latter insist that war cannot be avoided. As he dashes off into the breakers, she remains staring at the sea, perceiving in it a disturbing example of the disjointed justice of existence.

If attentiveness and indiscriminate appeal to all objects of desire around an individual are valid measurement of libidinal fitness, then Charles is, in contrast to Mathieu or Odette, a perfectly healthy sexual being. Sartre's usual scatological treatment of sexuality only serves to underscore the scandalous paradox of this invalid with a voracious hunger for sex. Unlike the able-bodied characters in *The Reprieve,* Charles's problems are not metaphysical, but, rather, material, physiological. Part of a colony of invalids packed off to inhale the salubrious air of Berck, he suffers from tubercular osteitis and is strapped to a gurney on which he is shunted about "like a flower pot" (OR, 758) by his nurse. His pseudo-predilection for fascism and sarcasm which those around him mistake for sadism are harmless expressions of frustration at the physical impediment to the satisfactory realization of desire. Yet through this desire-ridden body, hindered by infirmity, Charles fathoms better than Mathieu, Odette, or any of the other "standing ones" *[les debouts]* (759) certain ontological paradoxes that will forever remain enigmatic to them. In attributing this metaphysical knack to Charles, Sartre urges us to adjudicate upon his cast of characters and to decide that Charles alone deserves (in spite of his crudeness) to be rewarded by fulfillment of desire.

Sartre swings us from Odette to Charles, from southern to northern beach on a stylistic hinge composed of the noun "sea" modified by the stressed possessive adjective *"their"* (757). Fighting to shrug off Mathieu's words of insistent belief in the inevitability of war, Marcelle clings to the notion that economic power somehow enables her and her friends to control nature and thereby history: The Mediterranean before them is "so light, it reminded one of the sky turned upside down. What could anyone have against it?" (757). A lease on the waters firmly in hand, she and her fellow vacationers stand for the nation: their ability to pay the 100 franc per person pension should guarantee that the war cannot take place. For Charles, the sea "was clammy and glaucous, café au lait in color, so flat and monotone . . . smelling of iodine and medication" (757), and the third-person possessive in *"their* sea" emblematizes his incontrovertible *dispossession* from anything except perhaps his own wits. He knows, because he lives it, that the body is irretrievably plugged into the world around us. The narratological shift from Odette to Charles drives home the discrepancy between an illusory sense of control founded on the unspoken given of health and economic ease to an accurate sense of little or no control over events coursing through us. For Charles, the individual causes neither collective nor libidinal history to happen: these histories occur as randomly to the individual as the rivers flowing where gravity takes them.

An obstinate and obscene counterexample to the healthy protagonists of *The Reprieve,* Charles is living proof that the "standing ones" are neither tragic nor joyous enough to combat effectively contingency in the historical time and place where Sartre places them. The footloose manner of Mathieu's dash into the Mediterranean is as fake as the freedom rooted in ontological lightness that he defended in *The Age of Reason* and that so impresses Odette. Odette's confidence in peace is as flimsy as her belief that there is some means by which one can possess the sea: the concept of *"their* sea" *[leur mer]* is a lure *[un leurre].* With this implicit pun as fulcrum for the narratological transition introducing us to Charles, Sartre teaches that control and possession at Juan-les-Pins are as impossible as Marcel's conception of them at Balbec.

## FROM BERCK TO BOUVILLE[8]

The physical phenomena that overcome both Charles, in *The Reprieve,* and Roquentin, in *Nausea,* while they are in states of mental excitation, are related chiastically to the placenames *[noms de lieu]* where their stories unfold. If, as Beauvoir reported, Sartre's series of vignettes featuring an infirm's sexual obsessions unsettled readers of *The Reprieve,*[9] it was undoubtedly because Charles associates micturition and defecation with his frustrated yearning for commerce with women. While he waits to be loaded with his cohorts into a freight train for evacuation, Charles's battle to retain dignity over the bodily discomfiture of diarrhea alternates with and indeed magnifies his incessant thoughts of intercourse. When, after fantasizing that he was left behind at Berck with its "grey and naked sand as far as the eye can see" (OR, 921), the inevitable gets the best of him; Madame Louise's assistance in the clean-up touches off an explicitly announced erection imminent from the outset. Against his will to be disassociated from those who accept their illness as some preordained destiny, he is placed along with them, "a stone among stones" (946), in a bowel-like corridor to be shoved into the "gaping hole" of the train.[10] Once outside the convalescent hospital, he realizes that he is lying on the ground, "half indistinguishable from mud" (945), his body—indeed, his very being—having become indistinguishable from the gooey substance gurgling inside his intestines (955) as he yet persists in rising above subhumanity by desiring "fumelles" (944).[11]

Charles's struggle to preserve his integrity (one could also write *consistency*) as human occurs in a *place* whose *name* evokes not diarrhea but nausea.[12] With a name like *Berck*-Plage, Charles is in a site where one might more appropriately imagine a queasy Roquentin. Roquentin, the hero in whom everything including his own sexual obsessions inspires nausea, on the other hand, is stuck in Bouville—a place that affords no pleasant vista, no belvedere, nothing beautiful to see for Sartre's surrogate, Roquentin. Unlike Balbec or Berck, with their bright pebbly or sandy beaches, Bouville is situated at the mouth of a river depositing a sediment so pulverized, heavy, and mixed with organic substances that it accumulates along the shore and lines the depths of the estuary. Acutely aware that mud both stifles and fosters life, Sartre renews and amplifies its universal symbolism. Both stone and water, both organic and inorganic, the hybrid quality of mud would be to the in-itself what Adam's androgyny is to the for-itself.[13] The very name, Bouville, suggests what Roquentin discovers, to his horror, about the pebbles on its estuarial shore: they are hard and dry, as the superficial bourgeois mind might expect, but they hide a wet, muddy, slimy, and repulsive underside,[14] a feminine underside that no male can elude. As viscous substance, mud reveals to man what total being is because—in accordance with Sartre's description of slimy substances in the final chapter of *Being and Nothingness*[15]—man can create total being by coming into contact with it. But whereas in the 1943 text Sartre classified slime or "the viscous" as feminine, the mud of Bouville elicits thoughts of ambiguity in existence through its androgynous nature. And it is to this hybridity of existence that Sartre returns via the unlikely hero of *The Reprieve*.

Bouville is the concatenation of two cities in which Sartre actually dwelled: La Rochelle, where between 1917 and 1920 he coexisted miserably with his stepfather and discovered his own ugliness, and Le Havre, where during four academic years in the 1930s he fulfilled the unfulfilling function of *lycée* professor. A glance at the trusty *Guide Michelin* reveals that, at the muddy mouth of the Seine estuary, the masculine Havre conforms to our topographical vision of Bouville, while the feminine Rochelle is situated on a peninsula jutting forth between two channels *[pertuis]* and prolonged by the Ile de Ré. As composite of a *boue-ville* and a *bout-ville* projecting like a phallus into the sea, Bouville is emblematic of the frightening prospect of the two sexes united.

## BOUT À BOUE?—BEURK!

The vision of the open sea, its unpredictable viscosities, and the monsters that lurk within it keep the authorial vision alert to a truth deeper than that which can be made out from the shoreline. Just before reaching the Bouville Public Gardens for the climactic scene of *Nausea*, Roquentin surveys the situation at the seaside and thinks:

> La vraie mer est froide et noire, pleine de bêtes; elle rampe sous la mince pellicule verte qui est faite pour tromper les gens. . . . Moi je vois le dessous! les vernis fondent, les brillantes petites peaux veloutées, les petites peaux de pêche du bon Dieu pètent de partout sous mon regard, elle se fendent et s'entrebâillent.[16]

The explicit referent here hides an implicit one: puffed up pisciform bodies pop open like bivalves in a description that approaches the genital anatomy of the young girls for whom Roquentin lusts.[17] "The obscenity of the feminine sex is that of everything which 'gapes open.' It is *an appeal to being* as all holes are. In herself woman appeals to a strange flesh which is to transform her into a fullness of being by penetration and dissolution. . . . Beyond any doubt her sex is a mouth and a voracious mouth which devours the penis" (BN, 782). Like the muck into which Charles was dumped and the murky tunnel of the freight car waiting to whisk him away from the war zone, all passageways are, for Sartre, frighteningly feminine and yet inevitable in the experience of the male.[18]

To focus on why the prospect of male-female union is typically horrifying in Sartre's writings, I would like to amplify some points raised by Adrian van den Hoven concerning *Nausea* in relation to Sartre's childhood encounters with books.[19] Bolstering his conjecture that among the tomes found on the shelves of his grandfather's library Sartre pored through Jules Verne's *Twenty Thousand Leagues Under the Sea,* van den Hoven stresses not only the etymological connection between the title, *Nausea*, and Nautilus, the name of Nemo's submarine, but also the metaphorical relationship between Roquentin's sense of superiority *(supra)*, based on the putative ability to see below the surface of bourgeois life forms, and the underwater strolls taken by Nemo with Harvey and his crew. While I agree with van den Hoven that Verne's prophetic tale inspired the aqueous imagery in *Nausea*, I believe that Sartre drew this inspiration not so much from scanning the Hetzel edition *illustrations,* but more from *reading* the book filled with Verne's characteristically encyclopedic details and accuracy. As Sartre would underscore from *The Imagination* all the way to *The Family Idiot*, the power of consciousness to create the image *(imago)* surpasses any plastic image thrust before passive senses. In this, Sartre concurs with Proust who wrote, in the very passage introducing the little band of blossoming girls, that "to strip our pleasures of imagination is to reduce them to their own dimensions, that is to say nothing" (PW, 513). Moreover, the half of *The Words* where he informs us of the presence of Verne's works in his youthful experience is entitled "Reading."

Of all its fantastic episodes, "The Poulps" chapter of Verne's 1870 novel is the most terrorizingly memorable.[20] Augmenting suspense through rhetorical play, Verne lures the reader toward the narrative unveiling of a monster anticipated since the first page of the novel. Ned Land's ejaculation, "What a horrible beast!" (VV, 322), at that moment of revelation is echoed in Mathieu's repulsed invective at the thought of having conceived a child and in Roquentin's cries of "filth! what rotten filth!" (N, 134; OR, 159), when he awakens from an erotic dream following the experience with the chestnut tree. The Nautilus crew's initial sighting of actual giant squids was skewed by the inflated hearsay about krakens ("[w]hose tentacles could entangle a ship of five hundred tons, and hurry it into the abyss of the ocean" [VV, 3]) and about monstrous squids with "mouths like gulfs" and bodies "too large to pass through the Straits of Gibraltar" (VV, 321).

In pages Sartre claims he skipped over, Verne's sober scientificity combines with an unfailing sense for movement that brings a young reader's imagination within palpable reach of other-worldly, outlandish beasts. In discussing the possibility that such a creature as a poulp exists, Aronnax points out to Ned Land that *mollusk,* the phylum to which the cephalopod would belong, "indicates the relative softness of its flesh" (VV, 23). Yet the suction cups on the poulps' tentacles—analogous to the chestnut-tree root seen as a "suction pump" (OR, 153)—prove strong enough to rip one of the submarine's sheet metal panels off. Realizing that "electric bullets are powerless against the soft flesh, where they do not find resistance enough to go off,"

Nemo calls upon his men to "attack them with the hatchet" (VV, 324). How close the quality of the poulps' flesh is to the feminine "viscous" in *Being and Nothingness* and to the "passive resistance" (N, 130; OR, 154) of the stone on Bouville's beach! No sooner is Nemo's hatchet strategy hatched than two tentacles, "lashing the air, came down on the seaman stationed in front of Captain Nemo, lifting him up with irresistible power" (VV, 324). Losing his self-control and ability to obey Nemo's injunction against the use of any language other than English, this "unhappy man" cries for help in French, revealing to Aronnax his kinship through linguistic identity in a "heartrending cry" that the latter would remember the rest of his life (325).

In the final moments of struggle, as the men "buried [their] weapons in the fleshy masses," the squids unleash their ultimate defence mechanisms: "a strong smell of musk penetrated the atmosphere" and "the animal ejected a stream of black liquid" (325). In Bouville's Gardens, Roquentin complains: "my nostrils overflowed with a green, putrid odor" (N, 128; OR, 151) and describes black (by far the most frequently occurring color in the novel) as "a bruise or a secretion . . . an oozing . . . [an] amorphous, weakly presence" (130-31; 155). The Nautilus crew's only chance lay in their ability to hack off every one of the "slimy tentacles [that] sprang up like the hydra's heads" and stabbing whatever vital organs they might reach—the "staring eyes" or the "triple heart of the poulp" into which Ned plunged his harpoon (VV, 325). Overwhelmed by the sight of the chestnut trees, Roquentin writes: "I drop onto the bench between great black tree-trunks, between the black, knotty hands reaching towards the sky" (N, 126; OR, 149). Even as the giant squid attack was being assuaged, the survivors were engulfed by the beasts' severed tentacles from which life had not yet fully ebbed: "We rolled pell-mell into the midst of this nest of serpents, that wriggled on the platform in the waves of blood and ink" like the transformation of absurdity ("the key to Existence, the key to my Nauseas, to my own life") from a concept into "this long serpent dead at my feet, this wooden serpent" (N, 129; OR, 152-53). For the inconsolable Aronnax, "It was horrible," (VV, 325), while for Roquentin, this "horrible ecstasy" became an oxymoronic "atrocious joy *[jouissance]*" from which he could not free himself. Try as Roquentin might "to get rid of this filth," he *became* the root of the chestnut tree (N, 131; OR, 155) in which there were just "tons and tons of existence: endless" (134; 159). From the eyes of the evermeasured Nemo, this test wrenches ultimate proof of his susceptibility to compassion: "Captain Nemo, covered with blood, nearly 'exhausted . . . gazed upon the sea that had swallowed up one of his companions, and great tears gathered in his eyes" (VV, 325).

In *Twenty Thousand Leagues Under the Sea,* Verne thematizes the ostensibly undifferentiated substance that harbors invisible variations. The sea is not what it appears to the novice: although uniformly transparent, its waters are in constant movement. Currents, like the Gulf Stream, sometimes deep below the surface, dwarfing the greatest rivers, carry waters of diverse temperatures at uncanny speeds. Tides, swells, waves, tsunamis, and maelstroms lend the oceans a myriad of movements. Neither the density nor the viscosity nor the salinity of the sea is stable. Verne describes the slimy inconsistency and potential for suction in the poulps' fleshy tentacles in such a way as to have us believe that the giants are aberrant constructs of the very medium in which they dwell. These monsters of the "liquid masses" are the spongy and all-too-real concretization of the worst fears expressed with haunting regularity since the first pages of the novel: "Maybe the oceans also conceal mollusks of unimaginable size, crustaceans too fearful to contemplate, like 300-foot lobsters, crabs weighing 200 tons. Why not?" (VV, 11-12). Such proportions may be unimaginable, but what *can* be imagined is that Poulou, years before his experience with mescaline, already hallucinated about poulps through involuntary recollections of reading *Twenty Thousand Leagues Under the Sea.*

An outlandish contraption, the Nautilus itself conforms to the theme of difference within the same as well. To the eyes of sailors who search for it, it is virtually invisible within the transparent environment through which it moves. Swifter than the Gulf Stream, those who do sight it mistake it for Moby Dick or the mythical kraken.[21] The submarine's motto, *mobilis in mobile,* applies equally to a sea current. It was there, adrift through reading in his grandfather's library, already imagining himself a man among the other men and made of all of them, inside the Nautilus, itself a man-made mobile object within a mobile environment, that Poulou fostered the imagery that would express his theory of total being in terms of the fusion of two sexed beings in the final chapter of *Being and Nothingness.*

The influence such imagery exerted upon young Poulou's crude notions about sexuality and existence had to have been tremendous. As powerful as Pardaillan's heroism[22] and as ambiguous as the erotic undercurrents of *Moby Dick,*[23] Nemo's unexpected slippage from a measured tone to his nearly hysterical vow to "slaughter this vermin [by] fight[ing] them man to beast" (VV, 324) must have disconcerted and rivetted the young reader. This imagery is present for all who read Verne's 1870 novel: men dwarfed by their vehicle, *homunculi*—so many spermatozoa (young Sartre's "La Semence et le scaphandre"![24])—sealed in a cigar-shaped vessel, racing through a seamless aqueous environment, capable of slipping through the Straits of Gibraltar and penetrating the womb of the Mediterranean, men whose supreme battle before deliverance into freedom is with Medusa-like sea monsters. The poulps are phallic mothers whose viscous and interoceptive flesh, with enough strength to breach the bathyscaphe, can only be put to rest by means of a multiple castration. Their tentacles have the consistency of mud and writhe about like the roots of Roquentin's chestnut tree: "This veneer [of the individuation of things] had melted, leaving soft, monstrous masses, all in disorder—naked, in a frightful, obscene nakedness" (N, 127; OR, 151).[25]

True: in perusing Neuville's illustrations of the giant squid, Sartre could see the writhing configuration of tentacles, but only in reading Verne's text could he imagine fully the quality of the tentacular flesh. This is why it took Sartre's reading the text, a child's reading, one that is repeated over and over, to the points of saturation, memorization, and ventriloquy. "True: I did not know everything, I had not seen the seeds sprout, or the tree grow" (N, 129; OR, 153).

## FROM BOUVILLE TO TROUVILLE

The permutations, truncations, transpositions, and retellings of *The Sea Wall* that constitute the *œuvre* of Marguerite Duras inform us that, without ever necessarily reading Jules Verne, her life provided ample reason to fear water and to dread all that thrives or dies there.[26] Her mother's progressive madness, after thousands of crabs undermined the sea wall and allowed the Pacific to inundate her crops, caused Suzanne (Duras) to loathe crustaceans. The theme of aqueous environments in contemporary literature cannot be evoked without invoking the name of Marguerite Duras, who returned unfailingly with her writing (which was her life) to rivers, deltas, estuaries, and oceans.

In 1963, just before the turning point commonly identified by *The Ravishing of Lol V. Stein,* imbued with the intuition that "the feeling of love might come from a sudden crack in the logic of the universe, from an error, for example,"[27] Marguerite Duras leaves Neauphle and moves into an apartment purchased where Proust once kept a room: at Roches Noires in Trouville. Across the estuary from Le Havre, at the littoral, like Melville, Verne, Proust, Woolf, and Sartre before her, Duras brings into convergence physical, mental, or emotional illness with desire, its fulfillment, or unfulfillment in order to think the unthinkable fusion of feminine and masculine.

Duras's *Man Seated in the Passage,*[28] a paradigm of her reflection on this problem, will serve as link back to Sartre. Returning from a walk under a torrid summer sun, the woman lays out on her back—legs together, then spread—in the pathway leading to the house. The man, seated where the title demands that we envision him, fixes her with his blue desirous eyes, arises, moves out toward her, and, standing, ejaculates on her prostrate body. All the while, the narrator tells the woman, whose eyes remain closed, what she witnesses and, together, they orchestrate the subsequent acts. It is noted that, as the man returns to his cavernous domain, he casts his gaze upon the rolling hills before the river and the sea beyond without seeing them. Inside, "wasted by love and desire" (DM, 271; DH, 21), he lets "it" be taken by the woman's mouth: "she has what is usually food for thought in her mouth" (272; 27). Only the feminine pronoun, without antecedent, is used to designate the penis with its "crude and brutal shape" (272; 23), while the woman's genitals—described variously as slack *[étale]* or swampy *[marécageuse]*—are exposed "obscene[ly]" (269; 12). Her eyes still closed, the woman moves on from fellatio to a slow exploration of the cavernous regions of his body, "her face buried in the part of himself he knows nothing about, slowly breathing the fetid smell" (273; 29), "naming things, hurling insults, calling on words to come to her aid" (273; 31). Suddenly, amidst her tears, hetero-masculine penetration arrests these erotic peregrinations, and the text closes with a montage vacillating between the woman beaten by the man and the exterior with its fluviatile panorama.

Never before or since has Marguerite Duras brought the association of Eros and Thanatos so close to rendering the death-dealing results that Sartre cautioned us about at the conclusion of *Being and Nothingness*. Exposing the limits of what is tolerable in art, *The Man Seated in the Passage* is undoubtedly founded on a lived experience of which *Moderato cantabile* and *Hiroshima, mon amour* bear some sublimated marks. To locate the events that Duras has transformed, one would have to travel back upstream, against the force of gravity and history that brings the stone from mountain to shore.[29] There is no time. In a certain manner that only literature can render, the two women of the story—narrator and actor—dodge the male brutality: the one, gabbing at the sidelines, holds to the threshold of action; the other is projected beyond it by her metamorphosis into the ideal paradigm of beauty. The two feminine instances form a conspiracy to neutralize male violence by means of two topological feminizations: one local—that of the man's strangely invaginated domain, inside, outside, and on the threshold of which perversity is played out; and one distant—that of the river's mouth opening onto the sea. Of the first, he is becoming painfully aware; of the second, he remains ignorant.

The domain of the passageway into which an irresistible force returns the man is a uterine territory—similar, in a way, to those one finds throughout Beckett's work, but which Duras would never place directly above a grave in order to deliver her creations into death at the instant of birth. And this reprieve allows life the time to conquer death: if psychoanalysis posits the phallic woman harboring within her the signifier of desire, Duras, beginning with *The Man Seated in the Passage,* imagines a vaginal man—one whose entire being is associated with the womb. The man's cavern—the passage—is also an invagination of his body: an alternate route for eroticism that, when explored and aroused, brings him close to the woman in a manner unacceptable to him. As with the obvious ambiguity in the meaning of "cavern," it is fair to suppose that Duras plays on the homography between the French *verge*—the substantive behind the feminine pronoun—and the English noun "verge," associated with the concept of threshold.[30]

And thresholds there are: that between the house's passage and the outdoors, her vulva exposed as lasciviously as his anus remains hidden, and the threshold that embodies them all: the distant line where the river water meets that of the sea. Duras's subsequent texts will show that this man has already been led, through overdetermined vaginality, to an ontological threshold where she believes women dwell. The proof that he does not yet understand himself to have been neutralized by this displacement is underscored in the final movement of the text where the vista that imposes itself so patently to the reader is a vista that—within the diegesis—only the woman and the narrator/director can truly see for what it is.

The pen/camera embraces the panorama of the river, the estuary, and the sea under a hazy and violet sky, an ensemble that Sartre would have found sublime. This river mouth, this threshold between the fresh water of the Seine and the salt water of the Atlantic, joins all the others—the Mekong, the Magra, the Ota, the Gironde, the Ganges. The final scanning of the horizon universalizes the singularity and eternalizes the brevity of the passageway episode. The pornographic parable thus becomes the story of Anne-Marie Stretter, that of Lol V. Stein, that of Alissa, all the Anne's, the Anna's, and the she's. Lest we forget, Sartre's mother's name, Anne-Marie, combining the names of the putative grandmother and mother of Christ, was precious to Sartre's self-image. That parable projects into the future to become the story of all women and, I dare say, all men, of all being-on-the-threshold-of-the-other: the ethical *mitsein* that Sartre longed to institute in social reality, but could only point at in his prolific imagination.

## ABBREVIATIONS

BN: Jean-Paul Sartre, *Being and Nothingness*.
DH: Marguerite Duras, *L'Homme assis dans le couloir*.
DM: Marguerite Duras, *The Man Seated in the Passage*.
DV: Marguerite Duras, *La Vie matérielle*.
N: Jean-Paul Sartre, *Nausea*.
OR: Jean-Paul Sartre, *Œuvres romanesques*.
PW: Marcel Proust, *Within a Budding Grove*.
VV: Jules Verne, *Vingt Mille Lieues sous les mers*.

## NOTES

1. Duras denies Sartre the sacred appellation of writer, granting him only the lesser status of "idea-launcher" *[lanceur d'idées]* (Interview by Bernard Pivot, *Apostrophes*, Antenne 2, 28 September 1984) (my translation, as are all translations of the original French, unless otherwise indicated). She says that, on those rare occasions when she thinks of Sartre, a sort of "Solzhenitsyn of a country without Gulag" comes to mind; he appears to her "all alone in a desert built by himself" (*La Vie matérielle: Marguerite Duras parle à Jérôme Beaujour* [Paris: P.O.L, 1987], 119, henceforth abbreviated DV). There were virtually no professional contacts between the two writers: Duras wrote two short, hostile articles on Sartre; Sartre wrote nothing on her. Their signatures would occasionally appear together on the same petition. See also, Alain Vircondelet, *Duras* (Paris: François Bourin, 1991).
2. Michel Butor, *Illustrations III* (Paris: Gallimard, 1973), 76. See my translation and Jean-François Lyotard's discussion of this text in "False Flights in Literature," *Toward the Postmodern*, ed. Robert Harvey and Mark S. Roberts (Atlantic Highlands, NJ: Humanities Press, 1993), 125-42.
3. Marcel Proust, *Within a Budding Grove [A l'ombre des jeunes filles en fleur]*, trans. C. K. Scott Moncrieff and Terence Kilmartin, revised by D. J. Enright (New York: Random House, 1992), 502-16, henceforth abbreviated PW.
4. Denis Hollier, "L'Adieu aux plumes," in *Les Dépossédés* (Paris: Minuit, 1993), 179.
5. Jean-Paul Sartre, *Being and Nothingness*, trans. Hazel E. Barnes (New York: Philosophical Library, 1956), 234, 236, henceforth abbreviated BN.
6. Jean-Paul Sartre, *Le Sursis [The Reprieve]* (1945), in *Œuvres romanesques* (Paris: Gallimard "Pléiade," 1981), henceforth abbreviated OR.
7. One could speculate on the significance for Sartre of his grandfather's friend, Simonnot, in comparison to the significance for Marcel of Albertine, whose last name is Simonet.
8. Pierre Bost, "Proust devant une sonate, Sartre devant un air de jazz . . . ," *Le Figaro Littéraire* (8 January 1949): 1, 3; Robert Greer Cohn, "Sartre versus Proust," *Partisan Review* 28.5-6 (1961): 633-45; Rémy Saisselin, "Bouville ou

l'anti-Combray," *French Review* 33.3 (1960): 232-38; Eugenia Noik Zimmerman, "Some of These Days: Sartre's Petite Phrase," *Contemporary Literature* 11 (1970): 375-88; Eugenia Noik Zimmerman, "The Metamorphosis of Adam: Nausea and Things in Sartre and Proust" in George Stambolian, ed., *Twentieth Century French Fiction: Essays for Germaine Brée* (New Brunswick, NJ: Rutgers University Press, 1975), 54-71.
9. The "violently realistic" anecdotes of a friend who had been sent to Berck to convalesce "and the whole atmosphere [there] lent Sartre inspiration for an episode in *The Reprieve* that lofty souls reproached him for particularly." Simone de Beauvoir, *La Force de l'âge* (Paris: Gallimard, 1960), 322-23.
10. Charles also considers this "gaping hole" through which he is pushed to be *un jeu de massacre* ["a bean toss game"] (OR, 775). This exact image arises in Mathieu's nightmarish premonition of war: "'Draftable': Mathieu got small and round; Marcelle was waiting for him with her legs spread. Marcelle was a bean toss game and when Mathieu was all curled up like a ball, Jacques threw him and he fell into a black hole streaked by missiles, he fell into war" (898).
11. "Slang for females," according to the Pléiade notes (OR, 1996).
12. When repulsed by something, French children exclaim "Beurk!" or "Berk!" roughly equivalent to our "Yuk!" alluding onomatopoetically to vomiting.
13. Emmanuel Lévinas, whose *Théorie de l'intuition dans la phénoménologie de Husserl* (1930) introduced Sartre to phenomenology, continues to reflect upon this hypothesis as old as the rabbinic tradition. He writes, for example, in *Difficile liberté: essais sur le judaïsme* (Paris: Albin Michel, 1963): "Cette côte n'était-elle pas plutôt un côté d'Adam, créé comme être unique à deux faces et que Dieu sépara pendant qu'Adam, encore androgyne, sommeillait?" (56) ["Was this rib not a *side* of Adam, created as a single being with two faces that God separated while Adam, still androgynous, was sleeping?"]; *Difficult Freedom: Essays on Judaism*, trans. Sean Hand (Baltimore: Johns Hopkins University Press, 1990), 35.
14. OR, 6. In "L'Homme et les choses," a 1943 study of Francis Ponge's *Le Parti pris des choses*, Sartre restated his position on the project of consciousness (intentionality) and illustrated it with pebbles, shells, and other objects dear to Ponge: Ponge is not interested in describing qualities that might differentiate objects from humans, while *he is;* Ponge willingly goes to the heart of and even becomes things while *he* guards against such interiority. One can grasp the true essence of the stone—that it hides a fishy sliminess—only if one resists being sucked into it and perceives it from the outside, otherwise words retract into "word-things" (*Situations, I* [Paris: Gallimard, 1947], 308). See also Jean Pellegrin, "L'Objet à deux faces dans *La Nausée*," *Revue des Sciences Humaines* 113 (1964): 87-97.
15. Cf. Chapter 5 in Robert Harvey, *Search for a Father: Sartre, Paternity, and the Question of Ethics* (Ann Arbor: University of Michigan Press, 1991), 104-24.
16. The following English translation of this passage does not do justice to the alliteration I have emphasized: "The *true* sea is cold and black, full of animals;

it crawls under this thin green film made to deceive human beings.... I see beneath it! The veneer melts, the shining velvety scales, the scales of God's catch explode everywhere at my look, they split and gape." Jean-Paul Sartre, *La Nausée* (1938), OR, 147; *Nausea,* trans. Lloyd Alexander (New York: New Directions, 1964), 124, henceforth abbreviated N.
17. Books, for Poulou (the nickname Sartre's mother gave him, an individual I consider discrete from Sartre), were hermaphroditic objects whose feminine attributes are described similarly. See Jean-Paul Sartre, *Les Mots [The Words]* (Paris: Gallimard, 1964), 37.
18. Among many examples, Garcin cries at Estelle: "I don't want to sink down into your eyes. You're moist! You're soft *[molle]!* You're an octopus, you're a swamp." Jean-Paul Sartre, *Huis clos, Huis clos suivi de Les Mouches* (Paris: Gallimard "Folio," 1947), 84. See also, Josette Pacaly, *Sartre au miroir* (Paris: Klincksieck, 1980), 181-82.
19. Adrian van den Hoven, "*Nausea*: Plunging Below the Surface," in Ronald Aronson and Adrian van den Hoven, eds., *Sartre Alive* (Detroit: Wayne State University Press, 1991), 227-39.
20. Jules Verne, *Vingt Mille Lieues sous les mers [Twenty Thousand Leagues Under the Sea],* illustrated with 111 drawings by de Neuville (Paris: J. Hetzel, [1870]), henceforth abbreviated VV. "The Poulps" (*la poulpe* means "octopus" in French) is chapter 18 of 23 in the second and final part of the novel (Hetzel, 386-96).
21. "Leviathan is not the biggest fish;—I have heard of Krakens." Letter dated 17 November 1851 to Nathaniel Hawthorne.
22. Pardaillan was a paradigmatic hero of serial-story writer Michel Zévaco, whom the young Sartre read assiduously.
23. Verne drew explicitly from *Moby Dick.* Sartre wrote a short study of this "monument" by the "American Jules Verne" *[sic],* arguing that Melville's main concern was not the creation of a "universe of symbols," but one of things. "*Moby Dick* d'Herman Melville," in Michel Contat and Michel Rybalka, *Les Ecrits de Sartre* (Paris: Gallimard, 1970), 634-36.
24. In the immature story, Sartre transposed some of the tensions and issues involved in a rift that occurred between himself and his friend, Paul Nizan. See Jean-Paul Sartre, *Ecrits de jeunesse* (Paris: Gallimard, 1990), 140-87, and the "Notice" by Michel Contat and Michel Rybalka, 137-39.
25. On what constitutes "obscenity" for Sartre, refer to note 2 in OR, 1785.
26. Hydrophobia in literature is in no way unique to Sartre and Duras. Jules Verne's childhood was spent living on Ile Feydeau, in the Loire, west of Nantes. In the shape of a boat, as most river islands are, and subject to frequent floods, the boyhood home kept Verne in fear of floating out to sea were it ever ripped from its anchorage. While reading "The Poulps" episode, Sartre might have reassured himself by recalling that he lived nestled in the bosom of a city whose motto is *Fluctuat nec mergitur.*
27. Marguerite Duras, *La Maladie de la mort* (Paris: Minuit, 1982), 52.

28. Marguerite Duras, *The Man Seated in the Passage,* trans. Mary Lydon, in "Translating Duras," *Contemporary Literature* 24.2 (1983): 259-75 (translation of Duras's text, 268-75), henceforth abbreviated DM; *L'Homme assis dans le couloir* (Paris: Minuit, 1980), henceforth abbreviated DH.
29. Shortly before writing *Moderato cantabile* and *Hiroshima, mon amour,* Duras was on a Mediterranean beach with a man when she received the news of the death of her mother—the woman who bore her and who resisted the forces of colonial bureaucracy and the sea. With her lover, Duras traveled north, toward a town on the Loire where the burial was to take place. At Aurillac, in a hotel, perhaps in a passageway, the fucking (as "immoral," under the circumstances, as Meursault's "indifference") suddenly turned violent. Had Duras awakened in the man his anal eroticism? Had she revealed to him a homosexuality more fundamental than his heterosexuality? Had her proximity shown him his being-at-the-threshold-of-the-other without his being able to formulate that being in the theoretical language of men? Something on this order, I surmise, triggered the man's sadism luridly described in *The Man Seated in the Passage.* The biographical event is recounted in "Le Dernier Client de la nuit." But it took the exercise of fiction, the work of the writerly imagination, to move whatever discovery actually did take place into the universally recognized Durassian site of the ambiguity of our being: the estuary.
30. Mary Lydon discusses Duras's use of the feminine pronoun for the penis as well as the possible bilingual pun. Furthermore, she uses the idiomatic "to be on the verge of" several times in her translation.

# 10

## A Revisionary Account of the Apotheosis and Demise of the Philosophy of the Subject: Hegel, Sartre, Heidegger, Structuralism, and Poststructuralism

### Philip R. Wood

Why should it be necessary, in a volume devoted to Sartre, to invoke his successors at the center of philosophical topicality in France? Many different justifications could doubtless be provided. One reason would be that Sartre himself would have required it. According to his own Hegelian "progressive-regressive method," we must understand Sartre, we can only understand Sartre, today, on the basis of what has come after him.[1]

It would be a mistake, though, to believe that this might be grounds for beginning a "dialogue" between the positions involved: a revisionary historical perspective, say, that might conclude that the differences between Sartre, the structuralists, and the poststructuralists should be seen—precisely in some Hegelian fashion, in the light of an *Aufhebung*—as "a canceling while nonetheless preserving," an evolution in which some overarching continuity could be detected, "real differences notwithstanding." What really divides these figures is a shift so fundamental that it is not really plausible to argue—as his rare defenders (most recently Jameson) have often done—that Sartre's work already anticipates much of what comes after it and that the perceived differences and, consequently, the rejection of the older man's work by an unduly categorical younger generation, have been overdrawn.

Any account of Sartre in terms of the history of post-Sartrean philosophy in France will have to answer the following question: Why did the mainstay of modernity's thought since the Renaissance—humanism or, more broadly, a philosophy of the *subject* (which, as we shall see, contrary to a widespread misunderstanding, is by no means necessarily the same thing)—come under attack in structuralism and poststructuralism, culminating in the so-called "death of the subject"? Any attempt to answer this question, however, requires a preamble of preliminary distinctions and clarifications, for the demise of the philosophy of the subject has only rarely been correctly understood. Indeed, it is not until we have established in what subsequent French philosophy has consisted—and on exactly what grounds Sartre was repudiated by that philosophy—it is not until we have described the space in which our object, Sartre, appears today, that we can turn to Sartre himself.

For this reason, my argument has had to proceed by means of a series of deferments, with the result that Sartre himself does not always appear explicitly for extended stretches. Section I of this essay recalls the meaning of the term "subject" for Heidegger and Derrida (that is, not necessarily "consciousness" but, first and foremost, *ground* or *sub-iectum*, "that which underlies"). In this section, I also attack one of the more prominent, exemplary criticisms to which Sartre has been subjected (by Deleuze), as well as one of the better-known defenses he has enjoyed (by Jameson). Section II reviews the Hegelian system (primarily the *Science of Logic*) for two purposes: (1) to prepare the way for a clarification of the Derridean notion of *différance*—this by means of explaining Heidegger's objections to grounds and ontotheology and demonstrating *différance* "at work" in the Hegelian system itself; and (2) to lay the groundwork for an examination of structuralism and Sartre's *Critique of Dialectical Reason*. Section III demonstrates the failure of structuralism—primarily in the person of Althusser, but also in an early work by Deleuze—to move significantly beyond Hegelianism. I argue further that structuralism's residually "subjectivist" philosophy (for it has recourse to a ground or *sub-iectum*), and its ultimate failure, make it easier to discern in what the shift to *différance* consists, as a solution to this debacle. Finally, last but not least, Section IV engages Sartre's *Critique of Dialectical Reason* and seeks to elucidate the still imperfectly understood shift to poststructuralism in the work of Foucault and Derrida.

I

It has not always been grasped that by "subject" poststructuralism harks back to Heidegger's startlingly broad—but careful—usage, best exposed in his enormous *Nietzsche* study.[2] Here, the term subject does not necessarily refer to "consciousness" or what, in colloquial usage, we have in mind when we talk about "subjectivity" (although it may well do so, as we shall see), that is, when we distinguish ourselves as centers of awareness—endowed with the familiar panoply of human faculties (choice, agency, and so on)—from mere "objects," mere things. What Heidegger, or Derrida, means by subject is a *sub-iectum:* that which underlies, or is the *ground* of, beings, entities, or that which is.[3] Far from this faculty being restricted to humankind, Heidegger asserts that "up to the beginning of modern metaphysics with Descartes . . . *every being,* insofar as it is a being, is conceived as a *sub-iectum*" (HN, 96). Thus (prior to Descartes), "Stones, plants, and animals are subjects . . . no less than man is" (97). (Needless to say, the latter position did not entail endowing these entities with consciousness or spirit.)

It will be readily appreciated that this meaning of the term subject must radically alter the terms of any debate in which a putative "death of the subject" is discussed. So much so, indeed, that such debate as there has been up to now has mostly been beside the point, if not entirely otiose.

By contrast, what Heidegger means by humanism, or "the dominance of the subject in the modern age," is that "man" comes to exercise the function of sole *sub-iectum:* not only the ground of that which is, but that in terms of which all beings are judged and in sole terms of which the objectivity of objects is decided.[4] A prominent example of this "subjectivism" would be Kant's Copernican revolution, according to which "appearances"—what until recently we still called beings or entities—can only arise within space and time, the latter being forms of "pure intuition" that "exist in the mind."[5] Heidegger qualifies such a position as one for which "Beingness now means the representedness of the representing subject" (HN, 119). It is important to note, however, that Heidegger is careful to add the following qualification:

> This in no way signifies that the being is a "mere representation" and that the latter is an occurrence in human "consciousness," so that every being evaporates into nebulous shapes of mere thought. Descartes, and after him Kant, never doubted that the being and what is established as a being is in itself and of itself actual. But the question remains what Being means here and how the being is to be attained and made certain through man as one who has come to be a subject. (119)

The distinctive character of modern humanism, for Heidegger, becomes especially clear in his discussion of Protagoras's statement, "Man is the measure of all things." This, Heidegger argues, is not to be read anachronistically, in the light of philosophical modernity (i.e., Cartesian and post-Cartesian philosophy) as meaning that "a being becomes accessible when an 'I' as subject represents an object" (HN, 93). What Protagoras had understood, according to Heidegger—an understanding he is trying to revive—is that the accessibility of objects and our very capacity for what we ordinarily understand by the term subjectivity (consciousness of objects, etc.) may well be inextricably bound up with something that is "other" than "ourselves" (for Heidegger, "Being"; for Derrida, the "order" of *différance*), but does not constitute a new ground (an unconditioned foundation, *causa sui*), in its turn, that might be "outside of" Dasein.[6] (Being is not *separate from* Dasein [HN, 216-18].)

Clearly, then, the death of the subject cannot mean—or should not be taken to mean—the death of subjectivity, in the colloquial sense of the term ("consciousness," "agency," and so on). Although this is indeed how it has most often been understood. (This view has been most clamorously and bluntly expressed by Ferry and Renaut.)[7] Rather, what is entailed by post-structuralism is the death of *any* subject (and "man" in particular) as ground, as that which underlies.

Why there should be this objection to a ground of beings or entities, in the first place, we will see presently when we turn to Derrida's notion of *différance*; but we can perhaps anticipate what is to come to the extent of pointing out that, strictly speaking, the objection to any kind of ground of beings holds not only for "man," but equally for "structure," in Althusser's work for example. In other words, the objection to grounds on the part of Heidegger and Derrida is not merely, as some commentators (for example, Habermas)[8] have argued, a rehash of the familiar anti-foundationalism of *modernity*, which characterized Nietzsche's work, for instance, but (a fact that is often forgotten) is already a central objective of the Hegelian system, too. It is, rather, its intensification and extension into new areas in which a residual foundationalism lay hitherto undetected. A recent example will help explain this still very common misapprehension. In his otherwise excellent book, *Sociology of Postmodernism*, Scott Lash defines foundationalism as "the opposite of self or autonomous legislation. It is *heteronomous* legislation from another, universalist 'instance' such as nature, or reason, or the real, or God."[9] This describes perfectly a modern ideal of freedom and its counterpart, modernity's conception of foundationalism. Hegel, for example, would try matching the ideal of anti-foundationalism by making the self, reason, nature, the real, and God all meet in the absolute—that self for which there could be no other and therefore no heteronomy. As we shall see shortly, however, the very ideals of "self," "autonomy," and even ostensibly anti-foundationalist notions like "structure," which were expressly designed to shatter notions of selfhood, all work with a secret assumption of a ground. It is this demonstration that is the novelty of poststructuralism and that is still far from having been grasped.

With specific reference to Sartre himself, it should be noted that the attribution of a "philosophy of the subject" to him by Heidegger and the poststructuralists was not based on an erroneous belief, regularly attributed to them by his defenders, that the Sartrean "for-itself" was somehow a "substantial" or "essential" self (in the loose senses of these terms, interpretations that neglect the history of the terms in philosophy, i.e., as implying a *human nature*)—precisely the position Sartre had been concerned to dismantle in *The Transcendence of the Ego* and *Being and Nothingness*. This mistaken reading of Heidegger and the poststructuralists has been mobilized most recently by Fredric Jameson:

> Historical memory in our own time seems too short to have retained the lessons French existentialism once preached so passionately. . . . At any rate, long before Sartre's overtly political commitments . . . post-war existentialism . . . took as its protopolitical target a set of attitudes, values and practices very similar to those another generation would identify by way of anti-foundationalism and anti-essentialism. Indeed, the very slogan of existentialism—existence precedes essence—contained within itself all the elements of the later doctrine, and in particular the repudiation of whatever idea of a human nature, and the accompanying conclusion, namely that subjectivity is constructed. . . .[10]

This fails altogether to understand Heidegger's and the poststructuralists' indictment of a philosophy of the subject in Sartre's writings. It is correct to the extent that it points to Sartre's already having formulated an "anti-essentialism" (again, in the loose, nontechnical sense of the term) at the level of the human subject but irrelevant with regard to the poststructuralist complaints about their predecessor. In line with the repudiation of any philosophy of the subject (ground) in general and humanism in particular (as exemplar of the former), their criticisms bore on Sartre's sole attribution of the emergence of determination, or identity, to the capacity of the human "for-itself" (consciousness) for negation as a ground of identity and difference: all beings—and "being-in-itself" (tables, galaxies) as a whole—are able to emerge *qua* entities thanks to the fundamental negation of the human for-itself, which originally distinguishes itself from the mere "positivity" of being-in-itself.[11] Thus:

> If we envisage, for example, *destruction* . . . man is the sole being whereby a destruction can be accomplished. A geological fold, a

> storm do not destroy—or, at least, they do not destroy *directly:* they simply modify the distribution of masses of being. There is not *less* after a storm than before. There is *something else*. And even this expression is improper since, in order to posit alterity, there must be a witness who can retain the past in some fashion and compare it to the present in the form of the "no longer." (SE, 42-43)

For Sartre, identity and difference are grounded, originate, in the *"néantisation"* of the human for-itself. Even if the for-itself "is not," even if rather than something it is "nothing," it nonetheless constitutes a ground, more precisely a human ground, for the identity of entities: "If being-in-itself cannot be either its own ground *[fondement]* or that of other beings, the ground in general comes to the world through the for-itself. Not only the for-itself, as in-itself which has been nihilated *[néantisé],* founds itself but with it the ground appears for the first time" (SE, 124).

Before we explain why Heidegger and Derrida have considered any ground of identity and difference to be objectionable, there is one last, very widespread misreading of Sartre's early work that must be dispelled, because it is sometimes mistakenly believed that it is this aspect of his writing—transcended by his successors—that distinguishes him from the latter. This misreading consists of accusing Sartre of locating the negation of the for-itself—which establishes the identity and differences of entities—exclusively in the act of an *individual* human being and failing thereby to recognize the extent to which difference and identity might emerge from *collective* structures or "cultural constructions," as they say nowadays. A classic example of this misreading is implied in the following remarks by Gilles Deleuze:

> The mistake of philosophical theories [of the other *(autrui)*] is to reduce him either to a particular object or to another subject (and even a conception like that of Sartre limited itself in *Being and Nothingness* to uniting the two determinations, making of the other an object within my gaze, while allowing for the possibility for him to look at me in my turn and transform me into an object). But the other *[autrui]* is neither an object in my field of perception, nor a subject who perceives me: it is first and foremost a structure of the perceptual field, without which this field as an ensemble would not function as it does. That this structure may be actualized *[soit effectué]* by real characters, by different subjects, me for you, and you for me, does not prevent it from preexisting, as a condition of organization in general, the terms which actualize it in each organized perceptual field—yours, mine.[12]

These remarks constitute a significant blunder: they fail to take into account Sartre's manifest approval of a demonstration he attributes to Husserl, and adopts as his own position, that flatly invalidates Deleuze's criticism: "Whether I consider in solitude or in the company of someone else this table or this tree or this section of a wall, the other [autrui] is always there as a constitutive layer of significations which belong to the very object which I am considering" (SE, 288).

So, to resume the argument up to this point, the decisive difference between Sartre, on the one hand, and Heidegger and Derrida or Foucault, on the other—what the latter deride as the former's "philosophy of the subject"—consists neither in Sartre's attributing some "essentialist" Self or nature to the human subject nor in any failure on his part to recognize the "collective" or "cultural" origins of the identity of entities. The decisive difference consists in the for-itself—what later, in the *Critique de la raison dialectique* becomes *praxis* (even when alienated in the "practico-inert")—constituting an ultimate ground, or origin, of identity and difference. (If I may reiterate somewhat differently a point made immediately above, Sartre's position here is not individualism, although it is unquestionably *humanism*—I trust it is not necessary to argue this distinction.)

So what? What is the compelling objection to a ground or origin? Surely everything originates somewhere or somehow?

To understand the objections raised to grounds and origins—and thus to a *sub-iectum* or subject (whether human or otherwise) as that which underlies—we can turn to Derridean *différance;* for it is the latter that, more than any other notion of the period, makes the death of the subject—which we see must now be read as the impossibility of any *sub-jectum*—most vivid: *différance is* the death of the *sub-iectum* (a far more disturbing phenomenon than any attenuation of freedom, choice, agency, and so on—which *différance* emphatically does *not* entail—as will become apparent in due course).

To the extent that—by his own admission—Derrida's notion of *différance*, while explicitly mobilized against Hegel, is only infinitesimally, albeit crucially, distinct from the Hegelian system, we should begin with this distinction.[13] Unfortunately, this very difficult distinction—it has not generally been grasped—cannot really be drawn without a rather lengthy review of the Hegelian system, to which we shall proceed directly. This is all the more necessary to the extent that—in our attempt to establish precisely in what the shift from existentialist Marxism to structuralism and poststructuralism consists (as opposed to received opinion on the subject)—we need to reexamine Sartre's *Critique de la raison dialectique* in the light of its notorious dependence on the Hegelian system. I shall be arguing, however, that not only Sartre—who, as a Marxist, believed of course that he was moving beyond Hegel in important respects—but others who participated in that broad repudiation of Hegel of recent years initiated by structuralists (Althusser, for example, whom I shall be discussing below) failed markedly to take the full measure of the Hegelian system. The consequence for such figures (Sartre included), I shall argue, is that in the very instant in which they aggressively declared themselves to be anti-Hegelian, or post-Hegelian, they were at their most Hegelian. For this reason—and, as indicated, in order to distinguish *différance* from the Hegelian system by showing the latter to be "inscribed" in the former—the following review of the salient features of the Hegelian system, specifically in its formulation of the subject as ground of identity and difference, cannot be avoided.

## II

It will be recalled that, for Hegel, any entity—the perennial philosopher's table, for example—is what it is in relation not only to the chair, but in relation to the "infinite multiplicity" of everything else: from me to the stars and, ultimately, the totality of beings. As Hegel puts it, the "determinate being" or "quality" of any entity is "negatively determined" by opposition to an other: "Determinateness is negation posited as affirmative and is the proposition of Spinoza: *omnis determinatio est negatio.*"[14] Now, if the table or any other entity is what it is because it is not the chair and everything else in the universe, then each individual entity has its ground not in itself—it is not "self-standing" or "self-subsistent"—but in those "mediations" of its relations with everything else: what Hegel calls the "totality." The apparent self-subsistence of the entity, its "Appearance"—the presence of the table before me in all its incontestable and self-evidently vivid thinginess, its quiddity—is only an "essential illusory show" *[wesentliche Schein]* (HS, 501), or "the *simply affirmative* manifold variety which wantons in unessential manifoldness" (HS, 501). Now, the "law of Appearance," or the law of mediations—those negations that constitute and underlie the (illusory) subsistence of each Appearance—is what Hegel calls the "essential relation" (HS, 500). And, "The absolute itself is . . . that which constitutes in general the *ground* of the essential relation. . . . whole parts . . . these reflected determinations appear to ordinary thinking as a true being which is valid in and for itself; but the absolute as against them is the ground in which they have been engulfed" (HS, 530-31).

It is important to remember that Hegel's absolute is what we today would loosely call a "mind" (what Hegel, for important reasons we cannot go into, would prefer to call "Spirit") reflecting upon its own meditations and notions. In particular, as we have just seen, it is a mind as *ground* of that which is, of all beings (because it is the totality of determinations that has come to self-consciousness, in-itself and for-itself the whole). In this regard, as he himself pointed out, Hegel was doing no more than pushing Kant's "unity of apperception"—the unity of the "I think" or of self-consciousness—to its logical conclusion (HS, 584). (Kant had put it thus: "There can be in us no modes of knowledge with another, without that unity of consciousness which precedes all data of intuitions, and by relation to which representation of objects is alone possible" [KC, 136].) That the basis of the "essential relation" between entities is a mind, an "I think," is perhaps the most well-known single dimension of the Hegelian system; but it is a dimension that is always, quite suddenly, unaccountably, forgotten when writers (Marxists, for example) employ what is always (ultimately) a Hegelian dialectic which they think, because it is "shorn of its Idealism," is no longer metaphysical. (More of this presently. Suffice it to say, at this stage, that the objections of Heidegger and Derrida to Hegel are considerably more interesting, more challenging, than a reiteration of Marxism's complaints about Idealism.) Hegel himself was at least consistent and quite explicit in this regard. Thus, he insisted that it is not enough to engage in what he calls "a formal and unsystematic dialectic which . . . thinks vaguely of the absolute as the totality of determinations" (HS, 530). Rather, "the *exposition,* and in fact the *self*-exposition, of the absolute" is what is required (530). Furthermore, "the exposition of the absolute is, in fact, its *own* act, which *begins from itself* and *arrives at itself*" (532, Hegel's emphasis). So that, for the real to be rational, according to the famous formula, for a rational self-consciousness to be in-and-for-itself all reality, it must be able to recount not merely the "totality of determinations," but the latter as *one* adventure of Spirit coming to self-consciousness *exhaustively* or "without remainder" *(sans reste),* as Derrida puts it. Another way of saying this, of course, is that the absolute, as its name implies, is unconditioned, *causa prima* and *ens causa sui*—it has no "conditions of possibility" outside of itself—it is, in sum, what metaphysics calls "God," which is why, for Heidegger, and Derrida, Hegel's work constitutes the acme of "ontotheology."[15]

That the absolute is always Spirit, or mind, can be seen in Hegel's demonstration of the emergence of difference from simple identity (an example I choose among the many available, because it is to the structuralist and poststructuralist accounts of identity and difference that we shall next proceed). I shall begin by quoting extensively from Hegel's text before paraphrasing and explicating an argument that may seem somewhat impenetrable when lifted out of context.

In the *Science of Logic*, difference arises at the end of a process that begins with the "indeterminate immediacy" of "pure being," which "has no diversity within itself nor any with a reference outwards" (HS, 82). Hegel concludes that insofar as "There is *nothing* to be intuited in it . . . Being, the indeterminate immediate, is in fact *nothing*" (82). Being, *upon reflection* (this is the crucial moment), has "passed over" into its opposite: nothing. The two categories, while "each vanishes in its opposite," nonetheless remain distinct in their "*becoming*, a movement in which both are distinguished, but by a *difference* [my emphasis] which has equally immediately resolved itself" (83).

Very well. But let's try and make this plainer. Clearly, what we have just run through is a series of logical exercises that a *mind* has just engaged in with itself, along the lines of the following: "If I think of pure being—in which nothing can be distinguished and from which nothing else can be distinguished—I realize, upon reflection, in the next 'moment' of my thinking, that it is just the same as pure nothing. No sooner have I done this than I understand that there also now exists a third category—difference—which emerges from a distinction that, despite their similarity, can nonetheless be made between the first two (being and nothing): because if two things are 'the same' (similar) they are nonetheless not 'identical' (i.e., the very same thing within which all difference has disappeared definitively). For while I can indeed say that being and nothing are the same, I nonetheless continue to be able to distinguish them one from the other as different 'moments' in a dialectic that is in fact the process my own mind goes through when I reflect upon these matters," etc. Furthermore, the mind in question, in order to know these operations absolutely as one moment in "the totality of determinations" that constitutes all reality, must posit them as objects of its own thought, objects belonging to a totality by which it is not itself conditioned (like God, as creator of the universe)—even if it contains them within itself and even if, as Hegel puts it succinctly elsewhere, "Without the world, God is not God."[16]

It will be recalled that one of the objectives of this review of Hegel's *Science of Logic* is to establish what distinguishes Derridean *différance* from the Hegelian system. We have just seen that the Hegelian system requires a *sub-iectum*, a ground, to function, as do all metaphysics and ontology (including Marxism—claims to the contrary notwithstanding—as we shall see presently). With Derridean *différance*, by contrast, the identity of entities and their differences from one another are not the product of a subject-centered differentiation in which the chair is the chair because a subject (human or otherwise) has determined that it is not everything else in the universe—from the table to the Andromeda galaxy. One of the principal reasons for the misunderstandings that have bedeviled the reception of poststructuralism is that the reason for the emergence of a subjectless "order" of difference and identity has not been grasped.

One way of making vivid the necessity for the shift that has taken place is to point to the following incoherence at the heart of Hegel's system and any ontology (a problem that Hegel's system anticipates but does not quite succeed in conjuring away). If a subject determines that the table is what it is because it is not the chair and, ultimately, everything else, then the following problem arises: the corollary of this statement must be that the chair, in its turn, requires its difference from the table (and everything else) in order to be an object of comparison, and so on. The identity ("determination" by negation) of the table is, in other words, a prerequisite for the chair to be implicated in the identity of the table. The argument is circular. Put in terms of space and time—Kant's "pure forms of sensible intuition" without which nothing can appear to a subject—this is an impossibility because it defies their constraints: each entity would have to exist in its identifiable identity "before" it could be compared with the other, and "at a distance" from the other; and yet it is this very comparison that is supposed to establish such identity. In short, for any comparison between table and chair to take place, they must, as they say, "always already" present themselves to the subject in their identity and their difference. The system, or order, that makes them what they are must *exceed* the subject, must already be given all in one fell swoop.

Now, in some measure, Hegel acknowledged this by declaring, at the outset of the *Science of Logic,* that "the beginning must be an *absolute,* or what is synonymous here, an *abstract* beginning" (70), what he also describes as the "*logical* beginning" (68). He recognizes, in other words, at least implicitly, that the system of identity and difference cannot be founded in time or, more precisely, *in the course of* time (even if, of course, his explicit position is that it is indeed in the unfolding of time that the determinations, the Appearances, emerge—they are all "moments" of thought and the absolute itself is a "result," etc.). It all has to have already happened, as it were, "before" time begins.[17] For example, in order to start out, as above, with pure being, one has to presuppose the point of arrival, the absolute itself: "Logic, then, has for its presupposition the science of manifested spirit [i.e., *The Phenomenology of Spirit,* to which Hegel has just referred in the preceding sentence in the text], which contains and demonstrates the necessity, and so the truth, of the standpoint occupied by pure knowing and of its mediation" (HS, 68-69). If, in other words, Hegel is to write the *Science of Logic,* he has to assume, at the outset, the point of view of the absolute arrived at in *The Phenomenology of Spirit*. If we examine the latter, however, we find—despite statements to the effect that "the Absolute . . . is essentially a *result*"[18]—the absolute is nonetheless infiltrated very early on and clearly is the implicit starting point of *this* book that was supposed to ground the *Science of Logic*. Thus, in the opening few paragraphs of the introduction to the *Phenomenology*, Hegel is already dismissing the idea that cognition might be something separate from the absolute, an instrument or medium whereby one attains the latter, instead of its *already* being the absolute, an absolute that has simply failed to recognize itself as such because it has not yet passed through the immense travail of Spirit—"the seriousness, the suffering, the patience, and the labour of the negative" (10)—that work whereby "the whole . . . having traversed its content in time and space, has returned into itself, and is the resultant *simple Notion* of the whole" (7). And, indeed, only a short way into the preface, Hegel explicitly recognizes that the "end" must already be at the "beginning": "Only this self-*restoring* sameness, or this reflection in otherness within itself—not an *original* or *immediate* unity as such—is the true. It is the process of its own becoming, the circle that presupposes its end as its goal, having its end also as its beginning; and only by being worked out to its end, is it actual" (10).

Now, crucially, the "end" in Hegel's system, as is well known and as the above passage reminds us, is nonetheless not quite the same as the beginning:

> Thus the life of God and divine cognition may well be spoken of as a disporting of Love with itself; but this idea sinks into mere edification, and even insipidity, if it lacks the seriousness, the suffering, the patience, and the labour of the negative. *In itself* that life is indeed one of untroubled equality and unity with itself, for which otherness and alienation, and the overcoming of alienation, are not serious matters. But this *in-itself* is abstract universality, in which the nature of the divine life *to be for itself*, and so too the self-movement of the form, are altogether left out of account. (10-11)

Only the "working-out . . . of the whole wealth of developed form" enables the absolute, or "the life of God," to be true, to be "conceived and expressed as an actuality" (11). In sum, the "self-exposition" of the absolute cited earlier—Hegel's *Werke*—alone make God God, or the absolute absolute[19] (which is why Hegel has been able, legitimately, to be accused of writing, blasphemously, the autobiography of God). This is how Hegel puts it himself:

> Here it may indeed be said that every beginning must be made *with the absolute,* just as all advance is merely the exposition of it, in so far as its *in-itself* is the Notion. But because the absolute is at first only *in itself* it equally is *not* the absolute nor the posited Notion, and also not the Idea; for what characterizes these is precisely the fact that in them the *in-itself* is only an abstract, one-sided moment. Hence the advance is not a kind of *superfluity*; this it would be if that with which the beginning is made were in truth already the absolute; the advance consists rather in the universal determining itself and being *for itself* the universal, that is, equally an individual and a subject. Only in its consummation is it the absolute. (HS, 829)

To conclude with regard to Hegel: the "absolute absolute"—that which the mere absolute is not yet for as long as it has not yet revealed itself in its own self-exposition—has to preside at, precede, secretly ground its own self-exposition for the whole Hegelian system ever to get under way. Strictly speaking, this entails an infinite regress of grounds, or beginnings. The absolute is never a result, for it must have always presided, in its fullest development, at its own beginning: it was always already simultaneously both beginning and result, and therefore neither. It is this simultaneity of identical points of departure and arrival that disturbs the otherwise reassuring progression within circularity (a mounting spiral) of the Hegelian system: for the latter—talk of "logical" beginnings and "abstract" beginnings in Hegel is bogus—can only unfold in time. (Indeed, Hegel's entire extraordinary œuvre is best understood as an attempt to confront the eruption of history into thought.) Without its upward spiral—its movement of "becoming"—through its "moments" (aha! "pure being" has just "passed over" into "pure nothing"!), the Hegelian dialectic collapses.

The criticism of Hegel just elaborated is in fact the same argument as that developed earlier with the example of the difference between the table and the chair: a subject in space/time cannot ground difference and identity, whether the difference is that between chair and table or absolute (beginning) and absolute absolute (end). The subject is always preceded, or exceeded, by this difference. Or, as they say, the subject is always already "inscribed" in this difference. And no amount of circularity between beginnings and ends can change this.

This is perhaps the moment to interrupt, very briefly, our account of Hegel to emphasize that the incoherence in Hegel's system just elaborated should, under no circumstances, be attributed to his Idealism. The incoherence in question is not one that might conceivably have been avoided had Hegel been in a position to be, say, Marx before his time. No amount of taking into account his material or cultural conditions of possibility would have taken care of these inconsistencies. As I shall argue in the next section with regard to Althusser's structuralist Marxism, *any* metaphysics—and structuralism like Marxism is a metaphysics—engenders these incoherences. The latter are strictly the consequence of the subject's inscription within *différance*. One of the purposes of this review of Hegel's system, therefore, has been to demonstrate *différance* "at work." (Strictly speaking, we should perhaps say "at play," given the relations of complicity between work and *project* [and, thereby, a *subject*] for Derrida's masters—Nietzsche and Bataille. Indeed, we can take this opportunity to dismiss the pointless and uncomprehending hostility, so frequently expressed, toward the "irresponsibility" of this notion of "play" by recalling Bataille's rigorous demonstration of this complicity between project, work, and reason in Descartes and Hegel.)[20]

To return, however, to the *Science of Logic,* if, following Kant, we agree that a subject can only *be* a subject in relation to the "manifold of intuition" or "appearance"—thanks to space/time, then, because space/time makes the grounding of identity and difference by a subject impossible (as we have seen with the example of the difference between the table and the chair)—or, to put it differently, because space/time is a condition of the possibility of objects appearing to a subject rather than the reverse—whatever the order that sustains identity and difference is, it cannot be a subject (ground), it cannot be in space/time, and, furthermore, it cannot be some*thing* or an entity. It cannot even be the totality of relations between entities (we return thereby to the difficulties exposed in the example of the table and the chair). Hegel himself understood this, which is why his absolute—when it is still a beginning, an "unreflected immediacy," "the negation of all predicates and . . . the void," before it has passed over into "reflected immediacy" (essence) (HS, 531) and its long journey toward the Notion or Idea—must be thought of (impossibly) as "outside of" or "before" space/time (i.e., identity-and-difference, which are really just another name for the latter). This follows from the fact that "in it every determinateness of *essence* and *Existence,* or of *being* in general, as well as of *reflection,* has dissolved itself" (HS, 533). But, as we have seen, this "indeterminateness" can only be posited—is in fact grounded by—the already-exfoliated and developed system (the absolute as result), which itself presupposes space/time (the self-exposition of the absolute).[21] Otherwise it could never know itself and come to self-consciousness. It would persist as a mere "void." In short, it needs *Hegel* who is, of course, the *real* ground of the whole system!

## III

The above review of the Hegelian system was intended to clarify the Derridean notion of *différance* (because of Derrida's claim with regard to the latter's close affinity with the former) and to prepare the way for a discussion of Sartre's *Critique*. We have come some way toward achieving the first of these goals. There are two reasons, however, for postponing the realization of both objectives a little longer. The first is that our contemporary academic *doxa* makes us a little too swift to assume that we are all post-Hegelians and post-Sartreans. It is a little too easy, in other words, to think that the shortcomings of the *Science of Logic* do not apply to those of us working within that stew of French "theory," neo-Marxism, feminism, and postcolonial theory that constitutes "cultural studies" today. I shall attempt to demonstrate in this section, therefore, that Althusser (and hence Jameson, for example) continued to work within a philosophy of the subject (ground) ultimately under the aegis of Hegel. No doubt this is a provocative and surprising way to characterize the aggressively anti-Hegelian Althusser, but it is deliberately so. All the more so, to the extent that one of its consequences will be my suggestion that this residual Hegelianism is in part due to a failure to draw the lesson of the impasse at the heart of Sartre's more obviously Hegelian work. A comparison at this level illuminates both existentialist Marxism and structuralism in new ways insofar as these sworn enemies appear strangely, and unexpectedly, similar. While the opposition in terms of which the antagonists themselves cast their differences is doubtless valid, as far as it goes—humanism versus structure—it is not this distinction that is either interesting or decisive. Rather, it is the shared commitment of these writers to a philosophy of the subject (ground) that, once exposed, most sharply delineates the limits of their texts. Furthermore, I shall describe these failures, this common impasse, in such a way as to show how Derrida's notorious notion of *différance* emerges as a solution to them to the very extent that it constitutes the most thorough-going repudiation of these figures' most fundamental presuppositions.

From the point of view of Heidegger (after the "turning") or Derrida, a fundamental mistake has been committed by Marxists—from Althusser to Jameson—and by other writers frequently represented as more advanced than the latter and erroneously described as poststructuralists—among whom one could cite a considerable number of our current "cultural constructionists." This fundamental mistake has been to believe that the Hegelian system could be transcended by making, with regard to identity and difference, what we can call the "structural move."

The necessity for this structural move—which does indeed begin to recognize the flaws in Hegelianism and is compelling as far as it goes—is eloquently stated by Deleuze. In the course of criticizing Saussure and Troubetzkoy for discussing the differences between elements of language in terms of negations and oppositions, he says, "Isn't this a way of reintroducing the point of view of actual consciousness and of actual representation . . . ?"[22] We can certainly agree with this: we have just seen how true it is, with regard to the Hegelian system, that negations and oppositions presuppose a consciousness (as ground) that posits them. Deleuze continues:

> The forms of the negative do indeed appear in the actual terms and real relations [as the latter appear to a consciousness], but only insofar as they are cut off from the virtuality which they actualize and from the movement of their actualization. . . . In short, the negative is always derived and represented, never original nor present; the process of difference and differentiation always precedes that of the negative and that of opposition. (267)

We can agree with this too: the "actual" and "real" terms in which the negative and the oppositions that accompany it present themselves are merely those that are directly accessible to a subject—indeed, they are the very stuff of lived human experience—and, as such, they are the site par excellence of what has so aptly been called *méconnaissance*. As Deleuze puts it: "it is in the very nature of consciousness to be a false consciousness. The fetish is the natural object of social consciousness as common sense or collective meaning *[sens commun]* or recognition of value" (269). No doubt, too, one can, as Deleuze does, always posit some "process of differentiation" that precedes the actual negations and oppositions insofar as the latter are merely the material of subjective experience. The predictable next step is to invoke some form of truth to which one might accede if one were in possession of the *modus operandi* of the process of differentiation:

> Social problems can only be grasped in a "rectification" when the faculty of sociability raises itself up to its transcendent exercise, and breaks the unity of the fetishistic common sense or collective meaning *[sens commun]*. . . . The practical struggle does not take place on the terrain of the negative, but on that of difference and its power to affirm; and the war of those who have justice on their side is the conquest of the highest power, that of resolving problems by restoring them to their truth, by evaluating this truth over and beyond the representations of consciousness and the forms of the negative, by at last acceding to the imperatives on which they depend. (269)

To the mere "actuality" of negations and consciousness, Deleuze opposes the "virtual," the precise meaning of which, in Deleuze's text, need not concern us. It will suffice to recall that one sense of *virtual* is "that which has power or efficacy [without the material part]"—a meaning that is significantly related to the word's probable Sanskrit origin (*vira*: hero) and that reveals the term's subjectivist function in this text as ground of the structure. (It is homologous, in this regard, to the no less subjectivist "efficace" of Althusser's "structural causality" to which we will be turning shortly.) In the meantime, the importance of the following passage resides rather in its perfect articulation of the philosophical wall into which both structuralism and Sartre ran in their attempts to go "beyond" Hegel:

> The reality of the virtual consists in the elements and differential relations, and in the singular points which correspond to them. The *structure* is the reality of the virtual. . . . When the work of art lays claim to its origins in a virtuality in which it is plunged, it does not invoke any confused determination, but the completely determined *structure* which forms its differential genetic elements . . . the elements, the varieties of relations, the singular points coexist in the work or in the object, in the virtual part of the work or object, *without one's being able to assign a privileged point of view with regard to the others*, a center which would unify the other centers. *But how can one speak at the same time of complete determination, and only of a part of the object? The determination must be a complete determination of the object and yet only form a part of it.* (269-70, my emphasis)

Here we have arrived at the nub of the matter.

The structuralists may well, at first glance, have wrought a significant improvement over Hegel by locating the system of determinations that gives rise to identity and difference outside of the ambit of a consciousness. As Deleuze himself recognizes in the above passage, however, a fundamental problem remains—our familiar one of the ground: "the determination must be a complete determination of the object, and yet only form a part of it." In other words, if we take the notion of structure seriously—as a system all the elements of which depend for their identity on the differential relations among themselves as generated by the structure itself (however virtual, rather than actual these may be) and that determines the merely actual or "fetishistic" experience of human subjects (for example, the elements of a work of art as the latter presents itself to a consciousness)—then it is hard to understand how one part (virtual) can determine another (actual) without the former constituting a ground for the latter—

that is, constituting something that itself must escape the play of determinations of the structure in order to be a ground of the latter.

The difficulty evoked here is raised by the positions of most of the other major figures of the period. For example, Althusser, like Deleuze, is well aware of the shortcomings of the Hegelian system and so must represent Marx's use of the residually Hegelian notion of "contradictions" as a prescient fumbling toward something that will have to await Althusser's own formulation: "Marx [according to this view] thinks, by means of the Hegelian concepts of contradiction and development of the contradiction, something radically novel, the concept of which, according to this view, he would be incapable of formulating: namely, the mode of action of the structure as mode of action of the relations of production which govern it."[23] The problem of the ground emerges in Althusser's work in the shape of the entire mode of production as a "complex whole," an "articulated structure with a dominant" *[une structure articulée à dominante]*.[24] (The dominant contradiction here being that between forces of production and relations of production [AM, 214].) According to Althusser, the "economic" domain figures as merely one element (albeit a dominant one) of a whole that is constituted by the myriad relations among all the levels of the social formation: "each contradiction, each essential articulation of the structure, and the general relationship among the articulations in the structure with a dominant, constitute so many conditions of existence of the complex whole itself" (210). Furthermore: "the secondary contradictions are essential to the very existence of the principal contradiction ... they constitute in a real way the condition of existence of it, just as the principal contradiction constitutes their condition of existence" (211). The problem with this formulation is that, by conceding that the dominant contradiction owes its existence to all the others, the way is opened to one's wondering how that one contradiction can continue to be dominant—that is, to be a ground— or even how it could ever have been so in the first place. Disclaimers to the contrary notwithstanding, anything that is dominant within a structure— however much one insists upon the "relative autonomy" of substructures within the social formation, and even if the latter contribute in part to the dominant element's very dominance—is necessarily a ground: it must, ultimately, at some level or another, escape determination by, and therefore cannot owe its existence to, other, subordinate, structures.

I should specify that the objection raised here to a ground in the form of a *structure à dominante* (the dominant element being the economic "instance") is not merely a rehash of liberal bourgeois hostility to the so-called "reductionism" or "economism" of Marxist analyses. The humanism of that objection—and its secret class-motivation—make it altogether suspect.[25]

But perhaps we could do away with the dominant contradiction altogether and still talk about "structural causality." After all, the *structure à dominante* looms less prominently in *Reading Capital* than it had in the earlier *For Marx*.[26] Why don't we pass over the difficulties raised by a dominant contradiction and, in an attempt to salvage Althusser's position, see what happens to "structural causality" without a ground at all, without any preeminence given to an economic level? (This is Jameson's solution.[27]) Could we not, for example, invoke the famous account of structural causality as an "absent cause"—a "structure which is only a specific combination of its own elements, [which] is nothing outside of its effects"?[28]

This move may seem seductive, because it looks as if it might solve our problem; but there is one difficulty, which implies as its consequence—despite Althusser's claim to be going one better than Hegel—that structural causality does not, in the final analysis, constitute a decisive advance over the *Science of Logic*. Structural causality, no less than the Hegelian system, has to posit a whole, a *totality:*

> We know that the Marxist whole *[le tout marxiste]* is distinct without any possible confusion from the Hegelian whole: it is a whole whose unity, far from being the expressive or "spiritual" unity of the whole of Leibniz or Hegel, is constituted by a certain type of *complexity,* the unity of a *structured whole,* comprising what one can call levels or distinct and "relatively autonomous" instances which coexist in this complex structural unity, articulated with one another according to the specific modes of determination, fixed in the final instance by the level or instance of the economy. (AL1, 120-21)

Setting aside the problem of the economy as ground, as "determination in the last instance," the one thing the lengthy account of the *Science of Logic* above established was that one cannot posit a whole, a totality, and its "elements" without thereby, simultaneously, implicitly—however adamant one's disclaimers—positing a subject (*sub-iectum,* sub-stance) that totalizes that whole, that assigns elements and levels their place in that whole (or perhaps, even, generates them *in toto*). Even if one refines that "whole" out of existence—out of mere, vulgar thinginess—as an "absent cause," as a system of *relations,* one is ineluctably committing oneself to the efficacy (what Althusser calls *l'efficace*) of a totalizing agency, however inhuman. And once one has done this—and claimed to demonstrate the workings of the system of relations—one has also posited, implicitly, someone who can *know* the whole, someone who—again, disclaimers to the contrary notwithstanding—must stand outside the whole in order to be able to posit it and know its efficacy upon its levels and elements. In brief, one does not easily escape Hegel, the subject, and ontotheology.

Another way of demonstrating the ontotheological basis of structural causality is to return to the beginnings of the debate around these questions and invoke Aristotle's *Metaphysics*. Discussing the possibility of an "infinite series" of causes of something, Aristotle declares, rightly, that "if there is no first [cause] there is no cause at all."[29] If "an infinity of things" in the universe was causally necessary to "anything and everything else" (the reason for these scare-quotes will become apparent shortly)—which is what the ultimate consequence of causality by "infinite series" would be for us today—then one would run into a difficulty similar to one described earlier in the case of identity and difference in Hegel's system (the example of the table and chair): if entity A is the cause of B, then the reverse must also be true, which is circular and makes a mockery of space/time and, *a fortiori,* causality. Indeed, notions like "things," "everything," and so on, all become incoherent under such conditions.

This is why a First Cause, "eternal and unmovable and separate from sensible things" (AW, 1695), has to be posited if knowledge is ever to get off the ground.

Still another way of saying all this is that a totality, a whole—however "absent" and "structural"—because it circumscribes the infinite series of possible causes within limits in order to be able to mobilize causality, in order to make causality possible—partakes of the qualities of an entity, a being, just like the elements that compose it. We recall that one of the Greek terms for being was *ousia,* presence "in the sense of permanent presence, already-thereness."[30] Far from being an absent cause—this epithet must henceforth be read as a sign of *dénégation* (it secretly acknowledges that which it denies)—structural causality is a form of presence.

Now, there is one other form of presence, of being—other than, or in addition to, God—which causality and beings are designed to affirm: our own. Nietzsche put it the other way round, but the following remark ultimately comes to the same thing: "The concept of substance [sub-stance, *hypokeimenon,* sub-ject] is a consequence of the concept of the subject: not the reverse!"[31] (We can set aside the question as to whether it is substance that makes the emergence of a unified subject possible or vice versa—we are aware of contemporary predilections in this regard. Suffice it to say that this fatal pair always appear hand in hand.) Notwithstanding his animadversions against "the Chinaman of Königsberg," Nietzsche, like Hegel, is harking back to Kant's "unity of consciousness," otherwise known as "transcendental apperception" without which any knowledge of objects is impossible:

> If we were not conscious that what we think is the same as what we thought a moment before, all reproduction in the series of representations would be useless. For it would in its present state be a new representation which would not in any way belong to the act whereby it was to be gradually generated. The manifold of the representation would never, therefore, form a whole, since it would lack that unity which only consciousness can impart to it. If, in counting, I forget that the units, which now hover before me, have been added to one another in succession, I should never know that a total is being produced through this successive addition of unit to unit, and so would remain ignorant of the number. (KC, 133-34)

Kant continues: "There must, therefore, be a transcendental ground of the unity of consciousness in the synthesis of the manifold of all our intuitions, and consequently also of the concepts of objects in general, and so of all objects of experience, a ground without which it would be impossible to think any object for our intuitions . . ." (135-36).

Althusser's structural causality necessarily implies a human subject, a subject, furthermore, that has been correctly identified as aggressively "scientistic," "triumphalist," and so on. Furthermore, this subject is recognizably the product of a particular historical moment with its—thoroughly humanist—restriction of the structural causality to the domain of the "economy," "relations of production," and so on—that mundane (in the French sense of the term), modern, bourgeois domain par excellence—however "irreducible to any anthropological intersubjectivity" it may be (AL2, 53). (Why, in other words, restrict the structure to the arena in which *these* "levels" and "elements" enter into relation with one another? What is the justification for excluding—to take an example at random—the level of radiation generated by sunspots, which have been shown to be decisive in the meteorological cycles of rainfall and therefore, surely, a significant element in human behavior?)

To conclude this section on the structuralist move, inveighing against humanism and invoking a structural causality do not, of themselves, preclude a philosophy of the subject or, for that matter, ontotheology. To posit a totality automatically inscribes one within the position of an unconditioned subjectivity that, thereby, affiliates one with that long Christian tradition of a ground that is outside of the totality in question.[32]

All of the above can be applied with equal force to the work of Fredric Jameson. In *The Political Unconscious,* he formulates precisely the position I have mooted here: a modified Althusserianism, or structural causality *without* a "dominant" (35-37).

## IV

Sartre, *enfin!*

I began this essay by pointing to the necessity—according to Sartre's own "progressive-regressive method"—of reading him on the basis of his successors. I hope that this necessity will now, after the ostensibly disproportionate amount of space devoted to some of those successors, have become clear. For it is my hope that the interest, today, of engaging in such an exercise will be seen to reside not so much in the predictable conclusion that Sartre's work is marked by humanism, phallogocentrism, and so on (a judgment with which one can concur but which, to the best of my knowledge, has never been argued for so much as it has been flatly asserted) as in the demonstration that some of his most prominent successors—who sought in no small measure to establish their own identity on the basis of an aggressive repudiation of everything he stood for—neglected, in spectacular fashion, to draw the lessons they might have from the rigor and consistency of his Hegelianism and his consequent incoherence.

The problem that Sartre set himself to address in the *Critique of Dialectical Reason,* in its bluntest formulation, was the following: "Marxism is strictly true if History is a totalization; it is not so if human history disintegrates into a plurality of particular histories."[33] Clearly, what Sartre means by History, in general, is that modern history that has made of the planet what the economic historian Immanuel Wallerstein has called the "modern world system," that is, a global geopolitical network subordinated to the capitalist market. It is evidently something like the latter that Sartre has in mind when he invokes the notion of "totalization" in the following passage in which his philosophical ambitions find their most grandiloquent expression:

> These questions bring us at last to the real problem of History. If, in effect, the latter must in reality be the ongoing totalization of all the practical multiplicities and of all their struggles, then the complex products of the conflicts and the collaborations of these multiplicities which are so diverse must themselves be intelligible in their synthetic reality, that is to say they must be able to be understood as the synthetic products of *one* totalitarian *praxis.* Which amounts to saying that History is intelligible if the different practices which one can uncover and fix in one moment of the historical temporalization appear ultimately as partly totalizing and as joined together and fused in their very oppositions and their diversities by a totalization which is intelligible and from which there is no appeal.[34]

Nothing could be further from our contemporary predilections—with our principled hostility to "grand narratives"—than this statement of intent. Its ultra-Hegelianism jumps off the page. It may come as a surprise, however, given the broadly Heideggerian-Derridean cast to this essay, that I shall argue that Sartre was right to pursue his ultra-Hegelianism to its grandiose conclusion: the colossal wreck of the *Critique of Dialectical Reason*. Or, at all events, he was right to be wrong: wrong in the sense that the strictures formulated above with regard to Hegel and structuralism apply no less rigorously to the *Critique;* right insofar as he understood, better than his structuralist rivals did (Althusser in particular), that the moment one sets out to ground the emergence of identity and difference—whether by means of human praxis or a mode of production as structural causality—if one once does this, one is committing oneself to a subject, human or otherwise, that ineluctably performs a work of synthesis or totalization. It is the greater degree of consistency with which Sartre pursued this consequence—the relentless rigor with which he drove himself into an impasse—that proclaims his superiority to structuralists as a thinker.

The assertion that structuralists worked implicitly with a notion of totalization flies in the face of everything we have been taught to believe about those writers. How could it be true?

Let us return to Althusser:

> the structure of the relations of production determine *places* and *functions* which are occupied and assumed by agents of production, who are only ever the occupiers of these places, insofar as they are the "bearers" (*Träger*) of these functions. The true "subjects" (in the sense of constituting subjects of the process) are therefore not these occupiers nor these functionaries, are not therefore, contrary to all the appearances . . . of the naive anthropology, the "concrete individuals" . . . —but the definition and the distribution of these places and functions. The true "subjects" are therefore . . . the relations of production (and the political and ideological social relations). But as these are "relations," one cannot think of them under the category of *subject*. (AL2, 53)

It is not a matter of disagreeing with any of this. On the contrary, to the extent that, if one is going to explain social reality, Marxism continues to be the most powerful and, in my view, the most compelling social narrative our particular culture possesses, all of the above strikes me as entirely persuasive, as "true" as we can get. How can one deny, however, that the above passage implies an activity by a subject (*sub-iectum*) that may well not be human but that certainly engages in a crucial dimension of what Sartre describes as totalization:[35]

> through the multiplicities, [totalization] continues that work of synthesis which makes each part a manifestation of the whole and which relates the whole to itself through the mediation of its parts. But it is an *ongoing* activity, which cannot cease without the multiplicity reverting to its original status. This act delineates a practical field which, as the undifferentiated correlative of *praxis*, is the formal unity of the ensembles which are to be integrated; within this practical field, the activity attempts to effect the most rigorous synthesis of the most differentiated multiplicity: thus, by a double movement, multiplicity is multiplied to infinity, each part is opposed to all the others and to the whole which is in the process of being formed, while the totalizing activity tightens all the links, making each differentiated element both its immediate expression and its mediation in relation to the other elements. (SC1, 138-39)

What does the "assigning" of people to "places" and "functions" entail if not the above?

Now, it is true that Sartre's characterization of totalization contains important residues of Hegelianism that one does not find in structuralism—terms like "expression" and "mediation"—which were anathema to structuralism because they imply a praxis that synthesizes a *preexisting* "practical field" (as Sartre puts it)—a preformed "multiplicity" of different elements re-presented by a consciousness. Whereas what was always the most interestingly novel (shocking to many) aspect of structuralism at its best—and more especially of poststructuralism (Foucault, for example)—was the sense, successfully conveyed, of the generation of entities, of difference and identity, by the structure (or discursive formations and archives, in the case of Foucault). This is precisely what should be the ultimate import of the insistence, by Althusser, on the "relations" as "subject" at the end of the above passage, an import that is not really grasped by Althusser, however, as his insistence on "assigning" and "distributing" makes plain. These terms—they stem from an older ontological discourse of the "whole" and of "causality"—imply already-constituted individuals or entities (constituted prior to the work of the relations) that are *subsequently* distributed to places in a structure.

The strikingly different case of Foucault illustrates this point. As a post-Marxist, he has proceeded further down the road from ontotheology:

unlike Althusser, he invokes neither a whole nor causality. As a result (notoriously, in the view of his critics), he is able to argue that "the object" (madness, for example) does not preexist its "discovery" by a discourse (of psychopathology) but is instead "formed" by the latter: "This formation is ensured by an ensemble of relations established between instances of emergence, of delimitation and of specification. . . . These relations are established between institutions, economic and social processes, behavioural patterns, systems of norms, techniques, types of classification, modes of characterization; and these relations are not present in the object. . . ."[36] This move was interpreted by critics as a semiotic version of idealism—a consequence of the erroneous assimilation of "discourse" to "language" (similar to the equally mistaken confusion of "text," in the reception of Derrida's work, with "language").[37] Correctly understood, however, this move—which has become so familiar to us over the last thirty years as to appear deceptively self-evident in its apparent simplicity—cuts a veritable Gordian knot. No ontology here: no attempt to establish what is, why it is the way it is, the relation of parts to whole and vice versa, and so on and so forth. The entire tormented tangle of difficulties evoked above in the examples of Hegel, Althusser, and Sartre melt away as if by magic. All that remains is the account of the discursive formations that determine and make possible both the emergence of objects for knowledge and knowing subjects (a practice that, in its eschewal of ontology, is driven by presuppositions similar to those that lead Derrida simply to deconstruct texts).[38] I do not mean to suggest that this work is either easy or obvious. On the contrary, the task is arduous, beset by difficulties and snares of its own. Nonetheless, the problems involved are so different as to leave one with a permanent sense of having entered a new world, a world to which most of us are still in the process of adapting.

In the wake of this move, it is almost with lassitude that one returns to Sartre. To continue where we left off, however, Sartre was right to be wrong—compared with the residually "subjectivist" structuralists—because of the greater degree of lucidity with which he pursued his philosophy of a subject. This project generated often fascinating investigations in the *Critique*: How can we speak of any human interaction—the violence of a boxing match, for example—as a strictly social phenomenon, as an incarnation of the violence of an entire class-riven society that pits members of the working classes against one another in order to defuse their potential contestation of the social order? How do we do this without reducing the "social totalization of envelopment" to a suprahuman "hyperorganicism" or the prize fight itself—as it unfolds here and now—to a singularization of a universal concept? How do we preserve its difference from the totalization of envelopment, the fact that it totalizes the latter in its turn? How can the anti-Semitic policy encouraged by Stalin at one point be simultaneously explained by "biographical" factors and the exigencies imposed on Stalin himself by the totalization of envelopment as, partly, the outcome of his own praxis? The treatment of these questions was consistently, dazzlingly, brilliant. That Sartre failed, however, to achieve the objectives outlined in his programmatic statement of intent quoted earlier is generally acknowledged. That he was reduced, in his account of the Soviet Union after the revolution, to locating the "totalization of envelopment" in the figure of Stalin himself speaks volumes for the "voluntarism" of the entire enterprise,[39] as does the failure to develop a totalization of envelopment for nondirectorial societies, what he calls *"des sociétés désunies"* (a difficulty merely evoked in the Annexes to the second volume).

This impressive impasse—impressive in both a positive and negative sense of the term—is to be attributed to Sartre's refusal to give up his location of the ground in the for-itself, formulated in *L'Etre et le néant*, quoted earlier, which derives ultimately from Hegel[40] and which therefore engenders the same incoherences as the Hegelian system. Only the for-itself—or some other human subject to whom you delegate your godlike faculties (like Stalin)—can totalize the multiplicity of determinations. The crucial "problem of the totalization without a totalizer," evoked on the penultimate page of the first volume of the *Critique*, is, significantly, never really addressed.

The lesson of this impasse is that History—as a narrative, in time and space, of an "infinite multiplicity" of entities, individuals, groups, and their relations—is not, ultimately, "intelligible"; the goal of the second volume of the *Critique* (and its subtitle)—"the intelligibility of history"—is unattainable because the philosophy of the subject upon which it depends is intrinsically incoherent.

It is the recognition of the necessity of thinking without a ground—of realizing, after ontotheology, that it is not possible to ground identity and difference—that marks our times. It is this necessity that the notion of *différance* addresses and that has been vividly characterized by Derrida as thinking the "structurality of structure" (the latter's "play") without a center, or ground—an outcome that, of course, is strictly speaking inconceivable because it entails the evaporation into thin air of the structure itself (cf. the discussion of causality in Aristotle's *Metaphysics* above).[41] It is this novel situation that motivates Derrida's—for many readers—by turns, infuriatingly precious, disingenuous, mystifying statements to the effect that *différance* is "neither a word nor a concept" (DD, 3), that it "is not," that "it commands nothing, reigns over nothing and does not exercise anywhere any authority" (DD, 22).

The similarity of resonance, in this evocation of *différance,* with Sartre's descriptions of the for-itself ("it is what it is not, and is not what it is," etc.) has been noted.[42] Both notions in their time have been charged, stupidly, with the ultimate sin of Christendom: *nihilism* ("i.e., the radical repudiation of value, meaning, and desirability," NW, 7). The irony of this accusation is that *différance,* which dissolves the for-itself as ground, as *sub-iectum,* which renders its pretensions null and void—and yet exists in a relationship of "almost absolute proximity" with the Hegelian system in which the for-itself articulated its divine *grandeur* in the most uncompromising terms—the irony is that, in the very act of the dissolution of the for-itself as ground, *différance* thereby opens the royal road to the supreme, untrammelled, deathless, and infinite *(unendliche)* freedom, *ek-stasis,* to which the for-itself has always aspired and which motivated its paranoid delusions in the first place.

But I shall have to tell that story another day.

## ABBREVIATIONS

AL1: Louis Althusser, *Lire le capital,* vol. 1.
AL2: Louis Althusser, *Lire le capital,* vol. 2.
AM: Louis Althusser, *Pour Marx.*
AW: Aristotle, *The Complete Works of Aristotle.*
DD: Jacques Derrida, "La Différance."
FA: Michel Foucault, *L'Archéologie du savoir.*
HN: Martin Heidegger, *Nietzsche,* vol 4.
HS: Georg Wilhelm Friedrich Hegel, *Science of Logic.*
KC: Immanuel Kant, *Critique of Pure Reason.*
NW: Friedrich Nietzsche, *The Will to Power.*
SC1: Jean-Paul Sartre, *Critique de la raison dialectique,* vol 1.
SC2: Jean-Paul Sartre, *Critique de la raison dialectique,* vol 2.
SE: Jean-Paul Sartre, *L'Etre et le néant.*

## NOTES

1. Sartre outlines his progressive-regressive method in the final section of *Questions de méthode,* the methodological preamble to the first volume of the *Critique de la raison dialectique.* His biographical study of Flaubert, *L'Idiot de la famille,* constitutes its extended implementation. Although I shall be reading Sartre on the basis of his successors, this will not be done in accordance with the progressive-regressive method.
2. It may seem strange to begin an account of Sartre in terms of his successors with an examination of Heidegger, an older figure who is generally thought of

as a predecessor. It is true that much of his *Nietzsche* study originated in the 1930s, well before Sartre's heyday at the center of French intellectual life. However, not only were other portions written during the early 1950s, but the book was reworked before publication in 1961. Besides which, when the impact of this work on the younger generation of French philosophers began to make itself felt in the 1960s, Sartre was already in eclipse.

3. Martin Heidegger, *Nietzsche,* trans. Frank Capuzzi (New York: Harper and Row, 1982), 4:96-97, henceforth abbreviated HN; see also 3:220-21.
4. This has, of course, not always been the case, and Heidegger does reserve other definitions of humanism for earlier periods in the "Letter on Humanism" (e.g., *homo humanus* under the Roman Empire). In the great study on Nietzsche, Heidegger uses the term "anthropomorphism" to designate what he calls elsewhere, and I have called here, "humanism." I have, in this regard, simply chosen to use the more familiar term generally used by poststructuralist writers.
5. Immanuel Kant, *Critique of Pure Reason,* trans. Norman Kemp Smith (London: Macmillan, 1978), 66, henceforth abbreviated KC.
6. See HN, 93-94.
7. Luc Ferry and Alain Renaut, *Heidegger et les modernes* (Paris: Bernard Grasset, 1988); see also their *La Pensée 68: essai sur l'anti-humanisme contemporain* (Paris: Gallimard, 1985).
8. Jürgen Habermas, *The Philosophical Discourse of Modernity,* trans. Frederick Lawrence (Cambridge: MIT Press, 1987), 408, n. 28.
9. Scott Lash, *Sociology of Postmodernism* (London: Routledge, 1990), 9.
10. Fredric Jameson, "The Sartrean Origin," *Sartre Studies International* 1.1-2 (1995): 11.
11. See, for example, Jean-Paul Sartre, *L'Etre et le néant,* (Paris: Gallimard, 1943), 128-29, henceforth abbreviated SE (translation of passages from this and other volumes in French, unless otherwise noted, are my own). Heidegger formulates the criticism of the kind of position expressed by Sartre in the "Letter on Humanism," (Martin Heidegger, *Basic Writings* [New York: Harper and Row, 1977], 237-38).
12. Gilles Deleuze, *Logique du sens* (Paris: Minuit, 1969), 356-57.
13. In "La Différance," Derrida talks of "the relations of very deep affinity which *différance* thus written sustains with the Hegelian discourse" (Jacques Derrida, "La Différance," *Marges de la philosophie* [Paris: Minuit, 1972], 15, henceforth abbreviated DD). See also *Positions* (Paris: Minuit, 1972), 60: "*Différance* must sign (at a point of almost absolute proximity with Hegel. . . ) the point of rupture with the system of the *Aufhebung* and the speculative dialectic."
14. Georg Wilhelm Friedrich Hegel, *Science of Logic,* trans. Arnold V. Miller (Atlantic Highlands, NJ: Humanities Press, 1989), 111 and 113, henceforth abbreviated HS.
15. See Martin Heidegger, *Essays in Metaphysics: Identity and Difference,* trans. Kurt F. Leidecker (New York: Philosophical Library, 1960), 46-47, and *Nietzsche,*

trans. Joan Stambaugh, David Farrell Krell, and Frank A. Capuzzi (San Francisco: Harper and Row, 1987), 3:241.
16. Georg Wilhelm Friedrich Hegel, *Lectures on the Philosophy of Religion* (New York: Humanities Press, 1978), 200.
17. This notwithstanding the statement that "the absolute itself is *absolute identity*; this is its *determination,* for in it all manifoldness of the world-in-itself and the world of Appearance, or of inner and outer totality, is sublated. In the absolute itself is no *becoming,* for it is not being . . . " (HS, 531). One might want to specify, therefore, that *this* absolute (the "beginning" absolute—the one which precedes the "labour of the negative")—that in which "all determinateness as such has become an utterly transparent illusory being, a difference which has *vanished in its positedness*" (531), the "ground in which they [determinations] have been engulfed" (531), "the negation of all predicates and . . . the void" (530)—is in reality preceded, necessarily presupposed, at the outset, by the "end"—the completely unfolded Notion in which the totality of determinations has accomplished its "self-exposition"—or what Hegel also calls the "absolute absolute" (of which more below).
18. Georg Wilhelm Friedrich Hegel, *Phenomenology of Spirit,* trans. Arnold V. Miller (Oxford: Oxford University Press, 1981), 11.
19. The latter, faintly ridiculous phrase, "the absolute absolute," in which Hegel veers into self-caricature, can indeed be found in the *Science of Logic,* 533.
20. See, for example, Georges Bataille, *L'Expérience intérieure,* in *Œuvres complètes* (Paris: Gallimard, 1973), 5:130, 131, 124-25, 59 and passim.
21. In the *Phenomenology of Spirit,* Hegel says of "Science, the crown of the world of Spirit" that "It is the whole which, having traversed its content *in time and space* [my emphasis], has returned into itself, and is the resultant *simple Notion* of the whole" (7).
22. Gilles Deleuze, *Différence et répétition* (Paris: Presses Universitaires de France, 1968), 264.
23. Louis Althusser, *Lire le capital* (Paris: Maspero, 1966), 1:143, henceforth abbreviated AL1.
24. Louis Althusser, *Pour Marx* (Paris: Maspero, 1965), 210, henceforth abbreviated AM. I prefer this translation of *structure à dominante* to the usual, slightly misleading, "structure in dominance."
25. Marxism is perfectly capable of generating accounts of social phenomena that preserve the specificity and singularity of the so-called cultural "superstructure" and the precious, quivering, unique sensibilities of human individuals. Indeed, this was precisely Sartre's unrivalled achievement, most impressively demonstrated in *The Family Idiot.*
26. I do not mean to suggest that it disappears: see, for example, volume 1, 120-21, and volume 2, 64.
27. Fredric Jameson, *The Political Unconscious* (London: Methuen, 1981), 35-37.
28. Louis Althusser, *Lire le capital* (Paris: Maspero, 1968), 2:65, henceforth abbreviated AL2.

29. Aristotle, *The Complete Works of Aristotle* (Princeton: Princeton University Press, 1985), 2:1570, henceforth abbreviated AW.
30. Martin Heidegger, *Introduction to Metaphysics,* trans. Ralph Manheim (New Haven: Yale University Press, 1959), 193.
31. Friedrich Nietzsche, *The Will to Power,* trans. Walter Kaufmann and R. J. Hollingdale (New York: Vintage Books, 1968), 268, henceforth abbreviated NW.
32. This Heideggerian argument is derived, of course, ultimately from Nietzsche. See, for example, NW, 12.
33. Jean-Paul Sartre, *Critique de la raison dialectique,* vol. 2 (Paris: Gallimard, 1985), 25, henceforth abbreviated SC2.
34. Jean-Paul Sartre, *Critique de la raison dialectique,* vol. 1 (Paris: Gallimard, 1960), 754, henceforth abbreviated SC1.
35. Let it be understood, my objection is not the one that was raised by humanist critics of structuralism in the sixties to the effect that the latter simply transposed human faculties ("agency," etc.) onto the "inhuman" (structures).
36. Michel Foucault, *L'Archéologie du savoir* (Paris: Gallimard, 1969), 60-61, henceforth abbreviated FA.
37. For an evocation of the historically novel relationship between "words" and "things" that Foucault is addressing, see the very helpful passage that begins at p. 66 of the French version of *The Archeology of Knowledge:* "from the kind of analysis that I have undertaken, *words* are as deliberately absent as *things* themselves. . . ." Personally, I have always found Baudrillard's early works—from *La Société de consommation* to *L'Echange symbolique et la mort*—the most helpful for enabling one to understand *why* the semiotic revolution took place, as part of a wider phenomenon including the social domain of everyday life—a new strange world in which words, things, and signs developed such startlingly new relationships to one another, often appearing to trade places.

    One might add that *différance* articulates in philosophical terms the overall feel of our historical situation ("postmodernity," "late consumer capitalism"), which is such today that any talk of entities per se, any talk that attributes to anything more than a fleeting, contingent, "constructed" existence—some kind of "thinginess" or quiddity—seems pitifully naive. It is this situation that has made the linguistic or textual paradigm—as an articulated order not among things but mere "marks," "traces," or signs (as the barest minimum of quiddity) in an untotalizable "order" (the term is Derrida's) or "code" (Baudrillard)—so irresistibly compelling to two generations of academics.
38. It should be specified that this practice does not entail a fresh, simply more sophisticated, attempt to survey the "determinations" or "conditions of possibility" of the place which one occupies oneself as a subject. Foucault is quite explicit that we cannot describe our own "archive" (FA, 171). Nor did it ever entail a death of the subject in the sense of the elimination of consciousness. (The end of Man, announced at the conclusion to *Les Mots et les choses,* referred to the end of humanism—humankind as *sub-iectum* or ground—not

consciousness.) On the contrary, the description of discursive formations demonstrated the "empty place[s] that may in fact be filled by different individuals," the places from which *one can be a subject* (FA, 125).
39. With important qualifications, it is true: "So what is the totalization of envelopment during the Stalinist phase of socialist construction? It is Stalin, if you will, but to the extent that he is *produced* and supported by the praxis of everyone as the sovereign unicity which must integrate its structures and contain its exteriority" (SC2, 243). This is certainly not individualism, but it does constitute subjectivism and voluntarism in Heidegger's sense of these terms.
40. This holds true for the *Critique*, the following passage notwithstanding: "These remarks enable us to understand an initial characteristic of the critical investigation/experiment: it is conducted *within* the totalization [of envelopment] and cannot be a contemplative comprehension of the totalizing movement; nor can it be an autonomous and singular totalization of the totalization [of envelopment] which is known, but it is a real moment of the totalization in movement *[totalisation en cours]*" (SC1, 140).
41. See the opening pages of Derrida's "La Structure, le signe et le jeu dans le discours des sciences humaines," in *L'Ecriture et la différence* (Paris: Seuil, 1967).
42. See, for example, Christina Howells, *Sartre: The Necessity of Freedom* (Cambridge: Cambridge University Press, 1988), chapter 9.

# NOTES ON CONTRIBUTORS

GEORGE H. BAUER was Professor of French and Comparative Literature at the University of Southern California, author of *Sartre and the Artist,* and co-editor of the Pléiade edition of Sartre's *Œuvres romanesques.* He specialized in gender studies and twentieth-century French literature and published articles on Duchamp, Delay, Robbe-Grillet, Sartre, Butor, and Barthes. He died while this book was in preparation and will be greatly missed by his friends and colleagues.

ANNA BOSCHETTI, of the Università di Venezia, Italy, is author of *Sartre et "Les Temps Modernes": une entreprise intellectuelle.* A specialist in sociological literary theory, she has written articles on twentieth-century French poetry and philosophy, including studies of Michel Leiris and Simone Weil.

JEAN-FRANÇOIS FOURNY, Associate Professor of French at Ohio State University, is the author of *Introduction à la lecture de Georges Bataille* and guest-editor of special issues of journals on Bataille, Mitterrand, the Occupation, and Foucault. He has also published articles on Surrealism, Sartre, Bataille, Breton, and Bourdieu.

RHIANNON GOLDTHORPE is Emeritus Fellow and Tutor in French at St. Anne's College, Oxford, and Honorary Professor at the University of Wales. She is the author of *Sartre: Literature and Theory* and *La Nausée* and has published articles on Mallarmé, Malraux, Sartre, Ricoeur, and Proust. She is also co-editor of *French Studies.*

MARIE-PAULE HA, Assistant Professor of French at Ohio State University, is a specialist in twentieth-century French literature, colonialism, and the postcolonial condition. She has written a dissertation entitled "'Cet autre qui n'en est pas un': Figuring the East in the Works of Victor Segalen, André Malraux, Marguerite Duras and Roland Barthes" and has published articles on Malraux, Duras, and Cardinal.

ROBERT HARVEY, Associate Professor of French at the State University of New York, Stony Brook, is author of *Search for a Father: Sartre, Paternity and the Question of Ethics*. He has co-edited a collection of essays by Jean-François Lyotard entitled *Toward the Postmodern* and has translated Michel Meyer's *From Metaphysics to Rhetoric*. He has also published critical essays on Sartre, French cinema, and contemporary French culture.

CHRISTINA HOWELLS is Fellow and Tutor in French at Wadham College, Oxford. She is the author of *Sartre's Theory of Literature* and *Sartre: The Necessity of Freedom* and has edited *The Cambridge Companion to Sartre* and a collection of essays entitled *Sartre*. She has also published articles on Sartre, Derrida, Lévinas, Kant, Freud, and Hegel and is a founding member of the *Groupe d'Etudes Sartriennes*.

NATASCHA HEATHER LANCASTER is Assistant Professor of French at Wayne State University. She specializes in the treatment of knowledge and philosophy in literature. She has written articles on Jabès, Sartre, and Michaux and is currently preparing a book entitled *Sartre libérateur du lecteur pariah*.

CHARLES D. MINAHEN, Associate Professor of French at Ohio State University, is author of *Vortex/t: The Poetics of Turbulence* and editor of *Figuring Things: Char, Ponge, and Poetry in the Twentieth Century*. He has also published articles on Descartes, Baudelaire, Rimbaud, Mallarmé, Debussy, Char, Ponge, and Sartre.

TORIL MOI, Professor of Literature and Romance Studies at Duke University, is author of *Sexual/Textual Politics: Feminist Literary Theory, Feminist Theory and Simone de Beauvoir*, and *Simone de Beauvoir: The Making of an Intellectual Woman*. She has edited *The Kristeva Reader* and *French Feminist Thought: A Reader* and has also published numerous articles on literary theory, postmodernism, and the sociology of culture.

PHILIP R. WOOD is Associate Professor of French Studies at Rice University. He is the author of *Understanding Jean-Paul Sartre* and of a forthcoming work on the rise and fall of Marxist existentialism entitled *Existentialism to Poststructuralism and the Coming of the Postindustrial Age*. He has also published articles on Mitterrand, Heidegger, Sartre, and Derrida.

# WORKS CITED

Abbas, Ackbar. "The Last Emporium: Verse and Cultural Space." Introduction to *City at the End of Time*, by Ping-Kwan Leung. Hong Kong: Twilight Books, 1992.
Adotevi, Stanilas. *Négritude et négrologues*. Paris: Union Générale d'Editions, 1972.
Alain-Fournier. *Le Grand Meaulnes*. Paris: Livre de poche, 1967.
Alter, Jean. "*Les Mains sales*, ou la clôture du verbe." In *Sartre et la mise en signe*. Edited by Michael Issacharoff and Jean-Claude Vilquin. Lexington, KY: French Forum, 1982.
Althusser, Louis. *Lire le capital*. Paris: Maspero, vol. 1, 1966; vol. 2, 1968.
———. *Pour Marx*. Paris: Maspero, 1965.
Apollinaire, Guillaume. *Œuvres poétiques*. Edited by Marcel Adéma and Michel Décaudin. Paris: Gallimard "Pléiade," 1959.
Appiah, Anthony Kwayne. *In My Father's House: Africa in the Philosophy of Culture*. Oxford: Oxford University Press, 1992.
Aristotle. *The Complete Works of Aristotle*. Vol. 2. Princeton: Princeton University Press, 1985.
Arnold, James A. *Modernism and Negritude: The Poetry and Poetics of Aimé Césaire*. Cambridge: Harvard University Press, 1981.
Ashcroft, Bill, Gareth Griffiths, and Helen Tiffin, eds. *The Post-colonial Studies Reader*. London: Routledge, 1995.
Barnes, Hazel A. *The Literature of Possibility: A Study in Humanist Existentialism*. Lincoln: University of Nebraska Press, 1959.
Barrère, Jean-Bertrand. *La Cure d'amaigrissement du roman*. Paris: Albin Michel, 1964.
Bataille, Georges. "L'Expérience intérieure." In *Œuvres complètes*. Vol. 5. Paris: Gallimard, 1973.
Bauer, George H. "Homo/textuality: Eating/The Other." In *Homosexualities and French Literature: Contexts and Criticisms*. Edited by George Stambolian and Elaine Marks. Ithaca, NY: Cornell University Press, 1979.
Beard, James. *James Beard's American Cookery*. Boston: Little, Brown, 1972.
Beauvoir, Simone de. *La Cérémonie des adieux, suivi de Entretiens avec Jean-Paul Sartre: août-septembre 1974*. Paris: Gallimard, 1981.
———. *Le Deuxième sexe*. Paris: Gallimard "Folio," 1949.
———. *La Force de l'âge*. Paris: Gallimard, 1960.
———. *La Force de l'âge*. Paris: Gallimard "Folio," 1960.

———. *La Force de l'âge*. Paris: Gallimard "Le Livre de Poche," 1960.

———. *La Force des choses*. Paris: Gallimard, 1963.

———. *L'Invitée*. Paris: Gallimard "Folio," 1943.

———. *The Prime of Life*. Translated by Peter Green. Harmondsworth, UK: Penguin, 1988.

———. *The Second Sex*. Translated by H. M. Parshley. Harmondsworth, UK: Penguin, 1984.

———. *She Came to Stay*. Translated by Yvonne Moyse and Roger Senhouse. London: Fontana, 1984.

Bleikasten, André. "Faulkner et le nouveau roman." *Langues Modernes* 60 (1966): 422-32.

Boros, Marie-Denise. "La Métaphore du crabe dans l'œuvre littéraire de Jean-Paul Sartre." *PMLA* 81.5 (October 1966): 446-50.

Boschetti, Anna. *The Intellectual Enterprise*. Translated by Richard C. McCleary. Evanston, IL: Northwestern University Press, 1988.

———. *Sartre et "Les Temps Modernes."* Paris: Minuit, 1985.

Bost, Pierre. "Proust devant une sonate, Sartre devant un air de jazz . . ." *Le Figaro Littéraire* (8 January 1949): 1, 3.

Bourdieu, Pierre. "L'Illusion biographique." *Actes de la Recherche en Sciences Sociales* 62-63.6 (1986): 69-72.

———. *Outline of a Theory of Practice*. Translated by Richard Nice. Cambridge: Cambridge University Press, 1977.

———. *Questions de sociologie*. Paris: Minuit, 1980.

———. *Les Règles de l'art*. Paris: Seuil, 1992.

Buffat, Marc. *Les Mains sales de Jean-Paul Sartre*. Paris: Gallimard, 1991.

Burgelin, Claude, ed. *Lectures de Sartre*. Lyon: Presses Universitaires de Lyon, 1986.

Butor, Michel. *Illustrations III*. Paris: Gallimard, 1973.

———. "Une Technique sociale du roman." *Sartre et les Arts*. Special issue of *Obliques* 24-25 (1981): 67-69.

Carpenter, Edward. *Selected Writings*. Volume I, *Sex*. London: G.M.P, 1984.

Carrouges, Michel. *André Breton and the Basic Concepts of Surrealism*. Translated by Maura Prendergast. University, AL: Alabama University Press, 1974.

———. *André Breton et les données fondamentales du surréalisme*. Paris: Gallimard, 1950.

Chabrol, Claude. *Une Affaire de femmes*. MK2 Productions, Films A2, Films du Camelia and La Sept, 1988.

Charmé, Stuart Zane. *Vulgarity and Authenticity: Dimensions of Otherness in the World of Jean-Paul Sartre*. Amherst: University of Massachusetts Press, 1991.

Chonez, Claudine. "Jean-Paul Sartre, romancier philosophe." *Marianne* (23 November 1938). In *Œuvres romanesques*, by Jean-Paul Sartre. Paris: Gallimard "Pléiade," 1981.

Claiborne, Craig. Letter to the *New Yorker* (14 February 1993): 72.

Clifford, James. "Partial Truths." Introduction to *Writing Cultures: The Poetics and Politics of Ethnography*. Edited by James Clifford and George E. Marcus. Berkeley: University of California Press, 1986.

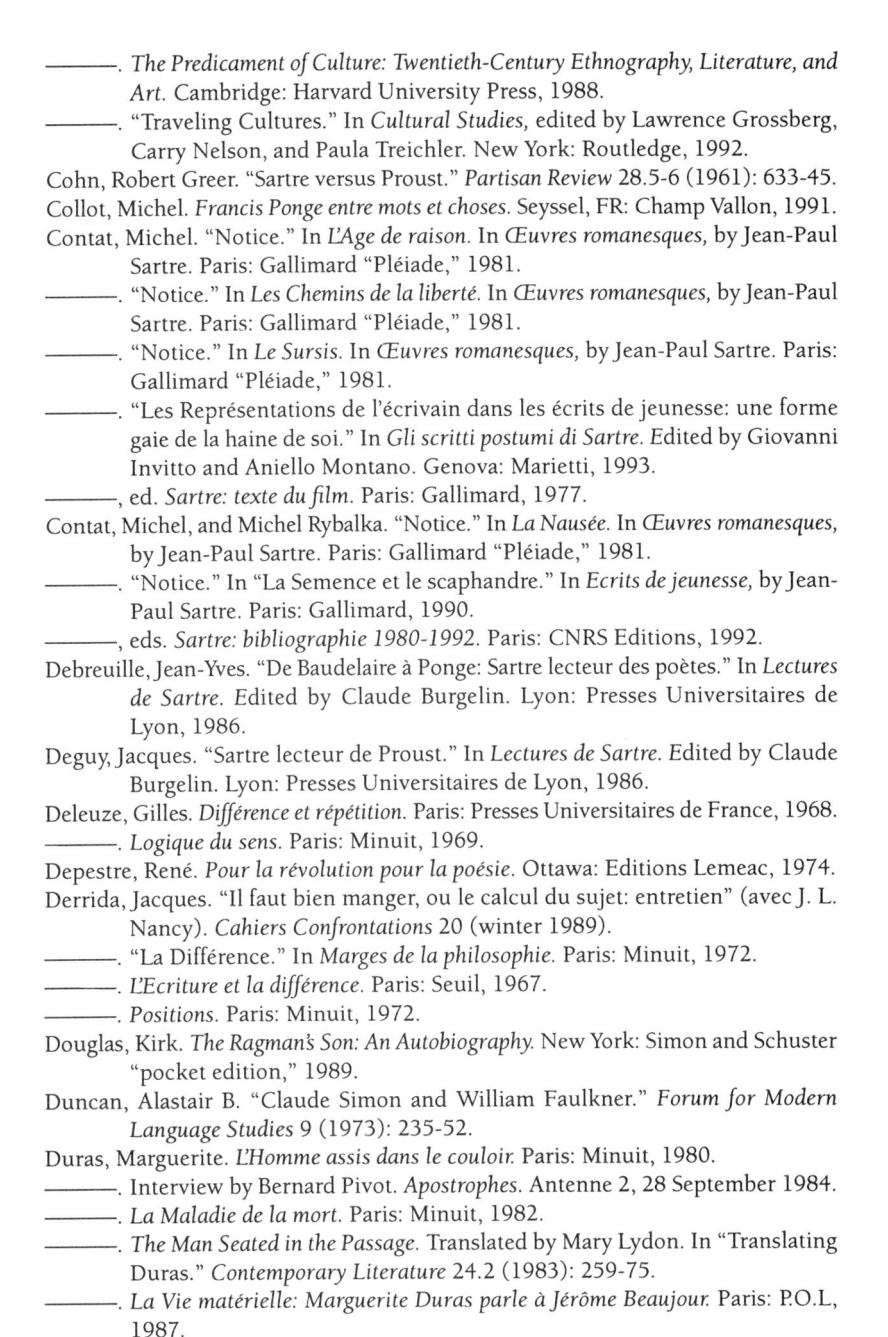

———. *The Predicament of Culture: Twentieth-Century Ethnography, Literature, and Art*. Cambridge: Harvard University Press, 1988.

———. "Traveling Cultures." In *Cultural Studies*, edited by Lawrence Grossberg, Carry Nelson, and Paula Treichler. New York: Routledge, 1992.

Cohn, Robert Greer. "Sartre versus Proust." *Partisan Review* 28.5-6 (1961): 633-45.

Collot, Michel. *Francis Ponge entre mots et choses*. Seyssel, FR: Champ Vallon, 1991.

Contat, Michel. "Notice." In *L'Age de raison*. In *Œuvres romanesques*, by Jean-Paul Sartre. Paris: Gallimard "Pléiade," 1981.

———. "Notice." In *Les Chemins de la liberté*. In *Œuvres romanesques*, by Jean-Paul Sartre. Paris: Gallimard "Pléiade," 1981.

———. "Notice." In *Le Sursis*. In *Œuvres romanesques*, by Jean-Paul Sartre. Paris: Gallimard "Pléiade," 1981.

———. "Les Représentations de l'écrivain dans les écrits de jeunesse: une forme gaie de la haine de soi." In *Gli scritti postumi di Sartre*. Edited by Giovanni Invitto and Aniello Montano. Genova: Marietti, 1993.

———, ed. *Sartre: texte du film*. Paris: Gallimard, 1977.

Contat, Michel, and Michel Rybalka. "Notice." In *La Nausée*. In *Œuvres romanesques*, by Jean-Paul Sartre. Paris: Gallimard "Pléiade," 1981.

———. "Notice." In "La Semence et le scaphandre." In *Ecrits de jeunesse*, by Jean-Paul Sartre. Paris: Gallimard, 1990.

———, eds. *Sartre: bibliographie 1980-1992*. Paris: CNRS Editions, 1992.

Debreuille, Jean-Yves. "De Baudelaire à Ponge: Sartre lecteur des poètes." In *Lectures de Sartre*. Edited by Claude Burgelin. Lyon: Presses Universitaires de Lyon, 1986.

Deguy, Jacques. "Sartre lecteur de Proust." In *Lectures de Sartre*. Edited by Claude Burgelin. Lyon: Presses Universitaires de Lyon, 1986.

Deleuze, Gilles. *Différence et répétition*. Paris: Presses Universitaires de France, 1968.

———. *Logique du sens*. Paris: Minuit, 1969.

Depestre, René. *Pour la révolution pour la poésie*. Ottawa: Editions Lemeac, 1974.

Derrida, Jacques. "Il faut bien manger, ou le calcul du sujet: entretien" (avec J. L. Nancy). *Cahiers Confrontations* 20 (winter 1989).

———. "La Différence." In *Marges de la philosophie*. Paris: Minuit, 1972.

———. *L'Ecriture et la différence*. Paris: Seuil, 1967.

———. *Positions*. Paris: Minuit, 1972.

Douglas, Kirk. *The Ragman's Son: An Autobiography*. New York: Simon and Schuster "pocket edition," 1989.

Duncan, Alastair B. "Claude Simon and William Faulkner." *Forum for Modern Language Studies* 9 (1973): 235-52.

Duras, Marguerite. *L'Homme assis dans le couloir*. Paris: Minuit, 1980.

———. Interview by Bernard Pivot. *Apostrophes*. Antenne 2, 28 September 1984.

———. *La Maladie de la mort*. Paris: Minuit, 1982.

———. *The Man Seated in the Passage*. Translated by Mary Lydon. In "Translating Duras." *Contemporary Literature* 24.2 (1983): 259-75.

———. *La Vie matérielle: Marguerite Duras parle à Jérôme Beaujour*. Paris: P.O.L, 1987.

Fanon, Frantz. *Black Skin White Masks*. Translated by Charles Mackmann. New York: Grove Press, 1967.

———. *Peau noire, masques blancs*. Paris: Seuil, 1953.

Fast, Howard. *Spartacus*. New York: Dell, 1951.

Fernandez, Dominique. *Il Mito dell'America negli intellettuali italiani*. Caltanissetta-Roma: Sciascia, 1969.

Fernandez, Ramon. *Messages*. First series. Paris: Gallimard, 1926.

Ferry, Luc, and Alain Renaut. *Heidegger et les modernes*. Paris: Bernard Grasset, 1988.

———. *La Pensée 68: essai sur l'anti-humanisme contemporain*. Paris: Gallimard, 1985.

Foucault, Michel. *L'Archéologie du savoir*. Paris: Gallimard, 1969.

———. *The Use of Pleasure*. Translated by Robert Hurley. New York: Pantheon, 1985.

Freud, Sigmund. In *The Interpretation of Dreams*. The Standard Edition of the Complete Psychological Works of Sigmund Freud. Vols. 4 and 5. London: The Hogarth Press, 1953.

———. In *Project for a Scientific Psychology*. The Standard Edition of the Complete Psychological Works of Sigmund Freud. Vol. 1. London: The Hogarth Press, 1966.

———. In *Studies on Hysteria*. The Standard Edition of the Complete Psychological Works of Sigmund Freud. Vol. 2. London: The Hogarth Press, 1955.

Genette, Gérard. *Figures III*. Paris: Seuil, 1972.

Gerassi, John. *Jean-Paul Sartre: Hated Conscience of His Century*. Vol. 1. Chicago: University of Chicago Press, 1989.

Glissant, Edouard. *Le Discours antillais*. Paris: Seuil, 1981.

Goldberg, David, ed. *Anatomy of Racism*. Minneapolis: University of Minnesota Press, 1990.

Goldthorpe, Rhiannon. *Sartre: Literature and Theory*. Cambridge: Cambridge University Press, 1984.

———. "Understanding the Committed Writer." In *The Cambridge Companion to Sartre*. Edited by Christina Howells. Cambridge: Cambridge University Press, 1992.

Habermas, Jürgen. *The Philosophical Discourse of Modernity*. Translated by Frederick Lawrence. Cambridge: MIT Press, 1987.

Harvey, Robert. *Search for a Father: Sartre, Paternity, and the Question of Ethics*. Ann Arbor: University of Michigan Press, 1991.

Hegel, Georg Wilhelm Friedrich. *Lectures on the Philosophy of Religion*. New York: Humanities Press, 1978.

———. *Phenomenology of Spirit*. Translated by Arnold V. Miller. Oxford: Oxford University Press, 1981.

———. *Science of Logic*. Translated by Arnold V. Miller. Atlantic Highlands, NJ: Humanities Press, 1989.

Heidegger, Martin. *Essays in Metaphysics: Identity and Difference*. Translated by Kurt F. Leidecker. New York: Philosophical Library, 1960.

———. *Introduction to Metaphysics*. Translated by Ralph Manheim. New Haven: Yale University Press, 1959.

———. "Letter on Humanism." In *Basic Writings*. New York: Harper and Row, 1977.

———. *Nietzsche*. Vol. 3. Translated by Joan Stambaugh, David Farrell Krell, and Frank A. Capuzzi. San Francisco: Harper and Row, 1987.

———. *Nietzsche*. Vols. 3 and 4. Translated by Frank Capuzzi. New York: Harper and Row, 1982.

Hill, Charles G. *Jean-Paul Sartre: Freedom and Commitment*. New York: Peter Lang, 1992.

Hollier, Denis. "L'Adieu aux plumes." In *Les Dépossédés*. Paris: Minuit, 1993.

Hoven, Adrian van den. "*Nausea*: Plunging Below the Surface." In *Sartre Alive*. Edited by Ronald Aronson and Adrian van den Hoven. Detroit: Wayne State University Press, 1991.

Howells, Christina. "Sartre and Freud." *French Studies* 33 (1979): 157-76.

———. *Sartre: The Necessity of Freedom*. Cambridge: Cambridge University Press, 1988.

Huston, John. *An Open Book*. London: Macmillan, 1981.

Idt, Geneviève. "*Les Chemins de la liberté*: les toboggans du romanesque." *Sartre*. Special issue of *Obliques* 18-19 (1979): 75-94.

———. "Les Modèles de l'écriture dans *Les Chemins de la liberté*." *Etudes sartriennes*, I. In *Cahiers de Sémiotique Textuelle* 2 (1984).

———. "*La Nausée*": Sartre, analyse critique par Geneviève Idt. Paris: Hatier, 1971.

———. "Préface." *Œuvres romanesques*, by Jean-Paul Sartre. Paris: Gallimard "Pléiade," 1981.

Irele, Abiole. *The African Experience in Literature and Ideology*. Bloomington: Indiana University Press, 1990.

———. "In Praise of Alienation." In *The Surreptitious Speech: Presence Africaine and the Politics of Otherness 1947-1987*. Edited by V. Y. Mudimbe. Chicago: Chicago University Press, 1992.

Izenberg, Gerald N. *The Existentialist Critique of Freud: The Crisis of Autonomy*. Princeton: Princeton University Press, 1976.

Jack, Dana Crowley. *Silencing The Self, Women and Depression*. Cambridge: Harvard University Press, 1991.

Jameson, Fredric. "On 'Cultural Studies.'" *Social Text* 34 (1993): 17-52.

———. *The Political Unconscious*. London: Methuen, 1981.

———. "The Sartrean Origin." *Sartre Studies International* 1.1-2 (1995).

Jones, Ernest. *Sigmund Freud: Life and Work*. Vol. 1. London: The Hogarth Press, 1953.

Judt, Tony. *Un Passé imparfait*. Paris: Fayard, 1993.

Junod, Tom. "On Men and Mollusks." *GQ* (May 1992): 170-73.

Kant, Immanuel. *Critique of Pure Reason*. Translated by Norman Kemp Smith. London: Macmillan, 1978.

Kauppi, Niilo. *French Intellectual Nobility: Institutional and Symbolic Transformation in the Post-Sartrian Era*. Albany: State University of New York Press, 1996.

Labriolle, J. de. "De Faulkner à Simon." *Revue de Littérature Comparée* 53 (1979): 358-88.
Lacan, Jacques. *Ecrits*. Paris: Seuil, 1966.
Laing, R. D. *The Divided Self, An Existential Study in Sanity and Madness*. Harmondsworth, UK: Penguin Books, 1965.
Laplanche, Jean, and Jean-Bertrand Pontalis. *The Language of Psychoanalysis*. Translated by Donald Nicholson-Smith. London: The Hogarth Press, 1973.
*Larousse dictionnaire moderne, français-anglais anglais-français*. Paris: Librairie Larousse, 1960.
Lash, Scott. *Sociology of Postmodernism*. London: Routledge, 1990.
Lavers, Annette. "Sartre and Freud." *French Studies* 41 (1987): 298-317.
Lecarme, Jacques. "Sartre lecteur de Maupassant?" In *Lectures de Sartre*. Edited by Claude Burgelin. Lyon: Presses Universitaires de Lyon, 1986.
Le Doeuff, Michèle. *L'Etude et le rouet: des femmes, de la philosophie, etc*. Paris: Seuil, 1989.
———. *Hipparchia's Choice: An Essay Concerning Women, Philosophy, etc*. Translated by Trista Selous. Oxford: Blackwell, 1991.
Lehmann, Rosamond. *Dusty Answer*. Harmondsworth, UK: Penguin, 1991.
Lévinas, Emmanuel. *Difficile liberté: essais sur le judaïsme*. Paris: Albin Michel, 1963.
———. *Difficult Freedom: Essays on Judaism*. Translated by Sean Hand. Baltimore: Johns Hopkins University Press, 1990.
Lionnet, Françoise. *Autobiographical Voices: Race, Gender, Self-Portraiture*. Ithaca: Cornell University Press, 1989.
Lyotard, Jean-François. "False Flights in Literature." In *Toward the Postmodern*. Translated by Robert Harvey. Edited by Robert Harvey and Mark S. Roberts. Atlantic Highlands, NJ: Humanities Press, 1993.
Magny, Claude-Edmonde. *L'Age du roman américain*. Paris: Seuil, 1948.
Masson, Pierre. "Sartre lecteur de Gide: authenticité et engagement." In *Lectures de Sartre*. Edited by Claude Burgelin. Lyon: Presses Universitaires de Lyon, 1986.
Metellus, Jean. "Sartre et la négritude." *Sartre*. Special issue of *Obliques* 18-19 (1979): 287-90.
Michaud, Régis. *Le Roman américain d'aujourd'hui*. Paris: Boivin, 1926.
Michel, Jean-Claude. *Les Ecrivains noirs et le surréalisme*. Québec: Editions Naaman, 1982.
Minahen, Charles D. "Crime: A Floating Signifier in Sartre's *Les Mouches*." In *Sartre*. Edited by Christina Howells. London: Longman, 1995.
Mohanty, Chandra Talpade. "Under Western Eyes: Feminist Scholarship and Colonial Discourse." *Boundary 2* 12.3-13.1 (spring-fall 1984): 333-58.
Moi, Toril. *Simone de Beauvoir: The Making of an Intellectual Woman*. Oxford, UK and Cambridge, MA: Blackwell, 1993.
Nietzsche, Friedrich. *The Will to Power*. Translated by Walter Kaufmann and R. J. Hollingdale. New York: Vintage Books, 1968.

*Le Nouveau Petit Robert*. Paris: Dictionnaires Le Robert, 1993.
Pacaly, Josette. *Sartre au miroir*. Paris: Klincksieck, 1980.
Paglia, Camille. *Sex, Art, and American Culture*. New York: Vintage Books, 1992.
Pellegrin, Jean. "L'Objet à deux faces dans *La Nausée*." *Revue des Sciences Humaines* 113 (1964): 87-97.
Ping-Kwan, Leung. *City at the End of Time*. Hong Kong: Twilight Books, 1992.
Ponge, Francis. *Le Parti pris des choses*. In *Tome premier*. Paris: Gallimard, 1965.
———. *Pièces. Le Grand Recueil 3*. Paris: Gallimard, 1961.
———. *The Power of Language*. Translated by Serge Gavronsky. Berkeley: University of California Press, 1979.
———. *La Rage de l'expression*. In *Tome premier*. Paris: Gallimard, 1965.
———. *Taking the Side of Things*. In *The Voice of Things*. Translated by Beth Archer. New York: McGraw Hill, 1972.
Pouillon, Jean. *Temps et roman*. Paris: Gallimard, 1946.
Prince, Gerald Joseph. *Métaphysique et technique dans l'œuvre romanesque de Sartre*. Geneva: Droz, 1968.
———. "On Narratology: Criteria, Corpus, Context." *Narrative* 3 (1995): 73-84.
Proust, Marcel. *Within a Budding Grove*. Translated by C. K. Scott Moncrieff and Terence Kilmartin. Revised by D. J. Enright. New York: Random House, 1992.
Pucciani, Oreste. "Sartre, Genet et l'homosexualité: ébauche d'une lecture homosexuelle du *Saint Genet*." *Les Temps Modernes* 46 (1990): 638-57.
Raimond, Michel. *La Crise du roman: des lendemains du naturalisme aux années vingt*. Paris: Corti, 1966.
Ricoeur, Paul. *De l'interprétation: essai sur Freud*. Paris: Seuil, 1965.
———. *Freud and Philosophy: An Essay on Interpretation*. Translated by Denis Savage. New Haven: Yale University Press, 1970.
Rivière, Jacques. "La Crise du concept de littérature." *La Nouvelle Revue Française* (1 February 1924).
Rosello, Mireille. *Littérature et identité créole aux Antilles*. Paris: Karthala, 1992.
Sage, Lorna. *Women in the House of Fiction: Post-War Women Novelists*. London: Macmillan, 1992.
Said, Edward. "Representing the Colonized: Anthropology's Interlocutors." *Critical Inquiry* 15.2 (winter 1989): 205-25.
Saisselin, Rémy. "Bouville ou l'anti-Combray." *French Review* 33.3 (1960): 232-38.
Sartre, Jean-Paul. "American Novelists in French Eyes." *The Atlantic Monthly* 178.2 (August 1946): 115.
———. "'Aminadab' or the Fantastic Considered as a Language." In *Literary and Philosophical Essays*. Translated by Annette Michelson. London: Rider and Company, 1955.
———. "'Aminadab,' ou du fantastique considéré comme un langage." In *Situations, I*. Paris: Gallimard, 1947.
———. *Anti-Semite and Jew*. Translated by George J. Becker. New York: Schocken Books, 1974.

———. "Autoportrait à soixante-dix ans." In *Situations, X*. Paris: Gallimard, 1976.
———. *Being and Nothingness: An Essay on Phenomenological Ontology*. Translated by Hazel E. Barnes. London: Methuen, 1958. Reprint 1972.
———. *Being and Nothingness: An Essay on Phenomenological Ontology*. Translated by Hazel E. Barnes. New York: Philosophical Library, 1956. Reprint Washington Square Press, 1966, 1972, 1992.
———. *Cahiers pour une morale*. Paris: Gallimard, 1983.
———. *Les Carnets de la drôle de guerre*. Paris: Gallimard, 1983.
———. *Critique de la raison dialectique (précédé de Questions de méthode), I: théorie des ensembles pratiques*. Paris: Gallimard, 1960.
———. *Critique de la raison dialectique, II: l'intelligibilité de l'histoire*. Paris: Gallimard, 1985.
———. *Critique of Dialectical Reason, I: Theory of Practical Ensembles*. Translated by Alan Sheridan-Smith. Edited by Jonathan Rée. London: New Left Books, 1976.
———. *Dirty Hands. No Exit and Three Other Plays*. Translated by Lionel Abel. New York: Vintage Books, 1955.
———. *Esquisse d'une théorie des émotions*. Paris: Hermann, 1965.
———. *L'Etre et le néant: essai d'ontologie phénoménologique*. Paris: Gallimard, 1943.
———. *L'Etre et le néant: essai d'ontologie phénoménologique*. Paris: Gallimard "Tel," 1943.
———. *Existentialism and Humanism*. Translated by Philip Mairet. New York: Haskell House Publishers, 1977.
———. *L'Existentialisme est un humanisme*. Paris: Nagel, 1946.
———. *The Family Idiot*. Translated by Carol Cosman. Chicago: University of Chicago Press, vol. 1, 1981; vol. 2, 1987; vol. 3, 1989.
———. "L'Homme au magnétophone." In *Situations, IX*. Paris: Gallimard, 1972.
———. "L'Homme et les choses." In *Situations, I*. Paris: Gallimard, 1947.
———. *Huis clos. Huis clos suivi de Les Mouches*. Paris: Gallimard "Folio," 1947.
———. *L'Idiot de la famille: Gustave Flaubert de 1821 à 1851*. Paris: Gallimard, vols. 1 and 2, 1971; vol. 3, 1972, revised ed., 1988.
———. *L'Imaginaire: psychologie phénoménologique de l'imagination*. Paris: Gallimard "Idées," 1940. Reprint 1966.
———. *Imagination: A Psychological Critique*. Translated by Forrest Williams. Ann Arbor: University of Michigan Press, 1962.
———. *Lettres au Castor et à quelques autres*. 2 vols. Edited by Simone de Beauvoir. Paris: Gallimard, 1983.
———. *Les Mains sales*. Paris: Gallimard, 1948.
———. *Mallarmé: la lucidité et sa face d'ombre*. Paris: Gallimard, 1986.
———. "*Moby Dick* d'Herman Melville." In *Les Ecrits de Sartre*, by Michel Contat and Michel Rybalka. Paris: Gallimard, 1970.
———. *Les Mots*. Paris: Gallimard, 1964.
———. *Nausea*. Translated by Lloyd Alexander. New York: New Directions, 1964.
———. *Nourritures suivi d'extraits de La Nausée*. Paris: Jacques Damase, 1949.

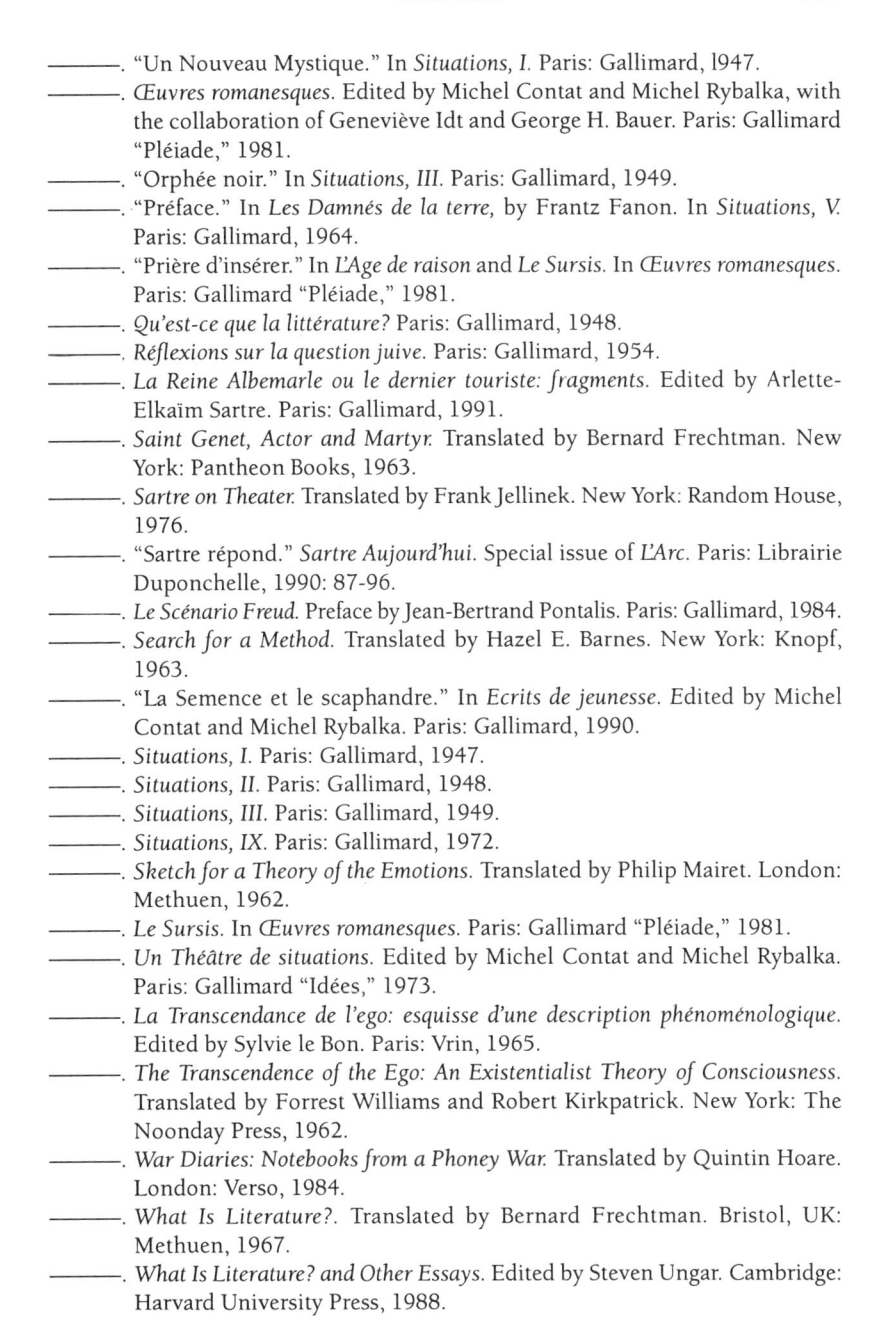

———. "Un Nouveau Mystique." In *Situations, I*. Paris: Gallimard, l947.
———. *Œuvres romanesques*. Edited by Michel Contat and Michel Rybalka, with the collaboration of Geneviève Idt and George H. Bauer. Paris: Gallimard "Pléiade," 1981.
———. "Orphée noir." In *Situations, III*. Paris: Gallimard, 1949.
———. "Préface." In *Les Damnés de la terre*, by Frantz Fanon. In *Situations, V*. Paris: Gallimard, 1964.
———. "Prière d'insérer." In *L'Age de raison* and *Le Sursis*. In *Œuvres romanesques*. Paris: Gallimard "Pléiade," 1981.
———. *Qu'est-ce que la littérature?* Paris: Gallimard, 1948.
———. *Réflexions sur la question juive*. Paris: Gallimard, 1954.
———. *La Reine Albemarle ou le dernier touriste: fragments*. Edited by Arlette-Elkaïm Sartre. Paris: Gallimard, 1991.
———. *Saint Genet, Actor and Martyr*. Translated by Bernard Frechtman. New York: Pantheon Books, 1963.
———. *Sartre on Theater*. Translated by Frank Jellinek. New York: Random House, 1976.
———. "Sartre répond." *Sartre Aujourd'hui*. Special issue of *L'Arc*. Paris: Librairie Duponchelle, 1990: 87-96.
———. *Le Scénario Freud*. Preface by Jean-Bertrand Pontalis. Paris: Gallimard, 1984.
———. *Search for a Method*. Translated by Hazel E. Barnes. New York: Knopf, 1963.
———. "La Semence et le scaphandre." In *Ecrits de jeunesse*. Edited by Michel Contat and Michel Rybalka. Paris: Gallimard, 1990.
———. *Situations, I*. Paris: Gallimard, 1947.
———. *Situations, II*. Paris: Gallimard, 1948.
———. *Situations, III*. Paris: Gallimard, 1949.
———. *Situations, IX*. Paris: Gallimard, 1972.
———. *Sketch for a Theory of the Emotions*. Translated by Philip Mairet. London: Methuen, 1962.
———. *Le Sursis*. In *Œuvres romanesques*. Paris: Gallimard "Pléiade," 1981.
———. *Un Théâtre de situations*. Edited by Michel Contat and Michel Rybalka. Paris: Gallimard "Idées," 1973.
———. *La Transcendance de l'ego: esquisse d'une description phénoménologique*. Edited by Sylvie le Bon. Paris: Vrin, 1965.
———. *The Transcendence of the Ego: An Existentialist Theory of Consciousness*. Translated by Forrest Williams and Robert Kirkpatrick. New York: The Noonday Press, 1962.
———. *War Diaries: Notebooks from a Phoney War*. Translated by Quintin Hoare. London: Verso, 1984.
———. *What Is Literature?*. Translated by Bernard Frechtman. Bristol, UK: Methuen, 1967.
———. *What Is Literature? and Other Essays*. Edited by Steven Ungar. Cambridge: Harvard University Press, 1988.

———. *The Words*. Translated by Bernard Frechtman. New York: Braziller, 1964.
Sartre, Jean-Paul, and Benny Lévy. "L'Espoir maintenant . . ." Parts 1-3. *Le Nouvel Observateur* 800 (10 March 1980): 18-19, 56-60; 801 (17 March 1980): 52-58; 802 (24 March 1980): 55-60.
Scharfman, Ronnie Leah. *Engagement and the Language of the Subject in the Poetry of Aimé Césaire*. Gainesville: University of Florida Monographs, 1980.
Schehr, Lawrence R. "Sartre as Midwife." In *Alcibiades at the Door: Gay Discourses in French Literature*. Stanford: Stanford University Press, 1995.
Scriven, Michael. "Television Images of Sartre." *French Cultural Studies* 3 (1992): 87-92.
Senghor, Léopold. *Liberté I: négritude et humanisme*. Paris: Seuil, 1964.
Siebers, Tobin. *Cold War Criticism and the Politics of Skepticism*. Oxford: Oxford University Press, 1993.
Simon, Claude. *L'Acacia*. Paris: Minuit, 1989.
Spiegelberg, Herbert. "Sartre's Last Word on Ethics in Phenomenological Perspective." In *Sartre: An Investigation of Some Major Themes*. Edited by Simon Glynn. Aldershot, UK: Avebury, 1987.
Sykes, Stuart. *Les Romans de Claude Simon*. Paris: Minuit, 1979.
Thibaudet, Albert. "Réflexions sur le roman." *La Nouvelle Revue Française* (1 August 1912): 9 f.
Ungar, Steven. "Sartre, Ponge and the Ghost of Husserl." *Sub-Stance* 8 (1974): 139-50.
Vercier, Bruno. "Traduit de l'étranger." In *La Littérature en France depuis 1945*. Paris: Bordas, 1974.
Verne, Jules. *Vingt Mille Lieues sous les mers*. Illustrated with 111 drawings by de Neuville. Paris: J. Hetzel, 1870.
Verstraeten, Pierre. *Violence et éthique: esquisse d'une critique de la morale dialectique à partir du théâtre politique de Sartre*. Paris: Gallimard, 1972.
Vircondelet, Alain. *Duras*. Paris: François Bourin, 1991.
Williams, Patrick, and Laura Chrisman, eds. *Colonial Discourse and Post-colonial Theory*. New York: Columbia University Press, 1994.
Williams, Raymond. *Marxism and Literature*. Oxford: Oxford University Press, 1977.
Wood, Philip R. *Understanding Jean-Paul Sartre*. Columbia: University of South Carolina Press, 1990.
Zimmerman, Eugenia Noik. "The Metamorphosis of Adam: Nausea and Things in Sartre and Proust." In *Twentieth Century French Fiction: Essays for Germaine Brée*. Edited by George Stambolian. New Brunswick, NJ: Rutgers University Press, 1975.
———. "*Some of These Days*: Sartre's Petite Phrase." *Contemporary Literature* 11 (1970): 375-88.

## INDEX

Alain-Fournier, 127 n. 17
Althusser, Louis, 9, 166, 178, 179, 181, 182-83, 185, 187, 188-89
Apollinaire, Guillaume, 73, 130, 132
Appiah, Anthony, 100, 102, 108 n. 10
Aragon, Louis, 74, 77, 87 n. 15
Aristotle, 184, 190

Bakhtin, Mikhail, 104
Barthes, Roland, 5, 144
Bataille, Georges, 59, 67 n. 9, 90 n. 30, 178, 193 n. 20
Baudelaire, Charles, 62, 64, 141
Baudrillard, Jean, 194 n. 37
Beard, James, 142
Beauvoir, Simone de (Castor), 2, 26 n. 1, 48 n. 4, 49 n. 5, 52 n. 21, 71, 72, 77, 111, 123-25, 135, 144
    **Works:**
    *La Cérémonie des adieux [Adieux: A Farewell to Sartre]*, 77, 86 n. 2, 91 n. 34, 129, 131-32, 134-35, 136-37, 141
    *Le Deuxième sexe [The Second Sex]*, 111, 124, 128 n. 19
    *La Force de l'âge [The Prime of Life]*, 71-72, 75, 76, 87 n. 14, 88 nn. 21, 24, 127 n. 17, 161 n. 9
    *La Force des choses [Force of Circumstance]*, 50 n. 8
    *L'Invitée [She Came to Stay]*, 7-8, 77, 88 n. 24, 111, 112, 117, 118-22, 128 n. 17
Bergson, Henri, 91 n. 30
Blanchot, Maurice, 59, 67 n. 9
Boethius, 50 n. 13
Du Bos, Charles, 79
Bourdieu, Pierre, 3, 4, 86 nn. 8, 9, 90 n. 28
Breton, André, 99, 108 n. 13
Breuer, Josef, 13, 17, 19, 21, 23, 24, 25
Brunschwicg, Léon, 82, 91 n. 30
Butor, Michel, 84, 148

Camus, Albert, 90 nn. 29, 30
Carpenter, Edward, 143
Caruso, Paolo, 48 n. 2
Céline, Louis-Ferdinand, 74, 87 n.15, 88 n. 22
Césaire, Aimé, 7, 108 n. 13
Chabrol, Claude, 127 n. 10
Charcot, Jean-Martin, 16, 19, 22, 24
Chonez, Claudine, 91 n. 34
Cicero, 40
Claiborne, Craig, 129-30, 142
Colette, 54-55
Contat, Michel, 49 n. 4, 73, 86 n. 6, 87 n. 10, 91 n. 34
Contat, Michel, and Michel Rybalka, 87 n. 15, 162 nn. 23, 24
Curtis, Tony, 137-38, 139

Deleuze, Gilles, 9, 166, 170, 171, 180-81, 182
de Man, Paul, 2, 5
Derrida, Jacques, 5, 37, 166, 167, 168, 170, 171, 173, 174, 178, 179, 189, 190-91, 192 n. 13, 194 n. 37, 195 n. 41
Descartes, René, 136, 167, 178
Dilthey, Wilhelm, 14, 16, 17, 27 nn. 8, 10
Dos Passos, John, 7, 71, 72, 74, 77-78, 82-83, 84, 88 n. 21, 90 n. 29, 91-92 n. 37
Dostoevski, Mikhail, 88 n. 24
Douglas, Kirk, 137-38, 139, 142
Duhamel, Georges, 86 n. 3
Duras, Marguerite, 8, 10 n. 9, 84, 147, 148, 157, 162 n. 26
  Works:
  *Hiroshima, mon amour*, 158, 163 n. 29
  *L'Homme assis dans le couloir* [*The Man Seated in the Passage*], 157-59, 163 n. 29
  *Moderato cantabile*, 158, 163 n. 29
  *La Vie matérielle* [*Practicalities*], 160 n. 1

Elkaïm-Sartre, Arlette, 39, 48 n. 4, 49 n. 5, 142

Fanon, Frantz, 7, 107 n. 3, 108 n. 9
Fast, Howard, 136, 137
Faulkner, William, 7, 71, 72, 74, 78, 82-85, 88 n. 21, 90 nn. 27, 29, 91-92 n. 37, 92 n. 39
Fernandez, Ramon, 79, 90 n. 27, 90 n. 29
Flaubert, Gustave, 18, 25, 29-36, 54-55, 62, 139, 191 n. 1
Fliess, Wilhelm, 13, 16, 17, 19, 21, 22, 23, 25
Foucault, Michel, 1, 3, 4, 5, 9 n. 1, 166, 171, 188-89, 194 n. 37, 194-95 n. 38
Freud, Jakob, 16, 17, 21-22, 25
Freud, Sigmund, 6, 11-25, 26 n. 5, 27 n. 10, 28 n. 12, 88 n. 22

Gaulle, Charles de, 4
Genet, Jean, 8, 62, 91 n. 34, 141, 144
Genette, Gérard, 90 n. 29
Gerassi, John, 39, 48 n. 4, 49 n. 5
Gide, André, 74, 78, 80, 87 nn. 11, 15, 136, 137, 143, 144
Giraudoux, Jean, 90 n. 30
Goethe, Johann Wolfgang von, 22
Guille, Pierre, 139, 141

Habermas, Jürgen, 168
Hammett, Dashiell, 72, 88 n. 24
Hawthorne, Nathaniel, 162 n. 21
Hegel, Georg Wilhelm Friedrich, 91 n. 30, 144, 168, 171-78, 179, 181, 183-84, 187, 189, 190, 193 nn. 17, 19, 21
Heidegger, Martin, 2, 8, 73, 75, 82, 84, 90 n. 30, 166-70, 171, 173, 179, 191-92 n. 2, 192 nn. 4, 11, 192-93 n. 15, 195 n. 39
Helmholtz, Hermann, 15,
Hemingway, Ernest, 71, 72, 74, 78, 83, 84, 88 n. 21
Herder, Johann, 101
Husserl, Edmund, 12, 29, 66 n. 2, 73, 82, 84, 171
Huston, John, 6, 11, 26 n. 1

Idt, Geneviève, 77, 86 n. 6, 87 nn. 11, 15

Jameson, Fredric, 9, 101, 165, 166, 169, 179, 183, 185
Jaspers, Karl, 14, 27 n. 10
Joyce, James, 74, 87-88 n. 17

Kant, Immanuel, 91 n. 30, 167, 173, 175, 178, 184-85

Lacan, Jacques, 5, 20, 33, 36-37
Laing, R. D., 59, 67-68 n. 11
Lalande, André, 82
Lanson, Gustave, 79
Larbaud, Valéry, 72-73
Lehmann, Rosamond, 127 n. 17
Lévinas, Emmanuel, 161 n. 13
Lévi-Strauss, Claude, 10 n. 9
Lévy, Benny, 39, 49 nn. 5, 6
Lyotard, Jean-François, 160 n. 2

Magny, Claude-Edmonde, 78, 83-84, 85, 91-92 n. 37
Mallarmé, Stéphane, 31, 141
Malraux, André, 72-73, 74, 78, 87 nn. 11, 15
Martin du Gard, Roger, 77

Marx, Karl, 8, 178, 182
Maupassant, Guy de, 54-55, 87 n. 11
Mauriac, François, 83, 84, 88 n. 24, 90 nn. 29, 30, 91 n. 34
Melville, Herman, 91 n. 34, 156, 157, 162 n. 23
Meyerson, Emile, 82
Meynert, Theodore, 13, 15, 16, 17, 19-21, 22, 23, 25
Michaud, Régis, 72
Morand, Paul, 71, 86 n. 3

Nietzsche, Friedrich, 168, 178, 184, 192 n. 4, 194 n. 32
Nizan, Paul, 8, 72, 81, 82, 83, 88 n. 22, 133, 136, 139, 141, 162 n. 24
*Nouvelle Revue Française* (*N. R. F.*), 72, 73, 79, 81, 90 n. 27

Olivier, Laurence, 138

Parain, Brice, 90-91 n. 30
Perec, Georges, 73, 85
Ping-Kwan, Leung, 106
Ponge, Francis, 7, 53-65, 91 n. 30
    **Works:**
    "La Lessiveuse" ["The Washing Machine"], 54, 57-58, 63
    "Le Mimosa," 62-63, 68-69 n. 17
    *Le Parti pris des choses* [*Taking the Side of Things*], 61, 66 n. 1, 68 n. 12, 129, 161 n. 14; "The Gymnast," 57; "Introduction to the Pebble," 55-56, 59, 60-61; "The Young Mother," 56-57
    "Some Reasons for Writing," 67 n. 7, 69 n. 19
Pouillon, Jean, 83, 90 n. 29
Protagoras, 167-68
Proust, Marcel, 8, 73, 74, 78, 81-83, 85, 87 nn. 11, 15, 140, 147, 148, 149, 150, 151, 154, 157

Ricoeur, Paul, 28 n. 12
Rimbaud, Arthur, 136
Rivière, Jacques, 79, 90 n. 27
Robbe-Grillet, Alain, 10 n. 9, 84
Romains, Jules, 74, 77, 87 n. 15
Rybalka, Michel, 146 n. 25

Said, Edward, 109 n. 26
Sarraute, Nathalie, 84
Sartre, Jean-Paul
    **Works:**
    *L'Age de raison* [*The Age of Reason*], 77, 143, 151
    "American Novelists in French Eyes," 77
    *Baudelaire*, 12

*Cahiers pour une morale [Ethics Notebooks]*, 28 nn. 15, 17, 39, 48 n. 4, 51 n. 13
"Le Carnet 'Dupuis,'" 28 n. 15
*Les Carnets de la drôle de guerre [War Diaries: Notebooks from a Phoney War]*, 16, 28 n. 15, 86 n. 9, 87 n. 15, 132-34
*Les Chemins de la liberté*, 77, 81, 87 nn. 11, 15, 91 n. 34, 136, 142, 144
*Critique de la raison dialectique [Critique of Dialectical Reason]*, 4, 12, 17, 166, 171, 179, 186-87, 189, 190
*Critique de la raison dialectique, I*, 188, 195 n. 40
*Critique de la raison dialectique, II*, 28 n. 15, 195 n. 39
*Drôle d'amitié*, 78, 142, 144
*Ecrits de jeunesse*, 162 n. 24
*L'Enfance d'un chef*, 76
*Esquisse d'une théorie des émotions [Sketch for a Theory of the Emotions]*, 12-13
*L'Etre et le néant [Being and Nothingness]*, 1, 7, 11, 12-13, 19, 20, 27 n. 7, 32-33, 37, 39, 43, 51 n. 13, 75, 79, 81, 82, 112-17, 120, 122, 123, 125, 131, 136, 152, 156, 158, 169-71, 190, 192 n. 11
*L'Existentialisme est un humanisme [Existentialism and Humanism]*, 117
*Huis clos [No Exit]*, 44, 162 n. 18
*L'Idiot de la famille [The Family Idiot]*, 2, 6, 16, 25, 29-32, 34-36, 37, 53, 135, 154, 191 n. 1, 193 n. 25
*L'Imaginaire [Psychology of the Imagination]*, 82
*L'Imagination [Imagination]*, 68 n. 13, 154
*Lettres au Castor*, 26 n. 1
*Les Mains sales [Dirty Hands]*, 6, 40-47, 48 n. 2, 50 n. 13
*La Mort dans l'âme [Troubled Sleep]*, 78, 142, 144, 146 n. 25
*Les Mots [The Words]*, 21, 72, 74, 140, 141, 154, 162 n. 17
*Les Mouches [The Flies]*, 50 n. 13
*Le Mur [The Wall]*, 84
*La Nausée [Nausea]*, 31, 75, 81, 84, 87 n. 15, 91 n. 34, 130, 134, 135, 136, 139-41, 151, 153-55, 157, 161-62 n. 16
*Nourritures*, 143
*Orphée noir [Black Orpheus]*, 7, 93-101, 102-4, 105, 107
*Qu'est-ce que la littérature? [What Is Literature?]*, 4, 62, 65, 67 n. 9, 69 n. 22, 74, 79, 90 n. 27, 124, 127 n. 12
*Questions de méthode [Search for a Method]*, 17, 191 n. 1
*La Reine Albemarle*, 142
*Saint Genet, Actor and Martyr*, 12, 53, 68 n. 16, 134
*Le Scénario Freud*, 6, 11-13, 16-25
"La Semence et le scaphandre," 146 n. 25, 156
*Situations*, 7
*Situations, I*, 74, 75-76, 77, 79, 80, 81-83, 84, 85, 88 n. 21, 88-89 n. 24, 90 nn. 27, 29, 90-91 n. 30, 92 n. 37; "Aminadab," 67 n. 9, 90 n. 29; "L'Homme et les choses," 53-65, 66 nn. 1, 2, 5, 67 n. 7, 67-68 n. 11, 161 n. 14; "Un Nouveau Mystique," 67 n. 9
*Situations, II*, 74, 75-76, 87-88 n. 17

*Situations, IX*, 27 n. 7; "L'Homme au magnétophone," 28 n. 20
*Situations, X*, 48-49 n. 4
*Le Sursis [The Reprieve]*, 77-78, 143, 149-52, 161 n. 9
*Un Théâtre de situations [Sartre on Theater]*, 48 n. 2, 50 n. 10
*La Transcendance de l'ego [The Transcendence of the Ego]*, 12, 29-30, 32, 33, 34, 169
Saussure, Ferdinand de, 180
Scudéry, Madeleine de, 148
Sembene, Ousmane, 105
Senghor, Léopold Sédar, 7, 93, 107
Simon, Claude, 1, 9 n. 2, 10 n. 9, 84, 85, 92 n. 39
Spitzer, Leo, 90 n. 29
Steinbeck, John, 78, 91 n. 37
Suarès, André, 79

Thibaudet, Albert, 79, 90 n. 27
Todorov, Tzvetan, 79
Trumbo, Dalton, 138, 139

Valéry, Paul, 89 n. 24
Verne, Jules, 147, 157, 162 nn. 23, 26
*Vingt Mille Lieues sous les mers [Twenty Thousand Leagues Under the Sea]*, 8, 153-56, 162 n. 20

Weber, Katherine, 129, 130
Woolf, Virginia, 54-55, 74, 84, 157

Zévaco, Michel, 162 n. 22
Zola, Emile, 83